Theōsis

Princeton Theological Monograph Series

K. C. Hanson, Editor

Recent titles in the series

Richard Valantasis et al., editors
The Subjective Eye: Essays in Honor of Margaret R. Miles

Byron C. Bangert
*Consenting to God and Nature:
Toward a Theocentric, Naturalistic, Theological Ethics*

Sam Hamstra Jr.
*The Reformed Pastor: Lectures on Pastoral Theology by
John Williamson Nevin*

David A. Ackerman
*Lo, I Tell You a Mystery: Cross, Resurrection, and Paraenesis
in the Rhetoric of 1 Corinthians*

Paul O. Ingram, editor
Constructing a Relational Cosmology

Caryn Riswold
Coram Deo: Human Life in the Vision of God

John A. Vissers
The Neo-Orthodox Theology of W. W. Bryden

Michael G. Cartwright
*Practices, Politics, and Performance:
Toward a Communal Hermeneutic for Christian Ethics*

Philip Harrold
*A Place Somewhat Apart: The Private Worlds of a Late
Nineteenth-Century University*

Mark A. Ellis, translator
The Arminian Confession of 1621

Theōsis
Deification in Christian Theology

Edited by Stephen Finlan
and Vladimir Kharlamov

Pickwick Publications
Eugene, Oregon

THEŌSIS
Deification in Christian Theology

Pickwick Publications
A Division of Wipf & Stock Publishers
199 W. 8th Ave., Suite 3
Eugene, OR 97401

ISBN: 1-59752-438-7

Cataloging-in-Publication Data

Theōsis: deification in Christian theology / edited by Stephen Finlan and Vladimir Kharlamov

x + 185 p.; 23 cm. (Princeton Theological Monograph Series; 52)

Includes bibliographical references.
ISBN 1-59752-438-7

1. Deification (Christianity). 2. Sanctification—History of doctrines. I. Finlan, Stephen. II. Kharlamov, Vladimir. III. Title. IV. Series.

BT767.8 T75 2006

Manufactured in the U.S.A.

Contents

Introduction

Stephen Finlan and Vladimir Kharlamov

Defining the Term

The closest English equivalent of theōsis is "deification." In Christian theology, theōsis refers to the transformation of believers into the likeness of God. Of course, Christian monotheism goes against any literal "god making" of believers. Rather, the NT speaks of a transformation of mind, a metamorphosis of character, a redefinition of selfhood, and an imitation of God. Most of these passages are tantalizingly brief, and none spells out the concept in detail.

Deification was an important idea in the early church, though it took a long time for θέωσις (theōsis) to emerge as the standard label for the process. The term was coined by the great fourth century theologian, Gregory of Nazianzus. Theologians now use theōsis to designate all instances where any idea of taking on God's character or being "divinized" (made divine) occurs, even when the term θέωσις is not used. And of course, different Christian authors understood deification differently.

It is difficult to define theōsis, but not difficult to cite several biblical passages that strongly suggest a process of heightened reflection of godly nature, which stimulated Christian deification discourse. The following

1

grouping of biblical passages is meant to bring out the logical development of the idea:

IMITATION OF GOD:
Be perfect, therefore, as your heavenly Father is perfect. (Matt 5:48)

The one who believes in me will also do the works that I do and, in fact, will do greater works than these, because I am going to the Father. (John 14:12)

Be imitators of God, as beloved children. (Eph 5:1)

TAKING ON GOD'S NATURE:
You . . . may become participants of the divine nature. (2 Pet 1:4)

You are gods, children of the Most High, all of you. (Ps 82:6)

Is it not written in your law, 'I said, you are gods'? (John 10:34)

INDWELT BY GOD:
Truly it is the spirit in a mortal, the breath of the Almighty, that makes for understanding. (Job 32:8)

The Spirit of truth . . . abides with you, and he will be in you. (John 14:17)

It is that very Spirit bearing witness with our spirit that we are children of God. (Rom 8:16)

BEING RE-FORMED BY GOD:
What is born of the Spirit is spirit. (John 3:6)

Be transformed by the renewing of your minds, so that you may discern what is the will of God—what is good and acceptable and perfect. (Rom 12:2)

Clothe yourselves with the new self, created according to the likeness of God in true righteousness and holiness. (Eph 4:24)

BEING CON-FORMED TO CHRIST:
He will transform the body of our humiliation that it may be conformed to the body of his glory. (Phil 3:21)

. . . . predestined to be conformed to the image of his Son. (Rom 8:29)

All of us, with unveiled faces, seeing the glory of the Lord as though reflected in a mirror, are being transformed into the same image from one degree of glory to another. (2 Cor 3:18)

When he [Christ] is revealed, we will be like him. (1 John 3:2)

FINAL DIVINIZATION OF THE KOSMOS:
The earth will be filled with the knowledge of the glory of the Lord, as the waters cover the sea. (Hab 2:14)

The effect of righteousness will be peace, and the result of righteousness, quietness and trust forever. (Isa 32:17)

When all things are subjected to him, then . . . God may be all in all. (1 Cor 15:28)

Although some of these passages concern the afterlife, or events connected with the return of Christ, all of them have implications for the present life of believers, suggesting an ongoing transformation, a progressive *engodding* of the believer, to use the endearing Old English phrase.[1]

Let us look at the implications of this grouping of biblical sayings. Imitation of God leads to a reception of the character traits of God, an idea that is standard throughout most of the Bible. The idea of being indwelt by a special spirit of God is found intermittently throughout the OT, and is a central idea in the NT. This is not synonymous with theōsis, but it is an indispensable element in any theology of theōsis. Without the constant guidance of God, we humans always go astray. Without "encouragement," the renewal of spiritual courage in our hearts, we constantly grow faint, like Peter after Jesus was arrested. But with a strong connection to inner guidance, believers "shall renew their strength, they shall mount up with wings like eagles" (Isa 40:31). "We do not lose heart. . . . our inner nature is being renewed day by day" (2 Cor 4:16). As Jesus said, "the kingdom of God is within[2] you" (Luke 17:21 NIV, KJV, TEV). This saying should not be marginalized just because it occurs in only one gospel. It is an indispensable part of the proclamation of Jesus, and is fully consistent with his teachings about an indwelling Spirit of Truth that "will be in you,"[3] and of a "light in you."[4]

---

[1] Pusey, *Lenten Sermon* 108, *Oxford English Dictionary* (Oxford: Clarendon, 1989) 5: 200.

[2] Heightening the social aspect of the gospel, NRSV offers "among," but "within" or "inside" are more accurate translations of ἐντός *entos*. C. H. Dodd points out, "When Luke means 'among' he says ἐν μέσῳ" (*The Parables of the Kingdom* [New York: Charles Scribner's Sons, 1936] 84 n.1).

[3] John 14:17; cf. 14:26; 17:23; 15:4.

[4] Matt 6:23; 5:16; Luke 11:35.

What surely suggests theōsis is the notion of being transformed by God, or taking on the divine nature. In the letters of Paul, in particular, this means being transformed into the likeness of Christ, who is the embodiment of God. Believers are "conformed to" and "transformed into" the image of Christ (Rom 8:29; 2 Cor 3:18; Phil 3:21), even having the "mind of Christ" (Phil 2:5; 1 Cor 2:16). One may, perhaps, suppress the divinizing implications of these passages, but not of those that say that believers will "become the righteousness of God" (2 Cor 5:21), and after death, "will also bear the image of the man of heaven" (1 Cor 15:49). *Theōsis* is central to the theology of Paul throughout.[5]

All of this depends upon, and revolves around, Christianity's central and unique idea: the *incarnation*—in Christ, God lived a human life. The incarnation is the definitive and unique doctrine of Christianity. Further, without the incarnation, there would be no theōsis. Christians are meant not only to learn from the life of the divine Son, but to reproduce the pattern of spiritual progress that he revealed, even to the point of taking on the character of God! A typical expression would be that of Didymus the Blind, who spoke of the soul's process of becoming "perfect [τελειοῦσθαι *teleiousthai*], becoming like [ὁμοιωθῆναι *homoiōthēnai*] God."[6] This is a staggering idea, and one that certainly needs to be connected with a mature and well-balanced theology.

This is more than just the longing for union with the divine, which is a central goal for most religions. Not all religions take it so far as to develop a concept of theōsis while still preserving human personal identity, as Christianity does. But it is not always well-defined. Deification played an important,[7] but not definitive, role in early Patristic theology. Despite Patristic fascination with deification, the fathers do not develop a "doctrine" of theōsis. Nor do the doctrinal controversies and decisions of the Church Councils deal with the subject.

The popularity of the idea is matched by a lack of precise definition. The church fathers argue for, rather than spell out, deification. Theōsis

---

[5] See also the deification concepts in Col 1:9, 27; 2:10; 3:10; Eph 3:19; 4:23–24; 5:1.

[6] *Commentary on Ecclesiastes* on 3:19; from *Didymos der Blinde. Kommentar zum Ecclesiastes*, pt. 2, ed. M. Gronewald (Bonn: Habelt, 1977) 99, located using TLG 8.0 (electronic database) © 1999 Silver Mountain Software.

[7] "Deification was the ultimate and supreme thought" (Adolf von Harnack, *History of Dogma*, tr. Neil Buchanan [New York: Dover, 1961 (1900)] 3:164 n.2).

concepts are closely related to soteriology, Christology, and anthropology. Doctrines about baptism and the Eucharist, the resurrection of the dead, eternal life, the image of God in human beings, redemption, and sanctification contain themes that relate to theōsis. But simply replacing theōsis with *sanctification* is an attempt to supplant Patristic theology with standard Reformation language. Deification was often seen as the *telos* (goal) of human existence and of salvation.

The church fathers of the late second to fourth centuries (Irenaeus, Clement of Alexandria, Origen, Athanasius, Gregory of Nyssa, and Gregory of Nazianzus) make theōsis a major theme, yet none of them defines the term,[8] or discusses it at sufficient length to clear up ambiguities; they seem to assume that its content is common knowledge in the Christian community.

The first theological definition of theōsis was given in the sixth century by Pseudo-Dionysius, but it is general and inexact: "Divinization consists of being as much as possible like and in union with God."[9] The meaning of theōsis varies throughout Patristic theology, sometimes even within the same author.[10] Some scholars project later developments of theōsis onto earlier church fathers, underestimating the role of specifically second-century themes. The articles here by Kharlamov will try to clarify how the theological concerns of the Apostolic Fathers and Apologists situate and shape their deification concepts.

Terminology of Theōsis

A great variety of terms are used to communicate the idea of deification. Ben Drewery sums up "the *content* or *attributes* of deification" as

---

[8] Jules Gross, *The Divinization of the Christian According to the Greek Fathers* (Anaheim, Calif.: A & C Press, 2002) 271–72.

[9] *Ecclesiastical Hierarchy* 1.3; *Pseudo-Dionysius: The Complete Works*. The Classics of Western Spirituality (New York: Paulist Press, 1987) 198; in the original Greek: *Corpus Dionysiacum, Patristische Texte Und Studien*, Bd. 36, ed. Beate Regina Suchla (Berlin: de Gruyter, 1991) 66.

[10] Donald F. Winslow proposes a "six-fold dimension" for *theōsis* in Gregory of Nazianzus alone: as a spatial, visual, epistemological, social, ethical, or "progressive union" metaphor (*The Dynamics of Salvation: A Study in Gregory of Nazianzus* [Cambridge, Mass.: Philadelphia Patristic Foundation, 1979] 193–98).

"τελείωσις *teleiōsis* (ethical perfection), ἀπάθεια *apatheia* (exemption from human emotions or passions), ἀφθαρσία *aftharsia*, ἀθανασία *athanasia* (exemption from mortal corruption or death)."[11] Among the conceptual equivalents for deification are union, participation, partaking, communion/partnership, divine filiation, adoption, recreation, intertwined with the divine, similitude with God, transformation, elevation, transmutation, commingling, assimilation, intermingling, rebirth, regeneration, transfiguration. The preferences of particular authors vary greatly.

Considering the language of theōsis, special attention should be given to vocabulary groups in all their grammatical forms, of words for union— ἕνωσις *henōsis*; participation—μετουσία *metousia* (from μετέχω *metechō*), μέθεξις *methexis*, μετάληψις *metalēpsis* (from μεταλαμβάνω *metalambanō*); partaking—μέτοχος *metochos*; and communion— κοινωνία *koinōnia* (from κοινωνέω *koinōneō*). In English, "partaking" and "sharing" suggest a distinction of the part from the whole, and connote a limited possession of the whole. In Greek, *metousia, methexis,* and *metalēpsis* convey the idea of "having together" or "obtaining a certain quality." *Metalēpsis*, in addition, can imply "harmonious mutual existing" or "acting together." *Koinōnia* and *metousia* express the idea of "communion" or "union." Also, we need to be aware that the terms listed above are not only applicable to deification; they could refer to other issues as well.

There are five groups of Greek words that explicitly point to making into a god or deifying: 1) ἀποθεόω/ἀποθειόω—ἀποθέωσις *apotheoō/ apotheioō-apotheōsis* 2) θεοποιέω—θεοποιία—θεοποίησις—θεοποιός *theopoiēsis-theopoios*; 3) ἐκθεόω/ἐκθειόω—ἐκθέωσις—ἐκθεωτικός *ektheoō/ektheioō-ektheōsis-ektheōtikos*; 4) θεόω—θέωσις[12] *theoō–theōsis*; 5) ἀποθειάζω—ἐκθειάζω *apotheiazō ektheiazō*.[13] The subject-verb sets θεὸς εἰμί *theios eimi* ("to be god") and especially θεὸς γίγνομαι *theos gignomai* ("to become god") were extensively used. Here, we purposefully use the word "god" with the lower case letter "g" to indicate that the deified human person never stops being human. Here we should point

---

[11] Benjamin Drewery, "Deification," in *Christian Spirituality: Essays in Honour of Gordon Rupp*, ed. Peter Brooks (London: SCM, 1975) 38.

[12] Although coined in the fourth century, θέωσις *theōsis* did not become the standard designator for deification until after Pseudo-Dionysus in the sixth century.

[13] See Norman Russell, *The Doctrine of Deification in the Greek Patristic Tradition* (Oxford: Oxford University Press, 2004) 333–44.

out that not all Greek words for deification connote a strong literal meaning of "becoming a god" or being "deified." Often it is the *qualities* of Godliness that are being emphasized.

A favorite word of Athanasius, θεοποιέω *theopoieō*, with the element ποιέω *poieō*, "to make," "to produce," implies agency, something done to someone. It can be translated, "to make god." Athanasius derives the noun θεοποίησις *theopoiēsis* and the adjective θεοποίητος *theopoiētos* from this verb. A mortal being made god is a paradox for Christian theology, where only God is without beginning or ending (ἀγένητος *agenētos*—"uncreated," "unoriginated"). Of course, the mortal was generated or created (γεννητός *gennētos*), and so is not God. Athanasian θεοποίησις *theopoiēsis* connotes the idea of passive deification: the human is acted upon, so God retains primacy and infinity.

Gregory of Nazianzus, in his poetry, uses θεὸν τεύχω *theon teuchō* ("to make/produce god"),[14] θεὸν τελέω *theon teleō* ("to complete/accomplish god"),[15] and τυκτὸς θεός *tyktos theos* ("created god").[16]

The extraordinary richness of Greek language offered Patristic writers a broad selection to choose from. Even though θεοποίησις *theopoiēsis* and later θέωσις *theōsis* became the choice expressions for Christians, other deification vocabulary was retained.

There is less diversity in deification terminology in Latin than in Greek. Some Latin writers simply transliterate Greek θέωσις *theōsis*, as we continue to do in English. Greek ἀποθέωσις *apotheōsis* was often rendered in Latin as *consecratio* or visa versa. The Latin *consecratio* was the official term used for declaring the deceased emperor, or any other figure, as *divus*.[17] Reflecting this widespread pagan usage, the English term "apotheosis" usually signifies an exaltation or a metaphorical glorification, usually without any Christian content.

Some English language authors make a distinction between divinization (taking on godly qualities) and deification (become a godlike being); others do not. Of course, all Christian authors made such a distinction *conceptually*, whether or not they make it terminologically.

---

[14] *Carm.* 1.1.3.4.

[15] *Carm.* 1.2.14.92.

[16] *Carm.* 1.2.9.132.

[17] Russell, *Doctrine of Deification*, 22.

When Latin writers came up with the term *deificatio*, derived from the verb, *deificare*, they were not making a distinction from "divinization," but providing another word for it. It was already obvious, from the standpoint of Christian theology, that no mortal becomes God.

History of Scholarship

The Eastern Orthodox Church has retained theōsis as a concept for theological reflection, while the Western churches—separated by time, language, and philosophy from the Greek thinkers of the early church—have dropped it. In fact, theōsis simply does not exist for most contemporary Western theologians. In lay theology the term is usually perceived as either blasphemous or absurd.[18] Some Protestants try to assimilate it to familiar Western concepts such as "sanctification by grace" or "justification by faith," trying to connect the Reformation directly to the Bible, as though the intervening centuries had no significance. We hope to show that the lines of continuity and transmission through the centuries of Christian thought are essential to Christian understanding at any one time and place. The near disappearance in Western Christendom of an idea that was widely accepted for over a thousand years (including by Latin theologians like Augustine), is a serious loss for the Christian thought and hope.

A significant line of modern scholarship adopts the thesis of Adolf Harnack about the Hellenization of early Christianity, the transformation of the living faith "into the creed to be believed," with theōsis considered to be "creedal" rather than "living." This is said to be the change of "the glowing hope of the Kingdom of heaven into a doctrine of immortality and deification."[19] M. Werner,[20] B. Drewery,[21] and many others follow

---

[18] E.g., Francis J. Hall, *The Incarnation* (New York: Longman, Green and Company, 1915) 192; Donald E. Gowan, *When Man Becomes God: Humanism and Hybris in the Old Testament* (Pittsburgh, 1975) 1.

[19] Adolf von Harnack, *History of Dogma*, tr. Neil Buchanan (New York: Dover, 1961 [1900]) 1:45.

[20] M. Werner, *Formation of Christian Dogma* (New York: Harper, 1957) 168.

[21] Drewery, "Deification," 49–62.

the line of Harnack's thinking, categorizing theōsis with decline and with doctrinal hardening.

At the opposite pole are theologians who build their entire theology upon a Christian concept of theōsis, including Vladimir Lossky,[22] Panayiotis Nellas,[23] and C. Stavropoulos,[24] who create the impression that there is nothing more important in Christian theology than deification, and, further, that Eastern Orthodoxy holds a "copyright" on it. Jean Daniélou exposes the anachronism of their approach, their interpreting the early fathers in light of later fathers.[25]

A Renewed Discussion

Between the polarized views—deification is either a pagan idea or the essential Orthodox doctrine—we find more moderate and historically oriented scholarly works. In 1938, Jules Gross published an extensive study of divinization in the Greek fathers,[26] providing the first comprehensive and chronological analysis of the notion, looking at Patristic, Hellenistic, mystery religion, biblical, and postbiblical sources.[27] More recently, new

---

[22] Vladimir Lossky, *In the Image and Likeness of God* (Crestwood, N.Y.: St. Vladimir's Seminary Press, 1974); *The Mystical Theology of the Eastern Church* (Crestwood, N.Y.: St. Vladimir's Seminary Press, 1976, 1998); *The Vision of God* (Crestwood, N.Y.: St. Vladimir's Seminary Press, 1983).

[23] Panayiotis Nellas, *Deification in Christ: Orthodox Perspectives on the Nature of the Human Person*, tr. Norman Russell (Crestwood, N.Y.: St. Vladimir's Seminary Press, 1987). First published in Greek in 1979.

[24] C. Stavropoulos, *Partakers of Divine Nature* (Minneapolis: Light of Life, 1976).

[25] Jean Daniélou, "Introduction," in *La Déification de l'homme, selon la doctrine des Pères grecs*. The book is authored by Myrrha Lot-Borodine (Paris: Editions du Cerf, 1970) 15.

[26] Jules Gross, *La divinisation du chrétien d'après les pères grecs: Contribution historique à la doctrine de la grâce* (Paris: J. Gabalda, 1938). Published in English as *The Divinization of the Christian According to the Greek Fathers*, tr. Paul A. Onica (Anaheim, Calif.: A & C Press, 2002).

[27] See also Edouard des Places, I. H. Dalmais, and Gustave Bardy, "Divinisation" (*Dictionnaire de spiritualité ascétique et mystique*, original eds., M. Viller, F. Cavallera, and J. de Guibert. Continued by Charles Baumgartner. Vol. 3, Paris: Beauchesne, 1957) 1370–98 and H. Rondet, "La divinisation du chrétien," *Nouvelle Révue Théologique* 17 (1949) 449–76, 561–88.

attention to theōsis was stimulated by the work of John Meyendorff [28] and through ecumenical dialogue.[29] A number of dissertations that deal with the history of theōsis or with theōsis in the works of particular figures, were produced.[30] In addition, several articles and books have appeared recently.[31] The first International Academic Conference on theōsis,

---

[28] John Meyendorff, "Theōsis in the Eastern Christian tradition," in *Christian Spirituality: Post-Reformation and Modern,* eds. Louis Dupré and Don E. Saliers (New York: Crossroad, 1989) 470–76. The theme of deification is widely scattered throughout Meyendorff's works.

[29] For instance, Paul R. Hinlicky, "Theological Anthropology: Toward Integrating Theōsis and Justification by Faith," *Journal of Ecumenical Studies* 34 (1997): 38–73; Tuomo Mannermaa, "Justification and *theōsis* in Lutheran-Orthodox perspective," in *Union with Christ* (Grand Rapids: Eerdmans, 1998) 25–41; Jouko Martikainen, "Man's Salvation: Deification or Justification? Observation of Key-Words in the Orthodox and the Lutheran Tradition," *Sobornost* series 7, no. 3 (Summer 1976): 180–92; *Salvation in Christ: A Lutheran-Orthodox Dialogue,* eds. Robert Tobias and John Meyendorff (Minneapolis: Augsburg, 1992) and Michael McDaniel, "Salvation as Justification and *Theōsis,*" in the same volume.

[30] Here we list just some of the Ph.D. dissertations: Isaac Chae, "Justification and Deification in Augustine: A Study of His Doctrine of Justification," Trinity Evangelical Divinity School, 1999; Caren F. Calendine, "Theōsis and the Recognition of Saints in Tenth Century Byzantium," University of Wisconsin, 1998; Arkadi Choufrine, "Gnosis, Theophany, Theōsis: Studies in Clement of Alexandria's Appropriation of his Background," Princeton Theological Seminary, 2001 (published by Peter Lang in 2002); J. A. Cullen, "The Patristic Concept of the Deification of Man Examined in the Light of Contemporary Notions of the Transcendence of Man," Oxford University, 1985; Jeffrey Finch, "Sanctity as Participation in the Divine Nature According to the Ante-Nicene Eastern Fathers, Considered in the Light of Palamism," Drew University, 2001; Maurice Fred Himmerich, "Deification in John of Damascus," Marquette University, 1985; Nancy Joyce Hudson, "Theōsis in the Thought of Nicholas of Cusa: Origin, Goal, and Realized Destiny of Creation," Yale University, 1999; Keith Edward Norman, "Deification: The Content of Athanasian Soteriology," Duke University, 1980; Eric David Perl, "*Methexis*: Creation, Incarnation, Deification in Saint Maximus Confessor," Yale University, 1991; N. Russell, "The Concept of Deification in the Early Greek Fathers," Oxford University, 1988; Elena Vishnevskaya, "*Perichoresis* in a Context of Divinization: Maximus the Confessor's Vision of a 'Blessed and Most Holy Embrace,'" Drew Unviersity, 2004; Kenneth Warren Wesche, "The Defense of Chalcedon in the 6th Century of the Doctrine of 'Hypostasis' and Deification in the Christology of Leontius of Jerusalem," Fordham University, 1986; Anna Ngaire Williams, "Deification in Thomas Aquinas and Gregory Palamas," Yale University, 1995.

[31] We mention just a few among most recent: George D. Dragas, "Exchange or Communication of Properties and Deification: Antidosis or *Communicatio Idiomatum*

"Partakers of the Divine Nature: Deification/*Theōsis* in the Christian Traditions," held at Drew University, Madison, New Jersey, on May 21–22, 2004, reaffirmed the significant academic and interdenominational interest in this aspect of Christian theology. It is gradually becoming a more appreciated topic in Western theological discourse.

While some articles in this collection discuss pre-Christian antecedents of theōsis, Greek and Jewish, most focus on particular Christian understandings. The article by Gregory Glazov examines OT covenant theology, with an emphasis on divine adoption, and on bearing the fruit of knowledge or attaining the stature of a tree of righteousness in Proverbs, Isaiah, and Sirach. The article by Stephen Finlan on 2 Pet 1:4 ("You may become participants of the divine nature") examines the epistle's apparent borrowings from Middle Platonic spirituality, Stoic ethics, and Jewish apocalyptic expectation. The epistle stresses "knowledge of Christ," which means cultivation of godly character and growing up into Christ.

Vladimir Kharlamov's first article examines the emergence of the deification theme in the Apostolic Fathers with its culmination in the passion mysticism of Ignatius of Antioch, who speaks of becoming a "Christ-carrier" and emphasizes the full integrity of human nature that participates in salvation and eternal life. The second article covers Apologists such as Justin Martyr (who considers the human being worthy to become a son of god, and even "god") and Theophilus of Antioch (for whom the human being reaches full maturity and is declared god through the therapeutic experience of death and resurrection).

Jeffrey Finch shows the integral connection between incarnational Christology and deification in the thought of two of the Church's most important theologians. For Irenaeus, the incarnation, the Recapitulation work of Christ, and deification of the believer are closely linked. For Athanasius of

and Theōsis," in *Greek Orthodox Theological Review* 43, no 1–4 (1998): 377–99; Nonna Verna Harrison, "Theōsis as Salvation: An Orthodox Perspective," in *Pro-Ecclesia* 6 (1997): 429–43; Steve McCormick, "Theōsis in Chrysostom and Wesley: An Eastern Paradigm on Faith and Love," *Wesleyan Theological Journal* 26 (1991): 38–103; Frederick W. Norris, "Deification: Consensual and Cogent," *Scottish Journal of Theology* 49 (1996): 411–28; Norman Russell, *Doctrine of Deification;* Kenneth Paul Wesche, "Eastern Orthodox Spirituality: Union with God in Theōsis," in *Theology Today* 56 (1999): 29–43; Anna Ngaire Williams, *The Ground of Union: Deification in Aquinas and Palamas* (New York: Oxford University Press, 1999).

Alexandria, the intimate contact between humanity and divinity in the incarnation of the Word enabled the possibility of human deification.

Robert Puchniak reminds readers of the importance of deification ideas to Augustine, including (but not exclusively) in some recently discovered letters. The God who "justifies," also "deifies" the Christian. Elena Vishnevskaya summarizes the systematic doctrine of theōsis in Maximus the Confessor, delineating the roles of the divine initiative and the human response, which together make divinization possible. The liturgy provides a glimpse of future divinization.

Myk Habets spells out the role of deification in Luther, Calvin, and the important evangelical writer, T. F. Torrance. Luther, for instance, taught that Christians are *made*, not just *deemed*, righteous. Stephen Finlan's article on the brilliant Russian philosopher, Vladimir Soloviev, who stimulated much discussion of deification, examines Soloviev's humbled thinking in his later years, and his warnings against false theōsis and false Messiahs. Soloviev provides a Trinitarian philosophy of divine goodness, truth, and beauty penetrating human life.

Although these articles stretch from the antecedents of Christian theōsis to the distinctive shaping of the concept by particular Christian thinkers, they all shed light on the divinization concept, the only idea that is adequate to describe the linkage between inward and outward, personal and universal, spiritual progress.

Bibliography

Bakken, Kenneth L. "Holy Spirit and Theōsis: Toward a Lutheran Theology of Healing." *Saint Vladimir's Theological Quarterly* 38 (1994): 409–23.

Calendine, Caren F. "Theōsis and the recognition of saints in tenth century Byzantium." Ph. D. diss., University of Wisconsin, 1998.

Chae, Isaac. "Justification and Deification in Augustine: A Study of His Doctrine of Justification." Ph.D. diss., Trinity Evangelical Divinity School, 1999.

Choufrine, Arkadi. *Gnosis, Theophany, Theōsis: Studies in Clement of Alexandria's Appropriation of his Background.* New York: Lang, 2002.

Cullen, J. A. "The Patristic Concept of the Deification of Man Examined in the Light of Contemporary Notions of the Transcendence of Man." Ph. D. diss., Oxford University, 1985.

Daniélou, Jean. "Introduction." In *La Déification de l'homme, selon la doctrine des Péres grecs,* edited by Myrrha Lot-Borodine, 9–18. Paris: Cerf, 1970.

Didymus the Blind. Commentary on Ecclesiastes. From *Didymos der Blinde. Kommentar zum Ecclesiastes,* pt. 2. Edited by M. Gronewald. Bonn: Habelt, 1977. Quotation taken from TLG 8.0 (electronic database) © 1999 Silver Mountain Software.

Dodd, C. H. *The Parables of the Kingdom.* Rev. ed. New York: Scribner, 1936.

Dragas, George D. "Exchange or Communication of Properties and Deification: *Antidosis* or *Communicatio Idiomatum* and Theōsis." *Greek Orthodox Theological Review* 43 (1998) 377–99.

Drewery, Benjamin. "Deification." In *Christian Spirituality: Essays in Honour of Gordon Rupp.* Edited by Peter Brooks, 33–62. London: SCM, 1975.

Finch, Jeffrey. "Sanctity as Participation in the Divine Nature According to the Ante-Nicene Eastern Fathers, Considered in the Light of Palamism." Ph. D. diss., Drew University, 2001.

Gowan, Donald E. *When Man Becomes God: Humanism and Hybris in the Old Testament.* Pittsburgh: Pickwick, 1975.

Gregory of Nazianzus. *Carmina.* PG 37.

Gross, Jules. *La divinisation du chrétien d'aprés les péres grecs: Contribution historique à la doctrine de la grâce.* Paris: J. Gabalda, 1938. Published in English as *The Divinization of the Christian According to the Greek Fathers,* trans. Paul A. Onica. Anaheim, Calif.: A & C Press, 2002.

Hall, Francis J. *The Incarnation.* New York: Longman, Green and Company, 1915.

Harnack, Adolf von. *History of Dogma.* Translated by Neil Buchanan. New York: Dover, 1961 [1900].

Harrison, Nonna Verna. "Theōsis as Salvation: An Orthodox Perspective." *Pro-Ecclesia* 6 (1997) 429–43.

Himmerich, Maurice Fred. "Deification in John of Damascus." Ph. D. diss., Marquette University, 1985.

Hinlicky, Paul R. "Theological Anthropology: Toward Integrating Theōsis and Justification by Faith." *Journal of Ecumenical Studies* 34 (1997) 38–73.

Hudson, Nancy Joyce. "Theōsis in the Thought of Nicholas of Cusa: Origin, Goal, and Realized Destiny of Creation." Ph. D. diss., Yale University, 1999.

Lossky, Vladimir. *In the Image and Likeness of God.* Crestwood, N.Y.: St. Vladimir's Seminary Press, 1974.

————. *The Mystical Theology of the Eastern Church.* Crestwood, N.Y.: St. Vladimir's Seminary Press, 1976, 1998.

————. *The Vision of God.* Crestwood, N.Y.: St. Vladimir's Seminary Press, 1983.

Mannermaa, Tuomo. "Justification and Theōsis in Lutheran-Orthodox Perspective." In *Union with Christ: The New Finnish Interpretation of Luther.* Edited by C. E. Braaten and R. W. Jensen. Grand Rapids: Eerdmans, 1998.

Martikainen, Jouko. "Man's Salvation: Deification or Justification? Observation of Key-Words in the Orthodox and the Lutheran Tradition." *Sobornost* 7. 3 (1976) 180–92.

McCormick, Steve. "Theōsis in Chrysostom and Wesley: An Eastern Paradigm on Faith and Love." *Wesleyan Theological Journal* 26 (1991) 38–103.

McDaniel, Michael. "Salvation as Justification and Theōsis." In *Salvation in Christ: A Lutheran-Orthodox Dialogue.* Edited by Robert Tobias and John Meyendorff, 67–84. Minneapolis: Augsburg, 1992.

Meyendorff, John. "Theōsis in the Eastern Christian tradition." In *Christian Spirituality: Post-Reformation and Modern.* Edited by Louis Dupré and Don E. Saliers, 470–76. New York: Crossroad, 1989.

Nellas, Panayiotis. *Deification in Christ: Orthodox Perspectives on the Nature of the Human Person.* Translated by Norman Russell. Crestwood, N.Y.: St. Vladimir's Seminary Press, 1987. First published in Greek in 1979.

Norman, Keith Edward. "Deification: The Content of Athanasian Soteriology." Ph. D. diss., Duke University, 1980.

Norris, Frederick W. "Deification: Consensual and Cogent." *Scottish Journal of Theology* 49 (1996) 411–28.

Perl, Eric David. *"Methexis:* Creation, Incarnation, Deification in Saint Maximus Confessor." Ph.D. diss., Yale University, 1991.

Places, Edouard des, I. H. Dalmais, and Gustave Bardy. "Divinisation." In *Dictionnaire de spiritualité ascétique et mystique,* 1370–98. Originally edited by M. Viller, F. Cavallera, and J. de Guibert. Continued by Charles Baumgartner. Vol. 3. Paris: Beauchesne, 1957.

Pseudo-Dionysius. *Ecclesiastical Hierarchy.* In *Pseudo-Dionysius: The Complete Works.* The Classics of Western Spirituality. New York: Paulist Press, 1987. In the original Greek: *Corpus Dionysiacum, Patristische Texte Und Studien;* Bd. 36. Edited by Beate Regina Suchla. Berlin: de Gruyter, 1991.

Rondet, H. "La divinisation du chrétien," *Nouvelle Révue Théologique* 17 (1949) 449–76, 561–88.

Russell, N. *The Doctrine of Deification in the Greek Patristic Tradition.* Oxford: Oxford University Press, 2004.

Stavropoulos, C. *Partakers of Divine Nature.* Minneapolis: Light of Life, 1976.

Tobias, Robert and John Meyendorff, editors. *Salvation in Christ: A Lutheran-Orthodox Dialogue.* Minneapolis: Augsburg, 1992.

Vishnevskaya, Elena. *"Perichoresis* in a Context of Divinization: Maximus the Confessor's Vision of a 'Blessed and Most Holy Embrace.'" Ph.D. diss., Drew University, 2004.

Werner, M. *Formation of Christian Doctrine: An Historical Study of the Problem.* Translated by S. F. G. Brandon. San Francisco: Harper & Bros., 1957.

Wesche, Kenneth Warren. "The Defense of Chalcedon in the 6th Century the Doctrine of 'Hypostasis' and Deification in the Christology of Leontius of Jerusalem." Ph.D. diss., Fordham University, 1986.

————. "Eastern Orthodox Spirituality: Union with God in Theōsis." *Theology Today* 56 (1999) 29–43.

Williams, Anna Ngaire. "Deification in Thomas Aquinas and Gregory Palamas." Ph.D. diss., Yale University, 1995.

————. *The Ground of Union: Deification in Aquinas and Palamas.* New York: Oxford University Press, 1999.

Winslow, Donald F. The Dynamics of Salvation: *A Study in Gregory of Nazianzus.* Cambridge, Mass.: Philadelphia Patristic Foundation, 1979.

Theōsis, Judaism, and Old Testament Anthropology

Gregory Glazov

The purpose of this reflection is to explore why Old Testament and Hebraic biblical models are relevant to the study of the Christian concept of theōsis and to explore the form and relevance of models underpinning biblical covenant theology and wisdom literature. I write from a Roman Catholic perspective.

Theōsis is not only a major principle in Eastern Orthodox theology, it has roots in both the Old and New Testaments, and in Jewish theology. There is some continuity between Patristic interests in "embodied theōsis" and second temple Jewish conceptions that touch on messianic thought and on angelomorphic glorification of human beings through mystical vision before the Throne of God and through liturgies.[1] But there are serious difficulties for current interplay between Jewish and Christian theology.

---

[1] Cf. Alexandre Golitzin, "Scriptural Images of the Church: an Eastern Orthodox Reflection," 2001, published on the web at www.marquette.edu/maqom/church.

Theōsis and Old Testament Biblical Theology

Accustomed by doctrine and tradition to "put a hedge around the Torah," the Jew, confronted by Christian doctrines of Trinity, incarnation, and theōsis, feels little interest in qualifying and adapting these concepts so as to make them consistent with the incommensurability between the divine and the human. To qualify and nuance something that seems idolatrous is to remove the hedge.[2] It is thus difficult to know what Christians may hope to obtain from scholarly demonstrations that Christian concepts such as theōsis are rooted in intertestamental Judaism and other developments in postbiblical Judaism. If Christians hope that such demonstrations will eventually constitute biblical support, the question is: for whom? For Orthodox Jews, such texts may be simply analogous to what confronts Christians in the Gnostic gospels. For Christians, the New Testament evidence and Church teaching already suffice to ratify that which is presented as apostolic doctrine, which here includes the mystery signified by theōsis. But if this is the case, the reasons for seeking Old Testament grounding for such doctrines need to be clarified.

Utilizing the threads of the Old Testament to present itself as its fulfillment, the New Testament can hardly be understood without the Old. The New is the fruit growing from the ground of the Old. By His incarnation and Resurrection, the Christ reminds us (against certain Greek instincts) that it is eminently good to be incarnate, in this world and the next, thus grounding St. Irenaeus's famous saying that "God's glory is man fully alive." Without the penultimate word of the Old,[3] the proclamation and reception of Jesus as the Christ is meaningless and the

---

[2] The Christian doctrines of the Trinity and the incarnation may be regarded as idolatrous in Judaism (cf. Maimonides's commentary on the Mishna, *'Avodah Zarah* 1:3, and *Hilchot Akum* 9:4). This, coupled with the teaching that idolatry is prohibited by the Noahide law for the Gentile as well as for the Jew (Sanhedrin 63b), undergirds R. Moshe Feinstein's and R. Joseph Soloveitchik's influential instruction to American Orthodox Jewry to abstain from any Jewish-Christian dialogue lest it create appurtenance for idolatry in Israel and give occasion to Christian gentiles to reaffirm such beliefs (David Ellenson, "A Jewish Legal Authority Addresses Jewish-Christian Dialogue: Two Responses of Rabbi Moshe Feinstein" [Jacob Rader Marcus Center of the American Jewish Archives, 2001]. Available at www.huc.edu/aja/00-4.htm).

[3] Dietrich Bonhoeffer, *Letters and Papers from Prison* (New York: Macmillan, 1953) passim.

Eucharist, instituted by him in the context of a Jewish Pasch, identified by him with the priestly "blood of the covenant" and the prophetic "new covenant," is incomprehensible.[4] If the Christ is incomprehensible without the Old Testament, this must also be the case with theōsis.

The recent renewal of Catholic thought through *ressourcement*[5] in the Fathers of the Church has been fed by, and continues to precipitate, an interest in a rapprochement with Orthodoxy. The same can be said about *ressourcement* in Hebrew sources, and a rapprochement between Protestantism and Israel. But if *ressourcement* in the witness of the Hebrew Scriptures makes Christians feel secure, their footing is radically undermined by the Jewish repudiation of Christian exegetical claims. The quest for an Old Testament biblical theology is thus an attempt at securing a foothold, a grip on something fairly crucial to Christian security. Jewish biblical scholars, however, are uninterested in attempts to construct a dialogical biblical theology.[6] While explaining that this disinterest derives from the Jewish aversion to playing biblical Trivial Pursuit with Christologically loaded dice, Levenson argues that a common biblical theology between Jews and Christians is impossible since, by reading the First Testament through two different prisms (the New Testament and the Mishnah) Jews and Christians are effectively reading a different book.

Similarly, Eastern and Western Christians have been divided by a millennium of tradition. However, critiquing positions without reference to their internal context surely results in cross-purposed babble, and it is premature to despair of the fruits that may be yielded in the next millennium by serious attempts of groups engaged in religious dialogue to understand the internal context determining the views and readings of their rivals.[7] To preemptively declare that groups separated by millennia of tradition cannot

---

[4] Cf. Matt 26:28 and Mark 14:24 with Exod 24:8; Luke 22:20 and 1 Cor 11:25 with Jer 31:31 and all four with Isaiah 53; Joseph Cardinal Ratzinger, "Is the Eucharist a Sacrifice?" in *The Debate on Sacraments*. Concilium 4.3 (1967).

[5] A "re-sourcing," or rediscovery of sources.

[6] Jon D. Levenson, "Why Jews Are Not Interested in Biblical Theology," in *The Hebrew Bible, the Old Testament, and Historical Criticism: Jews and Christians in Biblical Studies* (Louisville: Westminster, 1993) 33–61.

[7] Hilarion Alfeyev, "The Patristic Heritage and Modernity," paper delivered at the *9th International Conference on Russian Monasticism and Spirituality,* Bose Monastery (Italy), 20 September 2001. Available at www.orthodoxeurope.org/print/11/1/2.aspx.

possibly agree over any area of biblical theology, even if granted another thousand years for the task, is simply to dodge one's rival's claims to one's spiritual patrimony. But, in biblical terms, the rival remains a brother and as such must be known and kept. Christians cannot abandon the quest for a biblical theology because it is the foundational witness to their Messiah.

In preparing to search for biblical models of theōsis, it would be interesting to take bearings from Jewish reflections and enquire what, in a definition such as that given by Kallistos Ware, may conflict or harmonize with Jewish theology:

> While God's inner essence is forever beyond our comprehension, His energies, grace, life and power fill the whole universe, and are directly accessible to us. . . . The essence signifies the whole God as he is in himself; the energies signify the whole God as he is in action. . . . The essence-energies distinction is a way of stating simultaneously that the *whole* God is inaccessible, and that the *whole* God in his outgoing love has rendered himself accessible to man. By virtue of this distinction . . . we are able to affirm the possibility of a direct or mystical union between man and God—what the Greek Fathers term the *theosis* of man, his "deification"—but at the same time we exclude any pantheistic identification between the two: for man participates in the energies of God, not in his essence. . . . Man still remains man.[8]

The essence-energy distinction seems to resonate with Fackenheim's insistence that in Judaism, "Grace is manifest in the gift of the commandment itself which, bridging the gulf between two incommensurables, makes a human community partner in a divine-human covenant," a covenant that, in contradistinction to Hegel's "absolute religion" and "divine-human identity . . . does not accept the identity of the Divine and the human."[9] What Fackenheim denotes as the incommensurability of God with man, Ware calls the indivisible Divine essence, non-admissive of any pantheistic identification. The role that

---

[8] Kallistos Ware, *The Orthodox Way* (Crestwood, N.Y.: St. Vladimir's Seminary Press, 1995) 22–23.
[9] Emil Fackenheim, "Demythologizing and Remythologizing in Jewish Experience: Reflections Inspired by Hegel's Philosophy," in *Myth and Philosophy*, ed. George F.

Ware accords to divine energies, Fackenheim accords to grace manifest in the divine commandment, and the role that Ware reserves for "union but not fusion or confusion," Fackenheim reserves to "covenant understood as community partnership." Could divine commandments, words, and energies be understood as commensurable realities? Could union and covenant be understood so as well? What are divine commandments if not energies able to either transfer a human subject into a covenantal relationship or transform one in such a relationship into something that the relationship is meant to nurture? On the other hand, even though Fackenheim is able to nuance his reading of Christianity to admit that it repudiates Hegel's implicit "divine-human identity" and pantheism,[10] it is a safe bet that Athanasius' dictum would prove too much for him.

What exactly is the scandalizing impediment that stands at the parting of the ways between rabbinic Judaism and the early church? It would seem that the Jewish repudiation of Jesus as the Only Son of God, Word of God, God's "I Am," the Messiah who renews the Law and Covenant is a gestalt. None of these ideas taken individually necessarily contradicts postbiblical Judaism. But judging from the thrust of the rhetoric in the Gospels, the chief scandal impeding the recognition of Jesus as Messiah even for those Jews who became Jesus' apostles and disciples is the idea of his incumbent and necessary suffering and death, coupled with the belief that entry into the Kingdom of God necessitates following him to the Cross.

Even though Judaism eventually found room for a suffering and dying Messiah, the Messiah ben Joseph, this recognition did not imply that the road to salvation necessarily involves everyone's participation in the Messiah's suffering and "birth-pangs." The Messiah was expected to restore sinners to the ways of righteousness and loving-kindness, to bring peace through the dissemination of divine understanding, to feed the hungry, heal the sick, give liberty to captives, melt swords into ploughshares, and restore the kingdom and glory of Israel (Acts 1:6). If St. John the Baptist could stumble in relating this list to what he saw and heard of Jesus (Luke 7:20, 23), it is no surprise that most Jews fail to see how the prophecy that

---

McLean, vol. 45 of *Proceedings of the American Catholic Philosophical Association* (Catholic University of America, 1973) 20, 22, 23.

[10] Fackenheim, "Demythologizing," 20.

the Messiah will melt swords into ploughshares relates to what Jews have experienced historically from Christian sovereigns.[11]

From this perspective, the root Jewish scandal over Jesus is nothing else than the scandal of the biblical Job and of Dostoyevsky's Ivan Karamazov who cannot square God with suffering "for nothing." It is not a specifically Jewish metaphysics that leads them to repudiate him as Messiah. The Jews in repudiating Jesus simply represent, with all the genius of their commitment to realism and the created order, the basic reasons why humanity would rather have bread and security than a suffering Messiah. If this is correct, it follows that the Christian understanding of the process of theōsis must also be intrinsically linked to a participation in Jesus' *via dolorosa,* to a concrete, organic immersion in His passion, in a way that grants a redemptive role to suffering and removes the scandal of what usually looks like a bloody mess.

In fact, were it not for this linkage between suffering and theōsis, the mysteries of the Kingdom, as preached by Jesus, would have been more immediately comprehensible and palatable to his apostles and audiences. Given that Jesus' parables of the Kingdom are aimed at resolving this problem,[12] the parables are another quarry for scriptural anthropological models grounding the Christian doctrine of theōsis. And to the extent that these parables are composed in Hebraic biblical terms, they can in turn serve to identify areas of Hebraic biblical narrative that anticipate and ground the Christian conception of the way into the Kingdom.

Theōsis and Old Testament Covenantal Anthropology

The importance of the covenant for this reflection emerges from the comparison of Kallistos Ware's and Emil Fackenheim's emphases on theōsis and covenant, respectively, in discussing their conceptions of divine-human union. Is there any common ground between these? The answer depends

---

[11] Cf. Moses Nachmanides (Ramban), Éric Smilévitch trans., *La dispute de Barcelone: suivi du commentaire sur Esaïe 52–53 (Vikuach ha-Ramban* [Lagrasse, France: Verdier, 1984]) passim.

[12] Cf. Dale C. Allison, Jr., *The New Moses: A Matthean Typology* (Minneapolis: Fortress, 1993) passim.

on the content of each concept. Having defined theōsis I turn to covenant.[13] St. Irenaeus taught that understanding salvation history "consists in showing why there are a number of covenants with mankind and in teaching what is the character of those covenants."[14] The centrality of the covenant to biblical narrative was axiomatic in theology and scholarship[15] until thirty five years ago when Perlitt's conclusion that the concept was of late Deuteronomistic origin (7th c. BC) signalled the collapse of the scholarly consensus regarding its traditio-historical centrality.[16] Consequently, the covenant could no longer be regarded as the root and ground of Israel's self-awareness. The conclusion is termed neo-Wellhausean because Julius Wellhausen, the father of higher Old Testament criticism, argued that the relationship with God was originally *"a natural one as that of son to father,"* but that "Jehovah and Israel came to be regarded as contracting parties of the covenant by . . . the Deuteronomic law."[17]

Scholars following Wellhausen often differed in explaining the origins of the covenant but predominantly agreed that it was secondary. Scholars rooted the sense of kinship in socio-political arrangements of confederalism[18] or in suzerain-vassal treaties.[19] When it became difficult to prove that such structures actually informed the Sinai pericope, Nicholson concluded that no covenant took place at Sinai as described in Exod 24:1–11 but only a ceremony of adoptive kinship, Yahweh as Father adopting Israel and giving them laws to understand the prerequisites of family union.[20]

The motif of kinship being primitive remains constant in all the scholarly observations regarding covenantal origins. What is also constant

---

[13] I do so in grateful dependence on Scott W. Hahn, "Kinship by Covenant: A Biblical Theological Study of Covenant Types and Texts in the Old and New Testaments" (Ph.D. diss., Marquette University, 1995).

[14] *Against Heresies,* 1.10.3.

[15] Walther Eichrodt, *The Theology of the Old Testament,* 2 vols. (London: SCM, 1961).

[16] Lothar Perlitt, *Bundestheologie im Alten Testament,* WMANT 36 (Neukirchen-Vluyn: Neukirchener Verlag, 1969).

[17] Julius Wellhausen, *Prolegomena to the History of Ancient Israel* (New York: Meridian, 1957 [1889]) 469.

[18] Max Weber, *Ancient Judaism* (New York: Free Press, 1952) 79, 118.

[19] George E. Mendenhall, *Law and Covenant in Israel and the Ancient Near East* (Pittsburgh, Penn.: The Biblical Colloquium, 1955) 26–36.

[20] Ernest W. Nicholson, *God and His People: Covenant and Theology in the Old Testament* (Oxford: Clarendon, 1986) 69, 295.

is resistance to the insight that covenantal categories underpin kinship motifs. This thesis was advanced in the late 60s and 70s by Dennis J. McCarthy, S. J.,[21] whose survey of ancient Near Eastern covenants including suzerain-vassal treaties inductively demonstrated that covenants in the ancient Near East principally served to forge relationships based on diverse degrees of kinship depending on the status of the contracting parties. Thus, if the parties were kings of equal status, they emerged from covenantal ceremonies as "brothers"; vassals in trusting relationships emerged as "sons" while vassals suspected of rebelliousness emerged as "servants" as attested in biblical examples of secular covenants.[22] Eminent authorities have rallied to this position[23] even though mainstream discussions of covenantal theology continue to rotate round Wellhausen.[24]

Divine-human covenants are unattested in human religious history except in Israel.[25] McCarthy's reconstruction not only legitimates the traditional understanding of the centrality of the Israelite covenantal idea but illuminates significant corollaries, such as salvation history being essentially a narrative explaining that history is the arena of God's recurrent attempts to restore humankind—that is, *Adam,* created in His image and likeness as His son—to family unity. The reason for the divine institution of successive covenants is the failure of preceding ones to realize God's purposes. As Israel falters via the Golden Calf incident to answer God's

---

[21] McCarthy, *Old Testament Covenant: A Survey of Current Opinions* (Richmond, Virg.: John Knox, 1972); idem, *Treaty and Covenant.* Analecta Biblical 21A, rev. ed. (Rome: Biblical Institute Press, 1978).

[22] See the kinship language in the covenants between Asa of Judah and Ben-Hadad of Damascus (1 Kgs 15:18–20); between Ahab of Israel and Ben Hadad of Syria (1 Kgs 20:31–34), and between Ahaz of Judah and Tiglath-pileser, king of Assyria (2 Kgs 16:7–9); Syrian examples of ANE covenants (McCarthy, *Treaty and Covenant,* 98).

[23] "The failure to recognize the rootage of the institution of covenant . . . in the structure of kinship societies has led to confusion and even gross distortion in the scholarly discussion of early Israelite religion" (Frank Moore Cross, *Canaanite Myth and Hebrew Epic: Essays in the History of the Religion of Israel* [Cambridge, Mass.: Harvard University Press, 1973] 14).

[24] A. D. H. Mayes and R. B. Salters, eds., *Covenant As Context: Essays in Honour of E. W. Nicholson* (Oxford: Oxford University Press, 2003).

[25] But for one possible exception: the Sumerian Urukagina text concerning the covenant between King (ensi) Urukagina of Lagash (ca. 24th c. B.C.) and his God Ningirsu discussed by McCarthy, *Treaty and Covenant,* 31.

call to become a kingdom of priests and minister to humanity as His firstborn son, and confirms its recalcitrance again by its harlotry at Beth Peor, Moses gives it a second covenant on the plains of Moab. Israel receives Deuteronomy on account of its hardness of heart, but the law aims to effect within them a cathartic circumcision of the heart and restore them to the status of sonship (Deut 30:1-7).[26]

This understanding of the centrality of the paternal-filial categories informing the representation of the divine-human covenant in Israel's creation theology and salvation history shows that some concept of real kinship, and thus of divinization or theōsis in some qualified sense underpins this theology and history, giving rise on occasion to the classical "son of God" passages that often puzzle interpreters (Gen 6:1-4; Exod 4:22; Exod 7:1; Deut 32:6; 2 Sam 7:14; Pss 2:7, 89:27, 82:6 [Matt 22:45, Mark 12:37, Luke 20:44]; Prov 30:4; Hos 11:1-3; Isa 45:9-11). Without understanding of the kinship terminology and the unity underpinning the structure of biblical narrative, these are misinterpreted as signifying "creatureliness, election and intimacy. It has no messianic connotation, and it is certainly not intended to signify divinity."[27]

One could begin to respond to such a conclusion by asking what the biblical authors and redactors wished to accomplish by designating the Israelite king as Son of God (2 Sam 7:14, Pss 2:7; 89:27). Nicholson says that Israel's covenantal ideology is developed precisely to demythologize primitive pagan beliefs and replace these by the idea that relationship with God can only be secured by ethical behavior (Pss 15, 24). But does ethical behavior create or arise from merely *metaphorical* sonship? Those who recognize that there is more than metaphor at play here suggest that the terminology is rooted in the language of Ancient Near Eastern (ANE) adoption customs.[28] But here too, the question arises as to whether the legal metaphors are fictions or whether they point at something real (as

---

[26] On the devout as sons or daughters of God, see Deut 14:1; Isa 1:2; 30:1; Hos 1:10.

[27] Herbert Haag, "'Son of God' in the Language and Thinking of the Old Testament," in *Jesus, Son of God? Concilium* 153.3 (1982) 36.

[28] M. W. Schoenberg, "HUIOTHESIA: The Adoptive Sonship of the Israelites," *AER* 143 (1960) 261–73; Gerald Cooke, "The Israelite King as Son of God," *ZAW* 73 (1961) 218–24; idem, "The Sons of (the) God(s)," *ZAW* 76 (1964) 22–47.

Hahn states, humans can only adopt other humans[29]), a true *imago Dei* inscribed into human nature that urges him to aspire for mature likeness unto God. Validating this argument leads Hahn to Mettinger's proposal[30] that the Israelite concept of royal divine sonship demythologizes ANE royal ideologies while transforming their mysterious religious idea through an *interpretatio israelitica* that combines elements of pagan symbolic rites with prophetically or sacerdotally mediated performative utterances that constitute something mysterious but real.[31] Thus, Israelite royal-sonship ideology, being both ethical and monotheistic, could have contributed to the later emergence of Christology and theōsis.

Theōsis and Old Testament Sapiential Anthropology

The second motif stressed by Fackenheim was that of commandment. Fackenheim sharply contrasts spirituality grounded on commandments with post-Enlightenment Kantian rationalism.[32] For Kant, the good is done only by him who understands what he is doing and wills it, and not by him who does it without understanding its inner reasons, i.e., only on faith. The problem with Kant's view is that it closes the individual in upon himself, for the ethical act is grounded on one's own understanding and will. Such grounds, it would seem, would provide no occasion for acts of love understood as sacrifices of one's own will, as self-surrenders to another. Fackenheim pleads for living on the basis of obedience because only such really opens and frees the self to respond to another. This validates the importance of circumcision of the heart and of an ascetical moment in the journey towards God, which is vital to the Christian understanding of theōsis.

---

[29] Hahn, "Kinship by Covenant," chap. 6.

[30] Tryggve N. D. Mettinger, *King and Messiah* (Lund: Gleerup, 1976) 254–93.

[31] Performative verbs or utterances, e.g.: "I hereby crown you" or "I confess," do not report or describe an action but perform or accomplish it. They cannot be true or false but require contexts, conventions, sincerity and uptake from the audience to be felicitous; cf. John L. Austin, *How to Do Things with Words* (Cambridge, Mass.: Harvard University Press, 1962) 130–39.

[32] Fackenheim, "Demythologizing," 16–27.

The core teaching of biblical wisdom literature, the principle that stands at the beginning, middle, and end of the book of Proverbs (Prov 1:7; 9:10; 15:33; 30:30) and at strategic points in Job, Ecclesiastes, and the so-called Deuteronomistic History, is the teaching that the fear of the Lord is the beginning of wisdom, and that understanding entails departure from evil. Alternatively it is the teaching that wisdom consists in the humble keeping and doing of God's words and commandments. These two formulations are synonymous inasmuch as one takes the commandments to heart by committing oneself to doing them, departing from evil. The fear of the Lord, humility and righteousness may be the root and initial stages of wisdom (Ps 111:10; Sir 1:18) but they are not its end. In scripture, *keeping* is normally a prerequisite for *knowing* (Gen 4:9; Exod 31:13; Deut 7:9; 8:2; Prov 3:1;[33] John 8:52, 55; 14:15; 2 Pet 1:8). For the end of keeping God's words is entry into their life-giving energies, into the joy of knowing and savoring their inner wisdom and goodness, gaining the ability to discriminate between things that lead to life and things that do not, and the capacity to bring peace-making judgment and to dispense life-sustaining counsel. Being ubiquitous in biblical wisdom, psalmody and salvation history, these patterns may be read back into the Garden of Eden story in Genesis 2–3 to help unravel the meaning of one of its multifold layers of wisdom.

The Hebrew Scriptures speak of man as being earth and dust (Gen 2.7; 3:19, 23; Job 34:15; Eccl 3:20; 12:7) and the LXX adds to this by describing man as "earthborn" and "kindred [to the] earth" (γηγενοῦς . . . ὁμοιοπαθῆ . . . γῆν, *gēgenous . . . homoiopathē . . . gēn*) in Wis 7:1, 3. This identification emphasizes humanity's lowly and humble origin, and is underscored by the observation that humanity turns into ashes, the residue of burnt wood or vegetation, so "human beings are dust and ashes" (Sir 17:32; cf. 10:9; Gen 18:27; Job 30:19; Wis 2:3).[34] The imagery suggests

---

[33] See also the connection between keeping and living, Prov 4:4; 7:1.

[34] The exegesis of scripture in this paragraph is largely indebted to Levi Khamor, *The Revelation of the Son of Man* (Petersham, Mass.: St. Bede's, 1989) passim, esp. 1–12, and *The Revelation of Bethlehem* (Petersham: St. Bede's, 1989) (authorship attributed to "Two Hermits") 37–41, 44–52. Summarizing these anthropological reflections is Gregory Glazov, "Biblical Anthropology and Medical Ethics," in *Proceedings of the 20th Anniversary of the Foundation of the Linacre Centre International Conference at Queen's College, Cambridge, 28–31 July, 1997*, ed. Luke Gormally (Linacre Centre Publications, 1999) 90–116.

that between the stages of initial dust and final dust and ashes, humanity exists in a more exalted state, which, carrying through the metaphor of vegetation, may be that of a lofty and glorious tree, or of something smaller like a vine, or even grain.

Such representations are invoked in scripture, especially in the sapiential and prophetic strata, to illustrate what von Rad calls the "nutshell of the Israelite theory of knowledge," namely, that the knowledge and wisdom of God begin with (Prov 1:7; 9:10; 15:33; 31:30; Job 28:28; Sir 1:13)—and are thus "rooted" in (Sir 1:18; Wis 3:15)—reverential fear of him who empowers humanity to depart from evil and to keep, in the face of all tribulation, His commandments and so, by righteousness, gain access to the waters of divine instruction (Psalm 1; Sir 24:23–33) enter into life (Deut 30:15–16).

Entry into life means transformation from lowly earth, that is, *soil*, into the full stature of an exalted tree of righteousness (Prov 11:30; Sir 24:13–19; Isa 61:3), a paradisal tree of life and knowledge (see the identification of the righteous with "the Lord's paradise, the trees of life" in *Pss. Sol.* 14:3, 4), or a fragrant vine of understanding (Sir 24:15, 17, 19), thus becoming capable of yielding the fruit of righteousness (Prov 3:9 LXX; Prov 13:2; *Pss. Sol.* 15:3; Hos 10:12), the fruit of knowledge and understanding of God (Isa 4:2; 27:6; 53:11; Sir 1:14; *4 Ezra* 8:6). Conversely, the tree that humanity is or is meant to be, however glorious or proud, withers or blows away (Ps 1:4; Isa 1:30; 27:10–11; Jer 17:6–10; Ezek 19:10–14), is cut down or burned up (Ezekiel 31; Isa 5:24; 6:13; Mal 4:1).

Even the Messianic hope is expressed in terms of the Branch from the stump of Jesse (Isa 11:1–2; Jer 23:5; 33:15; Zech 3:8; 6:12), the shoot and handiwork of God's hands that will repossess the land for all time (Isa 60:21 MT and LXX). The focus on humanity as soil and its transformation by diverse kinds of seed surfaces clearly in *4 Ezra* 4:29–39, which describes Adam's heart as "the field where the good has been sown" (4:29), which could have yielded a harvest of righteousness (v. 35) and understanding (8:6) had it held on to the good seed, but did not and still fails to do so because it is dominated by evil seed that was also sown in it "from the beginning" (4:30), and consequently burdening it with so much "fruit of ungodliness" (4:31). The sons of men spend their lives in the field from which Adam was taken (Gen 2:15, 3:23; cf. Matt 13:38). God has provided the seed and rain for joyous growth (Isa 55:10–13), but people often fail to receive it.

The anthropology informing this sapiential imagery may in turn be applied to the imagery and terminology of Genesis 2–3 to infer that Yahweh intended Adam, whom he fashioned from the dust of the earth and transferred into the Garden of Eden, to be transformed, via the holding and keeping, in righteousness, of the one simple word and commandment which he entrusted "upon him" into, as it were, a glorious and lofty paradisal tree of life and of knowledge, yielding the fruit of righteousness and knowledge of God. Adam's failure to enter into life and preserve the status of an "oak of righteousness" (Isa 61:3) derived not so much from a desire to "become like God," (God did, after all, create Adam in His own image and likeness), but, as in the case of the Pharaoh of Ezekiel 31, from the failure to become *really* like God by means of an inward, organic, transformative appropriation of godliness via holding onto God's words, opting, instead, to try to attain this status via an act that severs any organic link between what one does and what one is and thus to deny the ethically reflexive nature of human action (Prov 1:29–33; 12:14; Isa 3:10). By means of this process, he would not have become less human, just as soil does not become any less material by entering into the life of a seed that opens within it. But he would have become transhumanized—become more than he was—just as soil becomes more than it was, when it is transformed into a plant.

One may note a resonance with Jesus' explanation, by means of the Parable of the Sower (Matthew 13), of the principle for entering the kingdom of God—*receptivity* to the seed. As the understanding of this parable is prerequisite to understanding all the other parables (Mark 4:13), it provides the foundation for soteriology and theōsis. Theōsis begins with the humble opening up of oneself to the reception of God's word, and progresses through the keeping and cultivation, i.e., the doing of the word (James 1:22–27). Given the conditions of "life in the field" (Matt 13:38), this necessitates a certain watchfulness and asceticism with regard to whatever is noxious and injurious, but as a keeper perseveres in truth and righteousness, he matures in loving-kindness, fulfilling the potential of humble humanity by attaining to the full stature of divine sonship. Transformed, metamorphosed or divinized by the word, he remains human throughout. The source of the seed remains mysteriously near in the form of the agent who sowed the seed-word, but also transcendent inasmuch as the spiritual animating principle of any living organism transcends its matter.

The biblical anthropological models taken from covenant salvation history and wisdom narratives provide many bases for a biblical theōsis theology. Before evaluating their relevance to Christian theōsis theology, it is necessary to clarify how much, in fact, Christian theōsis was grounded not just on explicit texts about transformation and divine adoption, but on teachings about the hidden, seed-like transformative energies of divine words and the potencies of human covenantal obedience.

Bibliography

Alfeyev, Hilarion. "The Patristic Heritage and Modernity," Paper delivered at the *9th International Conference on Russian monasticism and spirituality,* Bose Monastery (Italy), 20 September 2001. Available at www.orthodoxeurope.org/print/11/1/2.aspx.

Allison, Dale C., Jr., *The New Moses: A Matthean Typology.* Minneapolis: Fortress, 1993.

Austin, John L. *How to Do Things with Words.* Cambridge, Mass.: Harvard University Press, 1962.

Bonhoeffer, Dietrich. *Letters and Papers from Prison.* Edited by Eberhard Bethge. Translated by Reginald H. Fuller. New York: Macmillan, 1953.

Bouyer, Louis. *The Christian Mystery: From Pagan Myth to Christian Mysticism.* Edinburgh: T. & T. Clark, 1989.

Cooke, Gerald. "The Israelite King as Son of God." *ZAW* 73 (1961) 218–24.

———. "The Sons of (the) God(s)." *ZAW* 76 (1964) 22–47.

Cross, Frank Moore. *Canaanite Myth and Hebrew Epic: Essays in the History of the Religion of Israel.* Cambridge, Mass.: Harvard University Press, 1973.

Golitzin, Alexandre. "Scriptural Images of the Church: an Eastern Orthodox Reflection" (unpublished, 2001, written at the request of the Ecclesiology section of Faith and Order, World Council of Churches; available at www.marquette.edu/maqom/church).

Eichrodt, Walther. *The Theology of the Old Testament.* 2 vols. Translated by J. A. Baker. London: SCM, 1961.

Ellenson, David. "A Jewish Legal Authority Addresses Jewish-Christian Dialogue: Two Responses of Rabbi Moshe Feinstein" (Jacob Rader Marcus Center of the American Jewish Archives, 2001. Available at www.huc.edu/aja/00-4.htm).

Fackenheim, Emil. "Demythologizing and Remythologizing in Jewish Experience: Reflections Inspired by Hegel's Philosophy." In *Myth and Philosophy*, 16–27. Edited by George F. McLean, OMI. Vol. 45 of Proceedings of the American Catholic Philosophical Association; The Office of the National Secretary of the Association; The Catholic University of America, 1971.

Glazov, Gregory. "Biblical Anthropology and Medical Ethics." In *Proceedings of the 20th Anniversary of the Foundation of the Linacre Centre International Conference at Queen's College, Cambridge, 28–31 July, 1997*. Edited by Luke Gormally. Linacre Centre Publications, 1999.

Haag, Herbert. "'Son of God' in the Language and Thinking of the Old Testament." *In Jesus, Son of God?*, 1–36. Concilium 153.3 (1982).

Hahn, Scott W. "Kinship By Covenant: A Biblical Theological Study of Covenant Types and Texts in the Old and New Testaments." Ph.D. Dissertation, Dept. Theology, Marquette University, 1995.

Khamor, Levi. *The Revelation of Bethlehem*. Petersham, Mass.: St. Bede's, 1989. Authorship attributed to "Two Hermits."

———. *The Revelation of the Son of Man*. Petersham, Mass.: St. Bede's, 1989.

Levenson, Jon D. "Why Jews Are Not Interested in Biblical Theology." In *The Hebrew Bible, the Old Testament, and Historical Criticism: Jews and Christians in Biblical Studies*, 33–61. Louisville: Westminster, 1993.

Mayes, A. D. H., and R. B. Salters, editors. *Covenant As Context: Essays in Honour of E. W. Nicholson*. Oxford: Oxford University Press, 2003.

McCarthy, Dennis J., SJ. *Old Testament Covenant: A Survey of Current Opinions*. Richmond, Virg.: John Knox, 1972.

———. *Treaty and Covenant*. Analecta Biblica 21A. Rev. Ed. Rome: Biblical Institute Press, 1978.

Mendenhall, George E. *Law and Covenant in Israel and the Ancient Near East*. Pittsburgh, Penn.: The Biblical Colloquium, 1955.

Mettinger, Tryggve N. D. *King and Messiah*. Lund: Gleerup, 1976.

Nicholson, Ernest W. *God and His People: Covenant and Theology in the Old Testament*. Oxford: Clarendon, 1986.

Moses Nachmanides (Ramban). Translated by Éric Smilévitch. *La dispute de Barcelone: suivi du commentaire sur Esaïe 52–53* (*Vikuach ha-Ramban*) Lagrasse, France: Verdier, 1984.

Perlitt, Lothar. *Bundestheologie im Alten Testament*. WMANT 36. Neukirchen-Vluyn: Neukirchener, 1969.

Ratzinger, Joseph Cardinal. "Is the Eucharist a Sacrifice?" In *The Debate on Sacraments*, 35–40. Concilium 4/3 (1967).

Schoenberg, M. W. "HUIOTHESIA: The Adoptive Sonship of the Israelites." *AER* 143 (1960) 261–73.

Ware, Kallistos. *The Orthodox Way.* Crestwood, N.Y.: St. Vladimir's Seminary Press, 1995.

Weber, Max. *Ancient Judaism.* Translated and edited by Hans H. Gerth and Don Martindale. Glencoe, Ill.: Free Press, 1952.

Wellhausen, Julius. *Prolegomena to the History of Ancient Israel.* New York: Meridian, 1957 (1889).

Second Peter's Notion of Divine Participation

Stephen Finlan

For a Christian writer around 100 CE to say, "you may become participants of the divine nature" (2 Pet 1:4), was to evoke not only biblical images, but also concepts of divinization that were central to the leading Hellenistic philosophies—Middle-Platonism and Stoicism. Of course, Second Peter's[1] is a Christian teaching, but here he uses terminology that is recognizable from the Greek philosophical traditions, and this should not be overlooked in studies of Second Peter.

Second Peter has no hesitancy about using Middle Platonic and Stoic religious concepts and terms to express his biblical monotheism, but what he envisions by "participation in the divine" is far from obvious. It is not clear whether it means the "divinization" of the believer. One should suspend bias, investigate the relevant biblical and nonbiblical texts, and examine the message of Second Peter itself.

I leave aside almost entirely the "apotheosis" or deification of heroes and emperors, since both Jews and Christians recoiled from these notions.

---

[1] I use the term "Second Peter" to designate both the unknown author, and the epistle itself.

In reality, there is probably not a strict dividing line between the respectable philosophies (Platonism and Stoicism) and the popular religions, but I will maintain this barrier anyway, since it was a barrier that the philosophers and theologians themselves tried to maintain, and which we can observe when we study Hellenistic influences on biblical authors.

Middle-Platonic Background

An important connection between Plato and 2 Pet 1:4 is in the latter's reference to "escap[ing] the corruption that is in the world because of lust." That last term is ἐπιθυμία *epithymia*, the same word that Plato uses to describe "appetite" or "desire," the lowest level of a human being.[2] Second Peter seems to share the Platonic instinct that there is a high and noble level associated with correct knowledge, and a lowly level associated with *epithymia*.

The superiority of soul to body is a constant theme in Plato's thought; the body is like a tomb for the soul.[3] He writes, "we ought to try to escape from earth to the dwelling of the gods as quickly as we can; and to escape is to become like God, to become righteous and holy and wise."[4] But it is a mistake to think of Plato as fundamentally escapist.[5] His most celebrated work, *The Republic*, affirms that, rather than ascending to more spiritual levels, the spiritual person has the higher duty of staying in human community and helping others.[6] Social obligation and virtue are the central focus of several of his works.[7]

But the afterlife involves real community with gods. The souls that have not been corrupted in this life, but "who truly love wisdom,"[8] go on to find "gods for companions and guides."[9] Even clearer is the expression

---

[2] *Republic,* 437.

[3] *Gorgias* 493A; cf. *Phaedo* 67A-E.

[4] *Theaetatus* 176B, from *Plato*, vol. 2, tr. H. N. Fowler. LCL (London: Wm. Heinemann, 1921) 129.

[5] As N. T. Wright does. See *The Resurrection of the Son of God* (Minneapolis: Fortress, 2003) 355.

[6] *Republic,* 519E.

[7] Certainly the *Meno, Republic, Statesman, Crito,* and *Laws.*

[8] *Phaedo* 82C.

[9] *Phaedo* 108B; cf. 111B.

found in Plato's *Laws*, despite his taking a generally down-to-earth approach in this work: his protagonist advises that "what god wants is that we should be as like him as possible."[10]

Imitation of God is a major theme of Middle Platonism, which seeks to systematize Plato's metaphysics and theology, and which heightens the notion of deification. These are articulated most vividly by the prolific authors Plutarch of Chaeroneia and Philo of Alexandria. Plutarch uses the same adjective that Second Peter uses in our key passage—θεῖος *theios*, "divine." Plutarch uses θεῖος *theios* to describe the incorruption, power, virtue, and reason of God.[11] Plutarch teaches that humans can take on the first three of these characteristics, "incorruption, power, and virtue; and the most revered, the divinest of these, is virtue."[12] The goal of life is to come to resemble God. In order to do this, it is necessary to repudiate sensuality and selfishness.[13] Spiritual progress means imitating God, taking on God's righteous, rational, controlled nature. This results in an actual transformation, even taking on God's incorruption.[14] God is the perfect model. Deification involves progress, and is available only for a few:

> A few good men, specially honoured by the deity, may themselves become Daemons and act as guardian angels to others. . . . The better souls undergo a transformation from men to heroes, from heroes to daemons, and from daemons, some few souls, being purified through prolonged practice of virtue, are brought to a participation in the divine nature itself.[15]

---

[10] *Laws* 715E; from Christopher Rowe, *An Introduction to Greek Ethics* (London: Hutchinson & Co., 1976) 97.

[11] James M. Starr, *Sharers in Divine Nature: 2 Peter 1:4 in Its Hellenistic Context.* Coniectanea Biblical 33 (Stockholm: Almqvist & Wiksell International, 2003) 128.

[12] *Aristides* 6.2–3; from L. Ann Jervis, "Becoming Like God through Christ: Discipleship in Romans," in *Patterns of Discipleship in the New Testament*, ed. Richard N. Longenecker (Grand Rapids: Eerdmans, 1996) 147.

[13] *Genio* 585A, 591D–E; *De virt* 442; *Profectus* 83F; Starr, *Sharers*, 139; cf. Plato, *Phaedo* 82C, 83B.

[14] Starr, *Sharers*, 137–38.

[15] Plu., *De Defectu* 415 B–C; from John Oakesmith, *The Religion of Plutarch* (London: Longmans, Green, & Co., 1902) 172.

Philo of Alexandria is, in my view, the most interesting Middle Platonic thinker, utilizing both Platonic and Stoic terms and allegorizing, while remaining connected to Jewish monotheism. Philo draws heavily upon Plato and the interpreters of Plato for ethics and metaphysics alike. Philo uses the adjective *theios* to speak of God's justice and mercy, as we might expect, but also to describe the special status of biblical figures, especially Moses, who was "a piece of work beautiful and godlike, a model for those who are willing to copy it."[16]

But imitation of God is possible for anyone: solitude is an opportunity for "those who . . . desire to find God . . . to become like his blessed and happy nature."[17] Those draw near to God "who regard it as their goal to be fully conformed to God who begat them."[18] People are "nearly related to God."[19] God "made man partaker of kinship with Himself in mind and reason"[20] ("kinship" here is συγγενεία *syngeneia*, not κοινωνός *koinōnos*). The human intellect is "an impression of, or a fragment or a ray of that blessed nature."[21]

More than the average person, however, the prophet is a "friend of God," and "would naturally partake [here it is κοινωνὸν *koinōnon*] of God himself."[22] Moses, again, was "full of the divine spirit and under the influence of that spirit."[23] This is not just spiritualizing language for a purely mental experience. Philo believes that the human mind is temporarily "removed . . . . at the arrival of the divine [θεῖον] Spirit, but is again restored to its previous habitation when that Spirit departs."[24] Thus, there are two kinds of theōsis in Philo: prophetic oraculation, which

---

[16] *Mos.* 1.158; from Jervis, "Becoming Like God," 148.

[17] *Abr.* 87.

[18] *Opif.* 144; from *Philo*, vol. 1, tr. F. Colson and G. Whitaker, LCL (Cambridge, Mass.: Harvard University Press, 1929) 115.

[19] *Mos.* 1.279.

[20] *Opif.* 77; LCL edition.

[21] *Opif.* 146; Hendrickson edition.

[22] *Mos.* 1.156.

[23] *Mos.* 1.175.

[24] *Her.* 265; cf. *QG* 3.9; *Spec.* 4.49. See Gregory E. Sterling, "'Wisdom Among the Perfect': Creation Traditions in Alexandrian Judaism and Corinthian Christianity," *NovT* 37 (1995) 381; Carl R. Holladay, *Theios Aner in Hellenistic-Judaism: A Critique of the Use of This Category in New Testament Christology*, SBL Dissertation Series 40 (Missoula, Mont.: Scholars, 1977) 158.

is an extraordinary but momentary divinization; and the gradual divinization or "conforming to God" that results from lifelong practice of reason and piety.

Stoic Growth in Virtue

Although having a weak theology (that is, concept of God), Stoicism was intensely religious, and had a strong concept of deification, or rather, of reunion with the Logos. Further, Stoicism had more followers, and at more levels of society, than did Middle Platonism, which was embraced mostly by the highly educated.

The Stoics believed that Reason (the Greek word is λόγος *Logos*) pervaded the world. Human reason is connected with this Logos;[25] it is "a part of the mind of God that has descended in to the body."[26] Epictetus said, "You are a principal work, a fragment of God Himself, you have in yourself a part of Him. . . . You bear God about with you, poor wretch, and know it not."[27]

There can be little doubt that Second Peter was living in "a pervasively Hellenistic environment."[28] Even his use of φύσις *fysis* in our key verse (1:4), like his use of φυσικός *fysikos* in 2:12, "employs the vocabulary of Hellenistic piety," specifically the Stoic variety.[29] To be "in agreement with Nature" (φύσις *fysis*) was the supreme virtue for a Stoic, because nature is ruled by reason, and reason is God, more or less.[30]

Some Stoics speak of God as a personal being, for instance Epictetus, who says, "Rational creatures . . . are by nature fitted to share in the society of God, being connected with Him by the bond of reason—why should he not call himself a citizen of the universe and a son of God?"[31]

---

[25] J. Daryl Charles, *Virtue amidst Vice: The Catalog of Virtues in 2 Peter 1*, JSNT Sup 150 (Sheffield: Sheffield Academic, 1997) 102, citing Epictetus, *Diss.* 1.20.5; 2.20.21.

[26] Starr, *Sharers*, 159, summarizing Seneca, *Epistle* 120.14.

[27] Epict. *Disc.* 2.8; from *The Stoic and Epicurean Philosophers*, ed., tr. Whitney J. Oates (New York: The Modern Library, 1940) 295.

[28] Charles, *Virtue amidst Vice*, 47.

[29] Charles, *Virtue amidst Vice*, 101, with note 17.

[30] Edwyn Bevan, *Stoics and Skeptics* (Oxford: Clarendon, 1913) 55.

[31] Epict., *Disc.* 1.9; *Stoic and Epicurean*, 240.

But the general thrust of Stoicism is pantheistic, identifying the divine with the active principle (Logos) and with Nature (which is run by the Logos). Most Stoics cannot be said to have a *personal* God; everything that happens in Nature is a manifestation of the Logos, so everything in Nature is equally divine. The Divine is the *active* principle behind Nature or Kosmos (world): the "seminal principle of the world," or a "designing fire" (πῦρ τεχνικόν *pyr technikon*).[32] Greek polytheism is made to fit into this system; the gods are seen (or explained away) as reflections of the Logos. Imitation of the gods is a paramount value for the Stoics. In fact, "the only sufficient worship of the gods is to imitate them."[33] However, one can argue that, "the theistic language is mere metaphor," and that, with these explanations, "the gods are abolished. . . . The Deity in which he [Cleanthes] truly believes is the cosmos."[34] But this is not sufficient to account for a Seneca or an Epictetus.

Some early Stoics had difficulty with the idea of progress. Their monism indicated that one was either in harmony or out of harmony with Logos, and if one was truly in harmony with reason, one was the equal of Jupiter.[35] The deification of the sage really grows out of Stoic "deification of human virtue"[36]; to be truly virtuous was the highest possible condition for god or human. And later Stoics allowed that there could be progress toward this goal. Still, it remains close to pantheism. Deification is really just reunion with the Divine. The soul will return to the Divine when it dies, although there is not much notion of individual identity; this is more like reabsorption into the All. Thus, "death is not a great change from what now is . . . . *You* will not be, but something else will be, of which the world has need"[37]—a very unselfish sentiment.

Although ostensibly materialist (that is, believing everything, even Logos, was physical), Stoic philosophy was rich with religious thought and feeling, including in its exhortation toward moral and mental

---

[32] Diogenes Laertius, *Lives* 7.134–37; Starr, *Sharers*, 152.

[33] Starr, *Sharers*, 158; citing Seneca, *Ep.* 95.50.

[34] Ludwig Edelstein, *The Meaning of Stoicism* (Cambridge, Mass.: Harvard University Press, 1966) 34.

[35] Jacques Maritain, *Moral Philosophy*, tr. Joseph W. Evans (New York: Scribner's, 1964) 55.

[36] Maritain, *Moral Philosophy*, 54.

[37] Epict., *Disc.* 3.24; taken from Cyril Bailey, *Phases in the Religion of Ancient Rome* (Berkeley: University of California Press, 1932) 242.

betterment. Everyone received "seeds of virtue" or "seeds of reason" at birth,[38] but virtue needs to be developed, perfected, or it only gets practiced intermittently. Reason may be inherent, but virtue is acquired. What is needed is a complete change in one's behavior, even a conversion of one's life purpose, accompanied by the joining of a new community,[39] ideas that resonate with Second Peter. But where a Stoic would say that one's inclinations must become more rational, Second Peter would say one needs to "grow in the grace and knowledge of our Lord"; in fact, that is his final exhortation (3:18). Knowledge is central, but it is a particular kind of knowledge.

As Stoics stress the necessity of choosing the mental over the sensual life, Second Peter articulates a choosing of "goodness . . . and self-control" (1:5–6) over "dissipation . . . adultery . . . . greed . . . . licentious desires" (2:13–14, 18). The virtues list in 2 Pet 1:5–7 is easily the "most Hellenistic of the NT ethical lists."[40] Some of its words are rare in the LXX, but common in Greek moralizing literature. After "faith" and "goodness," Second Peter lists γνώσει *gnōsei* or "knowledge," a common term in Hellenistic philosophy (as in *C.H.* 13[41]), and then ἐγκράτεια *egkrateia* or "self-control"—one of the principal Stoic virtues. Next come "endurance," "godliness," "mutual affection," and the list culminates on "love," the supreme Christian virtue, so it is safe to say that Christian distinctiveness is clearly evident in the first and last terms. Inside the list, however, are words that are as much or more at home in a Stoic list of virtues.

In 2 Pet 2:22 there is an evident reference to Prov 26:11 (a dog returning to its vomit), but Second Peter attaches a nonbiblical, "oriental proverb"[42] about a sow returning to the mud. Immediately after paraphrasing Ps 90:4 with "one day is like a thousand years" (3:8), Second Peter speaks of the heavens passing away, the elements being dissolved with fire (3:10, 12). This is a really fascinating conflation of influences, seeming to combine Jewish apocalyptic with Stoic apocalyptic, possibly

---

[38] Musonius Rufus, *Fr.* 2 and Seneca, *Ep.* 94.29, respectively; Starr, *Sharers*, 163.

[39] Troels Engberg-Pedersen, *Paul and the Stoics* (Louisville: Westminster John Knox, 2000) 102–9, 125.

[40] Richard J. Bauckham, *Jude, 2 Peter*, WBC 50 (Waco: Word, 1983) 187.

[41] Bauckham, *Jude, 2 Peter*, 186.

[42] According to Richard Bauckham's footnote in the *HarperCollins Study Bible* (1993) 2289.

using ἐκπύρωσις *ekpyrōsis*,[43] the Stoic technical term for the final conflagration. At any rate, Second Peter accepts the notion of a final, violent day of judgment, similar to what is described in Jewish apocalyptic works such as *First Enoch*. And the approach of the end "like a thief" has a Pauline sound (1 Thess 5:2). Second Peter's theology is consistent with biblical monotheism, not with Stoic pantheism. Still, a fiery destruction followed by a cosmic re-formation does have a Stoic overtone. Pagan Hellenism is a suggestion that refuses to go away, despite the presence of specifically Jewish influences.

Of course, in theology *per se*, Second Peter departs sharply from Stoicism: he affirms the sovereignty and free will of God (not an impersonal "reason" in the cosmos), and the certainty of a judgment day under a personal God, not a mechanistic collapse of all things. Second Peter is confident about the personal God having spoken through the prophets (1:19) and manifested Godself in the Lord Jesus Christ.

It is entirely possible that Second Peter is arguing against the allegorizing stories and re-interpreted myths told by the Stoics, when he argues against "cleverly devised myths" (1:16). He could be attacking those to whom he was formerly close, ideologically. Additionally, some scholars see an attack on Epicurean skepticism in 3:3–4, 9.[44] Second Peter may be distancing himself from his former philosophical comrades. Some of these comrades may have joined him in converting to Christianity, but then slid back to pagan philosophy, like a dog returning to its vomit (2 Pet 2:22). Second Peter 2 sounds somewhat Stoic (even if directed against Stoics), but sounds even more like the way that Jewish apocalyptic inveighs against sin.

The sharp contrast between godliness and the sensuality of the world found in Second Peter recalls similar rhetoric in Middle Platonic, Stoic,[45] and Hellenistic Jewish writings.[46] Anti-sensualism itself does not signal to

---

[43] There is significant variation among the ancient manuscripts for 2 Pet 3:10–12. They clearly speak of the heavens and the earth being dissolved or burned up, but only a minority of scholars argue for the Stoic term ἐκπύρωσις *ekpyrōsis* being present; Bauckham (*Jude, 2 Peter*, 317–18) mentions Olivier and Windisch.

[44] Charles, *Virtue amidst Vice*, 45–46; "Epicureans were known in terms of their denial of divine judgment" (Neyrey, *2 Peter, Jude*, 122).

[45] "You bear Him about within you and are unaware that you are defiling Him with unclean thoughts and foul actions" (Epict., *Disc.* 2.8; *Stoic and Epicurean*, 295); cf. *Disc.* 2.18; Diogenes Laertius, *Lives* 7.110, 113.

[46] *Testament of Reuben* 5–6; Philo, *Ebr.* 5–6; idem, *Spec.* 1.206; 4.89–91.

us whether the influence upon Second Peter's mind is "pagan" or Jewish. Second Peter repeatedly chooses terminology that is common in "pagan" Hellenistic literature, but his eschatology closely resembles that of apocalyptic Judaism.

Apocalyptic Judaism

Some scholars want to treat lightly all of the "Hellenistic garb" found in Second Peter, arguing that his apocalyptic shows biblical, not Hellenistic, roots.[47] While I think the Hellenism is more than merely "garb," I can accept the notion that the main Hellenistic influence upon the author is Hellenistic *Judaism*, especially the apocalyptic genre. The original meaning of the Greek word "apocalyptic" is "revelatory," but since much of the literature that spoke of revelation also spoke of God and God's angels separating the good people from the evil people, carrying out an end-time judgment, and re-making the world, the term "apocalyptic" has naturally taken on this implication of end-time catastrophe and judgment, and I am intending to include that implication when I use the term here.

Echoing the popular apocalyptic literature of the time, Second Peter promises that incineration is "coming to the ungodly" (2:6), who will be destroyed like animals (2:12), sent "to the deepest darkness" (2:17). Yet there is no hint of any knowledge of covenant thinking or of the importance of holy days, things one would expect from a Galilean Jew. Despite the reference to prophecy fulfilled (1:19), no specific prophecy is given; and despite a knowledge of biblical stories (in 2 Pet 2:4–8, 15–16), some details are peculiar (Balaam's father's name is misspelled in 2:15). These peculiarities in Jewish knowledge tend to suggest a pre-Christian identity as either a non-Palestinian Jew or a devout Gentile who was being instructed in Judaism.

Second Peter's apocalypticism bears resemblances to some passages in Isaiah, but with only one certain quotation.[48] But the allusions to the

---

[47] Charles, *Virtue amidst Vice*, 47 n.14, agreeing with R. Bauckham, E. Loevestam, and M. Green.

[48] The heavens rolling up (Isa 34:4), or vanishing like smoke (Isa 51:6), may be echoed in 2 Pet 3:10, 12, where the earth passes away, dissolves. The weakness of these parallels is strengthened, however, by the one actual quotation: the Lord executing judgment

influential apocalyptic book we call *First Enoch* are more obvious: 2 Pet 2:4 speaks of the rebel angels being "committed . . . to chains of deepest darkness to be kept until the judgment," which seems to derive from "Azazel" being "b[ou]nd . . . and throw[n] into the darkness," then covered with rocks until "he may be sent into the fire on the great day of judgment" (*1 En.* 10:4–6).[49] Second Peter goes on to speak of the judgment of the ungodly, lawless, and lustful (2:6–11), recalling the several Enochian chapters that speak of the punishment of the lustful and violent rebel angels, the "Watchers" (*1 Enoch* 9–14, 18, 21). The righteous believers are promised that they will "be partners with the good-hearted people of heaven" (104:6); God "and my son are united with them forever in the upright paths" (105:2). There will be a "new heaven" (94:16), a "new creation" (72:1).

Not all Hellenistic Jewish literature shares the same apocalyptic viewpoint, or uses the same philosophic strategies. There is a work very different from *First Enoch* which sheds light on 2 Pet 1:4. *Pseudo-Phocylides* is a moralizing teaching text, presenting both Jewish and Hellenistic ideas in a thoroughly Hellenistic guise, ascribing the authorship to a Greek writer (Phocylides[50]). Far from being an effort to persuade Gentiles to consider the "philosophy of Moses" (as with Philo), this is an effort to instill principles of right and wrong, without distinguishing Greek from Jewish philosophy. It has a divinization passage that seems to blend Jewish bodily resurrection with Platonic godlikeness. *Pseudo-Phocylides* 103–4 says, "We hope that the remains of the departed will soon come to the light . . . and afterward they will become gods [θεοὶ τελέθονται *theoi telethontai*]."[51] The sentences that immediately follow this one sound very Hellenistic, where the spirit is "on loan," and people are destined to "become gods."

---

with fire and making a new heavens and new earth (Isa 66:16, 22) is repeated in 2 Pet 3:7, 13. Most of the individual elements in 2 Pet 3:7–13 are independent of Isaiah.

[49] Translated by E. Isaac, in *The Old Testament Pseudepigrapha*, vol. 1, ed. James H. Charlesworth (New York: Doubleday, 1983) 17.

[50] An authority on ethics cited by Plato and Aristotle (*Rep.* 407a7; *Pol.* IV.II.1295b); John J. Collins, *Jewish Wisdom in the Hellenistic Age*, OTL (Louisville: Westminster John Knox, 1997) 159.

[51] P. W. van der Horst, *The Sentences of Pseudo-Phocylides: With Introduction and Commentary*, SVTP 4 (Leiden: Brill, 1978) 185.

Yet elsewhere *Pseudo-Phocylides* restates certain moral principles that can be found in the Pentateuch and Proverbs, without ever giving a hint that these are Jewish in origin. Since the whole piece is presented as a work of Greek wisdom, and Jewish ideas are never identified as such,[52] and since its divinization concept looks so Greek, its author seems to be interested in assimilating to Greek culture. In fact, there may be a significant parallel between conceptualization and socialization. The author's assimilation to Greek culture seems to be paralleled by his concept of assimilation to the Divine; one is drawn into God, much like one is drawn into the universal culture!

Second Peter is not assimilationist, nor does he speak of becoming gods or God, but of partaking of the divine *nature*, which seems to mean divine character, knowledge of the Savior, and proper self-controlled and ethical behavior. Second Peter has a different social strategy from *Pseudo-Phocylides*, but there is a point of similarity, in that both assert their truths as *universal* principles, not tied to the Jewish nation or the Mosaic covenant. In *that* sense, both are Hellenistic; Hellenism is characterized by the search for universal principles and universal community. Second Peter, however, has a particular ideology and social group—Christianity—distinct from popular Hellenistic culture, and in that sense is very different from *Pseudo-Phocylides*, though both use Hellenistic ideas.

Both of these works, as well as *1 Enoch*, envision the salvation of righteous Gentiles. *First Enoch* says that the Son of Man, the Chosen One, will be "the light of the gentiles and he will become the hope of those who are sick in their hearts. All those who dwell upon the earth shall fall and worship before him" (48:4-5). "He shall proclaim peace to you in the name of the world that is to become" (71:15).

For *1 Enoch* and 2 Peter, there is a severe dividing line between the good and the evil people, but this is an ideological and moral divide, not an ethnic one. *First Enoch* is still closely attached to Jewish identity, but the criterion of judgment that is spelled out is always ethical, not national. Those who are going to be punished are "governors, kings, high officials, and landlords" (*1 En.* 63:12), "those who amass gold and silver" (94:7), and the "powerful people who coerce the righteous" (96:8).

---

[52] Collins, *Jewish Wisdom*, 176.

Pseudo-Phocylides alerts us to a linkage between theology and sociology, but, of course, notions of deification can be had by people of greatly divergent social strategies and theologies. *First Enoch*, with its intense moral resentment of oppressive outsiders, strongly suggests a sectarian social profile, while *Pseudo-Phocylides'* instinct for moral education and ostensible Greek identity implies an assimilationist strategy. In the social dimension, Second Peter is closer to Enoch's sectarianism.

The lack of lofty intellectualizing in Second Peter blocks the application of the label "Platonic." The absence of even a hint of any notion that nature is to be identified with God, shows an ability to dispense with fundamental Stoic principles. The strong perpetuation of Jewish literary themes, along with the absence of any interest in the temple cult or holy days, suggests diaspora Judaism as the most likely social background for the author. But we cannot understand Second Peter if we do not explore his specifically Christian beliefs.

Pauline Parallels; Petrine Disputes

There is a peculiar kind of Pauline influence. Second Peter clearly borrows from certain portions of the letters of Paul, but shows no hint of any notion of justification, substitution, typology, fulfillment of promises made to Abraham, or Jesus as a Second Adam—the distinctive soteriology and salvation history of Paul, yet Second Peter does share some of Paul's ideas about the Second Coming, moral purification, and divinization of the believer. In any case, Second Peter's connections to the letters of Paul are much more numerous than his links to First Peter. Just a few of them are: salvation being "bought" (forms of the verb ἀγοράζω *agorazō*, 2 Pet 2:1; 1 Cor 6:20; and of course, this *is* a soteriological image); something "stored up" for destruction (forms of the verb θησαυρίζω *thēsaurizō*, 2 Pet 3:7; Rom 2:5[53]); being a slave to corruption (φθορά *fthora*, 2 Pet 2:19; Rom 8:21). One of the last theological points in Second Peter, being "found by him ... without spot or blemish (ἀμώμητος *amōmētos*)" (3:14), may owe something to Paul's "be blameless (ἄμεμπτος *amemptos*)

---

[53] Jerome H. Neyrey, *2 Peter, Jude: A New Translation with Introduction and Commentary*, AB 37C (New York: Doubleday, 1993) 133, where a number of other parallels are listed.

. . . at the coming of our Lord Jesus" (1 Thess 3:13; cf. 5:23; Phil 2:15). The words are formed from different roots, but they sound similar and have similar meanings.

Not all apparent connections to Paul, however, are certain. The image of "body" as "tent" (2 Pet 1:13-14: τὸ σκήνωμα; cf. 2 Cor 5:1, 4: τὸ σκῆνος) occurs as a metaphor in Greek (Hippocrates[54] and Hermeticism[55]) and Hellenistic Jewish literature (Philo[56] and Wisdom 9:15[57]).

But Second Peter does have connections to Pauline terminology. The term "participants" (κοινωνοὶ *koinōnoi*; 2 Pet 1:4) is common in Paul: "ye are partakers (κοινωνοὶ *koinōnoi*) of the sufferings" (2 Cor 1:7 KJV); "you share (συγκοινωνούς *sygkoinōnous*) in God's grace" (Phil 1:7). There is a conceptual, but not terminological, connection between taking on God's *nature* (2 Pet 1:4) and believers being "conformed (συμμόρφους *symmorfous*) to the image of his Son" and "conformed to the body of his glory" (Rom 8:29 and Phil 3:21, respectively), and to "this mortal body put[ting] on immortality" (1 Cor 15:53). Although Paul is largely referring to the afterlife, he does see the process beginning in this lifetime: believers reflect "the glory of the Lord," and are "being transformed into the same image from one degree of glory to another" (2 Cor 3:18). Christians "have the mind of Christ" (1 Cor 2:16), or *need* to have it (Phil 2:5). They can discern the will of God when they are "transformed by the renewing of your minds" (Rom 12:2).

Second Peter says that the ignorant do not correctly understand Paul, "to their own destruction" (3:16). Those who "exploit you" (2:3) were formerly on "the straight road" (2:15), and knew "the way of righteousness" (2:21), but now, "many will follow their licentious ways, and because of these teachers the way of truth will be maligned" (2:1). In Second Peter's opinion, these apostate Christians are sexually immoral, and are bringing the Christian message into disrepute. Though not assimilationist, Second Peter is sensitive to what outsiders think of Christians.

---

[54] *Aph.* 8.18; from Alfred Plummer, *A Critical and Exegetical Commentary on the Second Epistle of St. Paul to the Corinthians.* ICC (Edinburgh: T. & T. Clark, 1915) 142.

[55] *C.H.* 13.12, 15; David E. Aune, "Anthropological Duality in the Eschatology of 2 Cor 4:16–5:10," in *Paul Beyond the Judaism/Hellenism Divide*, ed. Troels Engberg-Pedersen (Louisville: Westminster John Knox, 2001) 225 and 312 n.55.

[56] Using, instead, the term *oikos* (*Somn.* 1.20); from Plummer, *Second Epistle*, 142.

[57] Aune, "Anthropological Duality," 225; Plummer, *Second Epistle*, 142.

There is clearly an intra-Christian fight over who is the true inheritor of the apostolic tradition, who presents "the way of truth." To claim to be Peter is certainly to make an authority claim.[58] Second Peter attacks the notion that "scripture is a matter of one's own interpretation" (1:20). He is attempting to foreclose interpretation by some people, equating "false prophets" of the past with "destructive opinions" in the present (2:1). Everything is at stake in interpretation; wrong interpretation leads to destruction (3:16).

Knowledge of Christ

The prime religious value in Second Peter, the key to spiritual transformation, is "knowledge of Christ." The principal summarizing passages all say something about knowledge. In 2 Pet 1:2, the author wishes "the knowledge (ἐπίγνωσις *epignōsis*)[59] of God and our Lord Jesus" on his readers. Ἐπίγνωσις was the word used in Hos 6:6 LXX for what God most desires—knowledge of God, the loss of which is deadly (Hos 4:1, 6).

Knowledge (γνῶσις *gnōsis*) is in the middle of Second Peter's virtue list, which begins with faith (1:5) and ends with love (1:7). Lack of these virtues means one is "near-sighted and blind" (1:9); such people "are like irrational animals [who] do not understand" (2:12). Christians "have escaped the defilements of the world through the knowledge (ἐπίγνωσις *epignōsis*) of our Lord and Savior Jesus Christ" (2:20). Escaping the corruption that is in the world is the primary religious need. For Second Peter, divinization means escaping such corruption, and taking on a Godly character.

This does not take place in a protected environment, but in treacherous waters. "Knowing Christ" requires successful navigation past "cleverly devised myths" (1:16) and "deceptive words"[60] (2:3), linked with a strange sensualist religiosity (2:10-19; 3:4) and with a distortion of Pauline teaching

---

[58] Charles tries to downplay the fact (*Virtue amidst Vice*, 35, 86).

[59] This word is used by Paul for "acknowledging" God (Rom 1:28) and for determining what is good, which probably means God's will (Phil 1:9). But ἐπίγνωσις *epignōsis* dominates Second Peter's discourse; this is not the case with Paul.

[60] Or "untrue tales" (NJB), or "stories they have made up" (NIV).

(3:16). Those who successfully avoid error achieve γνῶσις *gnōsis* of the Lord and Savior (3:18). Correct *knowing* and correct *behavior* go together.

The believer needs to reject corruption, learn about Christ, and take on his virtues. This is a *virtue soteriology*: one is saved by, and for, virtue. But it is virtue mediated through Christ; salvation and divinization are thoroughly Christological. God gives "life and godliness, through the knowledge of him who called us by his own glory and goodness" (1:3). These things are given "so that through them you may . . . become participants of the divine nature" (1:4). Divinization is progress into greater moral excellence; the means for achieving it are also a matter of choosing moral excellence.

Virtue is the beginning, the middle, and the end of the process: by "goodness," God "called" the believer (1:3); "effort" must be made to develop virtue (1:5); believers "ought to be . . . leading lives of holiness and godliness" (3:11); and God will create a world "where righteousness is at home" (3:13).

Doctrinal correctness is itself a virtue: not interpreting Scripture according to "human will" (1:21), not listening to "enticing" and "adulterous" religious teaching (2:14), being able to recognize "bombastic nonsense" and "error" (2:18). There seems to be a clearly sociological corollary to all this cognitive advice, namely: stay in the group, stay on "the straight road" (2:15). "Faith" can mean staying on the path, so correct membership, correct belief, and saving virtue go together: "support your faith with goodness, and goodness with knowledge, and knowledge with self-control" (we mentioned that ἐγκράτεια *egkrateia* was a principal value among Hellenist philosophers of all stripes, but it also was for Paul [Gal 5:23; 1 Cor 9:25; Acts 24:25]). Everything Hellenistic, however, is here Christianized. The values and the terms resonate with Hellenistic philosophy, but attaining these values requires loyalty to and "knowledge" of, Jesus, the Messiah, the Savior, the revelation of God.

How does divinization begin, for Second Peter? The necessary preconditions are ethical character and proper belief. When these are present, divinization commences, which then results in enhancement of one's ethical character, and establishment of one in proper belief! The means and the destination are quite alike.

Deification is linked with sobriety, humility, piety, and morality. There is no hint, in Second Peter, of spiritual ecstasy or vision, but only of these more cautious and communal virtues, similar to those advocated in the Pastoral Epistles: staying with "the sound teaching that you have followed" (1 Tim 4:6; 2 Tim 1:13); being "temperate, serious, prudent" (Titus 2:2); avoiding "idle talkers" and those with "itching ears" (Titus 1:10; 2 Tim 4:3); rejecting "profane myths and old wives' tales" (1 Tim 4:7). Second Peter and the Pastorals recommend an attitude of humility and teachability in community. Virtue includes conformity to the group—as long as it is the *right* group.

Second Peter has more to say about eschatology and epistemology than the Pastorals do, but the social message seems the same: stay in the orthodox community; cultivate cooperative and conformist virtues. Second Peter, however, places more emphasis on right perception or recognition (*epignōsis*). This focus on knowledge of God places Second Peter in continuity with the prophetic (Num 24:16; Hos 4:6; 6:6) and wisdom (Prov 2:5; Eccl 2:26) traditions, and with the Pauline understanding of Jesus as the doorway to knowledge of God (2 Cor 4:6), and of such knowledge as the gateway to deification:

> To know the love of Christ that surpasses knowledge, so that you may be filled with all the fullness of God. (Eph 3:19)

It is in such matters that Second Peter looks very close to the Pauline tradition: "knowledge of the Son of God" leads to "maturity," growing up "into Christ," and being able to resist wrong doctrine (Eph 4:13-15). One becomes like a new person; in fact, "the new self . . . is being renewed in knowledge according to the image of its creator" (Col 3:10). I think that deification in Second Peter finds its closest intellectual relatives in Ephesians and Colossians. In these three letters, deification means growing up into the likeness of Christ, although this is spelled out more clearly in Ephesians and Colossians than in Second Peter.

What Second Peter emphasizes is Jesus as *Savior*, a title that occurs five times, from the first to the last verse of the epistle, including that climactic advice to "grow in the grace and knowledge of our Lord and Savior Jesus Christ" (3:18; cf. 1:1, 11, 2:20; 3:2). Deification is spiritual growth directed by the Savior toward the inculcation of "the divine nature," which seems to mean character values. So what is divinized is one's character, but also one's "knowledge of God and of Jesus," who "give[s] us everything needed for life and godliness, through the knowledge of him who called us by his own glory and goodness" (1:2-3). Jesus and God are so blended as to be almost indistinguishable. So also are knowledge and character reciprocally related. To know God is to start becoming like God.

Abbreviations:

C.H. – *Corpus Hermeticum*, scripture of a Gnostic, Platonizing religious philosophy
LCL – Loeb Classical Library
LXX – The Septuagint, the Greek translation of the Jewish Scriptures
NT – New Testament
OT – Old Testament

Bibliography

Primary Sources:
Athanasius (English; two sources) *Contra Gentes and De Incarnatione.* Edited and translated by Robert W. Thomson. London: SCM, 1971. And *The Letters of St. Athanasius Concerning the Holy Spirit.* Translated by C. R. B. Shapland. London: Epworth, 1951.
Diogenes Laertius (English and Greek): *Lives of Eminent Philosophers*, vol. II. Translated by R. D. Hicks. Loeb Classical Library 185. Cambridge: Harvard University Press, 1931.
Epictetus (English): *The Stoic and Epicurean Philosophers.* Edited and translated by Whitney J. Oates. New York: The Modern Library, 1940.
First Enoch (English): *The Old Testament Pseudepigrapha*, vol. 1. Translated by E. Isaac. Edited by James H. Charlesworth. New York: Doubleday, 1983.
Philo (English; two sources): *The Works of Philo.* Translated by C. D. Yonge. Peabody, Mass.: Hendrickson, 1993. And (only for *Opif.:*) *Philo*, vol. 1. Translated by G. H. Colson and G. H. Whitaker. Loeb Classical Library. Cambridge: Harvard University Press, 1929.
Plato (English and Greek): (for *Phaedo* and *Theaetatus*) *Plato* vols. 1–2. Translated by Harold North Fowler. Loeb Classical Library. New York: Putnam, 1921, 1923.

PSUEDO-PHOCYLIDES (English and Greek): *The Sentences of Pseudo-Phocylides: With Introduction and Commentary.* P. W. van der Horst. SVTP 4. Leiden: Brill, 1978.

TESTAMENTS OF THE TWELVE PATRIARCHS (English): *The Old Testament Pseudepigrapha*, vol. 1. Translated by H. C. Kee. Edited by James H. Charlesworth. New York: Doubleday, 1983.

Secondary Sources:

Aune, David E. "Anthropological Duality in the Eschatology of 2 Cor 4:16–5:10." In *Paul Beyond the Judaism/Hellenism Divide*, 215–39. Edited by Troels Engberg-Pedersen. Louisville: Westminster John Knox, 2001.

Bailey, Cyril. *Phases in the Religion of Ancient Rome.* Berkeley: University of California Press, 1932.

Bauckham, Richard J. *Jude, 2 Peter.* Word Biblical Commentary 50. Waco: Word, 1983.

———. "2 Peter." *HarperCollins Study Bible.* New York: HarperCollins, 1993.

Bevan, Edwyn. *Stoics and Skeptics.* Oxford: Clarendon, 1913.

Charles, J. Daryl. *Virtue amidst Vice: The Catalog of Virtues in 2 Peter 1.* JSNT Sup 150. Sheffield: Sheffield Academic, 1997.

Collins, John J. *Jewish Wisdom in the Hellenistic Age.* OTL. Louisville: Westminster John Knox, 1997.

Edelstein, Ludwig. *The Meaning of Stoicism.* Cambridge: Harvard University Press, 1966.

Engberg-Pedersen, Troels. *Paul and the Stoics.* Louisville: Westminster John Knox, 2000.

Holladay, Carl R. *Theios Aner in Hellenistic-Judaism: A Critique of the Use of This Category in New Testament Christology.* SBL Dissertation Series 40. Missoula, Mont.: Scholars, 1977.

Horst, P. W. van der. *The Sentences of Pseudo-Phocylides: With Introduction and Commentary.* SVTP 4. Leiden: Brill, 1978.

Jervis, L. Ann. "Becoming Like God through Christ: Discipleship in Romans." In *Patterns of Discipleship in the New Testament*, 143–62. Edited by Richard N. Longenecker. Grand Rapids: Eerdmans, 1996.

Maritain, Jacques. *Moral Philosophy.* Translated by Joseph W. Evans. New York: Scribner's, 1964 (from the French edition, 1960).

Neyrey, Jerome H. *2 Peter, Jude: A New Translation with Introduction and Commentary.* AB 37C. New York: Doubleday, 1993.

Oakesmith, John. *The Religion of Plutarch.* London: Longmans, Green, & Co., 1902.

Plummer, Alfred. *A Critical and Exegetical Commentary on the Second Epistle of St. Paul to the Corinthians*. ICC. Edinburgh: T. & T. Clark, 1915.

Rowe, Christopher. *An Introduction to Greek Ethics*. London: Hutchinson & Co., 1976.

Starr, James M. *Sharers in Divine Nature: 2 Peter 1:4 in Its Hellenistic Context*. Coniectanea Biblical NT Series 33. Stockholm: Almqvist & Wiksell, 2003.

Sterling, Gregory E. "'Wisdom Among the Perfect': Creation traditions in Alexandrian Judaism and Corinthian Christianity." *NovT* 37 (1995) 355–84.

Wesche, Kenneth Paul. "ΘΕΩΣΙΣ in Freedom and Love: the Patristic Vision." In *The Consuming Passion: Christianity and the Consumer Culture*, 123. Edited by Rodney Clapp. Downers Grove: IVP, 1998.

Wolters, Al. "'Partners of the Deity': A Covenantal Reading of 2 Peter 1:4." *Calvin Theological Journal* 25 (1990) 28–44.

—————. "Postscript to 'Partners of the Deity.'" *Calvin Theological Journal* 26 (1991) 418–20.

Wright, N. T. *The Resurrection of the Son of God*. Minneapolis: Fortress, 2003.

Emergence of the Deification Theme in the Apostolic Fathers

Vladimir Kharlamov

In the writings of the Apostolic Fathers we do not see specific use of the terminology that was employed by later Christian writers to communicate the concept of deification. Nevertheless, this corpus of literature introduces many themes associated with this concept that are destined to receive fuller development in the theology of Irenaeus, Clement of Alexandria, Origen, Athanasius, and others. By concentrating attention on later development of the concept of theōsis, most scholars generally underestimate, and even overlook, the role of second century theology. This essay and the following one, "Deification in the Apologists of the Second Century," attempt to fill in this gap, and to show the importance of the formative aspects of the Apostolic Fathers' and Apologists' contribution, not only toward shaping the basic method of traditional Patristic theology and Christian spirituality, but also toward the early development of the concept of deification *per se*.

That humanity has a special place in the "economy" (household, salvation history) of God is a commonly assumed notion of Christian writers. It is one of the central themes of Jewish and Christian scripture. The Apostolic Fathers, following the New Testament understanding of a transformed God-human relationship, continue to elaborate on this theme. If in the OT, God was interacting with his chosen people and the rest of humanity through the mediation of the Torah and prophets, God was still distantly transcendent and hidden. With the coming of Christ, God reveals himself in human nature, *bringing reconciliation to all humankind.*

Reconciliation became possible because of Christ's incarnation, death and resurrection. His victory over the consequences of sin and death inaugurated a new kingdom of God that already started on earth, but will only be fully realized at the second coming. Eschatological expectations are the distinctive feature of this period, which can partially be seen in the incipient presence of the concept of deification as the transition from corruptibility, destruction, and death to immortality, new creation, and eternal life. The Apostolic Fathers saw immortality as a gift of God, not a natural property of the human soul. Immortality is connected with the event of Christ's resurrection, which presages the general resurrection. The Apostolic Fathers put significant emphasis on the resurrection of the flesh. As Christ ascended to heaven in the resurrected human body, so will we be in the presence of God in a condition similar to his.

Imitation of Christ is another concept that becomes a part of the deification theme. The goal of a believer is to emulate the life and actions of Christ as much as possible. Human ability to imitate Christ is sealed in the message of the incarnation, that also reveals the human potentiality to incorporate the divine.[1] Martyrdom is presented as the way to obtain likeness to Christ and immortality. Especially in Ignatius of Antioch, imitation of Christ leads to intimate union with the object of imitation, an incorporation into Christ.[2] This can be termed "Christification." It would not be long before the divinity of Christ would be firmly established in the Christian community, and the concept of identification with Christ would imply identification with God. So the concept of Christification would be substituted for the concept of deification.

---

[1] Eph 4:13; 1 John 3:2; 2 Pet 1:4.
[2] Incorporation into Christ, in the broader sense, was admission into the Church, the body of Christ. In a more narrow sense, it was participation of the individual in Christ both as an intimate personal union and as an eschatological relationship with Christ that continues beyond death.

In the period of the Apostolic Fathers, imitation of Christ and deification are expressed more in terms of "economy" than of ontology. Later trinitarian and Christological controversies would put more emphasis on ontological aspects. In the Apostolic Fathers, it is best not to read in any theological anthropology that is not explicitly spelled out, and definitely not spelled out in ontological terms. The aspects of deification that are predominant for the Apostolic Fathers are practical: involving salvation, morality, and eschatology. The emphasis is not on what happens with human nature when it is deified, but rather on what should be done to allow deification to take place. Their language of deification is metaphoric, not metaphysical. When the Apostolic Fathers refer to the image of God in a human being, this has a more practical than ontological meaning. However, they understand the image of God to entail human freedom of will, an ability to understand and to know, and an ability to communicate with God.

Contrasting images of light and darkness, life and death, corruption and incorruption, perishable and imperishable, theologically introduced by the Apostolic Fathers as the supporting terminology of deification, find congenial use in Christian vocabulary. God becomes more accessible because of the incarnation of Christ. It is through Christ that God, according to Clement of Rome, "called us from darkness to light, from ignorance to the knowledge of the glory of his name."[3] This glorified state of the entire human being[4] in the presence of God ultimately becomes the goal of salvation in the Eastern Fathers. Some later fathers saw this salvific transformation effecting not only humanity but also all creation. Already the *Epistle of Barnabas* speaks about the Sabbath, the rest of creation, as the eighth day—"the beginning of another world."[5]

---

[3] *1 Clem.* 59.2; English translations of the Apostolic Fathers are from J. B. Lightfoot and J. R. Harmer, tr., ed., rev., Michael W. Holmes, *The Apostolic Fathers* (Grand Rapids: Baker Book House, 1989).

[4] In spite of some similarity with the Hellenistic concept of the higher part of a human person (the soul) having a natural kinship with the divine, Christian authors emphasized glorified perfection for the *whole* of human nature, including materiality. It is not a *part* of the human that ultimately reaches the state of deification, but the entire human being.

[5] *Barn.* 15. 8–9.

Didache

The strong belief of the primitive church in the imminent second coming of Christ, the *parousia,* finds expression in early liturgical development as well.[6] An example of this can be seen in the exclamation *"maranatha!"*[7] For Aloys Grillmeier, this exclamation signifies evidence of the early worship of Christ as the Lord,[8] and marks the transition from regard for the "pre-Easter, earthly Jesus" to the "post Easter community." This transition signifies progress "from lived experience to the preached gospel, the *kerygma,* then leads further from *kerygma* to dogma, without implying any opposition between them."[9] The Christ-figure and Christ-event are the cornerstones of the Christian message.

The shift to the "post Easter community" has not only christological, but also anthropological and eschatological significance for the development of the concept of deification. Raised from the dead, Christ not only manifests his divine power over death as the Son of God, but also embodies transformed and redeemed human nature as the Son of Man. The conditions of the resurrected human body would later receive more theological attention. The resurrection of Christ, as an already fulfilled fact of salvation history, prefigures the general resurrection that is expected by the Christian community at the end of time. Though not elaborated in any depth, these facets of Christian thought play a very important role in the emergence of deification concepts.

Aramaic *maranatha* is traditionally translated as "our Lord, come," but it can also be translated "our Lord has come" or "our Lord is now

---

[6] *Did.* 9–10. The *Didache,* or the *Teaching of the (Lord through the Twelve) Apostles (to the Nations),* was an early work on Christian discipline. It was discovered by P. Bryennios in 1873. Some parts of the *Didache's* content were alrseady known in such compilations as the *Apostolic Constitutions* (7:1–32) and the *Epistle of Barnabas* (18–20). Starting with Eusebius of Caesarea we find a number of patristic references to a writing or writings called the "Teaching(s)" of the Apostles wheather was it the same work as *Didache* or similar works is beyond historic verification. Therefore a date for *Didache* varies from as early as 70 CE to the end of the third century.

[7] 1 Cor 16:22; *Did.* 10.6.

[8] Aloys Grillmeier, *Christ in Christian Tradition. Vol. 1: From the Apostolic Age to Chalcedon (451)* (Atlanta: John Knox, 1975) 11.

[9] Grillmeier, *Christ,* 8.

present."[10] Grillmeier links *maranatha* of 1 Cor 16:22 with the eucharistic declaration of Christ's second coming in 1 Cor 11:26 and the eschatological proclamation of Rev 22:20. In all three instances *maranatha* points toward the eschatological future. The penitential aspect of *maranatha* in 1 Cor 16:22 comes together with the sacramental (eucharistic) and eschatological aspect of 1 Cor 11:26 in *Did.* 10.6. The post-eucharistic prayer in the *Didache* 10 lists knowledge, faith, immortality, and the divine indwelling (10.2) as gifts given by God through Jesus, "your servant" (10.3), who *is* "Grace" (10.5), and who can sanctify the church (10.4). Finally, there is the prayer for the Lord to come (10.6).

The proclamation of the actual presence of Christ the Lord at the Eucharist indicates the fellowship of the Christian community as "sharers in what is imperishable,"[11] and the linkage of this with the believer's reception of knowledge and immortality, has deification implications. Believers will be saved at the resurrection of the dead, and it may be that some will accompany Christ in the *parousia* (16.6–7), which certainly has deification implications.

The Epistle of Barnabas

The Epistle of Barnabas is probably the earliest document of the post apostolic period.[12] The relationship of Christianity to Judaism occupies the mind of the author. How should Christians appropriate the prophecies of the OT? This epistle provides one of the first examples of the use of the allegorical method of interpretation of Jewish Scripture for purposes of

---

[10] See, K. G. Kuhn, "Μαρανα θά" in *Theological Dictionary of the New Testament*, ed. Kittel, 6:466–72.

[11] *Did.* 4.8; cf. *Barn.* 19.8.

[12] It seems that this epistle as a whole is the work of one author, who, however, stays anonymous. Patristic tradition, starting with Clement of Alexandria, attributes this work to Barnabas, one of the affiliates of the apostle Paul described in the book of the *Acts*, but modern scholarship disputes this attribution. Since the epistle refers to the destruction of the Jerusalem temple (*Barn.* 16.3) it was written after 70 CE, but probably before 135, when the emperor Hadrian built a Roman temple on the site, because *Barn.* 16.4 expects the Jerusalem temple to be rebuilt, and certainly before 190—when the first indubitable use of this epistle was made by Clement of Alexandria.

the Christian community. The letter tries to establish the notion that everything that Christ did was predicted in the OT. It points to the pre-existence of Christ, his participation in the process of creation of this world,[13] and to the necessity of the incarnation as an example of righteous life.[14] The divinity of Christ is entailed in the statement that he is the Son of God.[15] Christ's death was not only predicted, but necessary for the forgiveness of sins, redemption,[16] and destruction of death through the resurrection.[17] The concepts of "life" and "death" are particularly interesting for us, as they provide the background for the entire letter. They are aimed at the notion of the regenerated and fruitful eternal life of the eighth day of creation—an eschatological fulfillment of the whole of creation that had already begun with Christ's resurrection. The incarnation was like the beginning of a new creation. God "will create the beginning of an eighth day, which is the beginning of another world."[18] The "eighth day" signifies Christ's resurrection and ascension.[19]

Barnabas does not specifically bring up the issue of deification. This epistle does, however, point to one aspect of Christ's incarnation that is important for theōsis: its connection to the divine indwelling. Precisely because of incarnation, Christ can "dwell in us" (6.14). Thus does he make "a holy temple" out of "this little house, our heart" (6.15). In this "little house . . . dwells God" (16.8). The incarnation and the divine indwelling are also the promise of that future goal "when we ourselves are so perfected as to become heirs of the Lord's covenant" (6.19).

In Christ, believers have this "hope of life, which is the beginning and the end of our faith" (1.6), and the epistle ends with a confrontation between the way of light/life and the way of darkness/death, between the power of "light-giving angels of God" and "angels of Satan" (18.1). The "Two Ways" section of this letter is the largest and the most influential piece of tradition in *Barnabas,* and again it comes close to theōsis: Christians

---

[13] *Barn.* 5.5.
[14] *Barn.* 5.10.
[15] *Barn.* 5.11; 12.10.
[16] *Barn.* 5.1, 11; 6.7.
[17] *Barn.* 5.6.
[18] *Barn.* 15.8.
[19] *Barn.* 15.9.

are called to be "sharers in what is incorruptible" (19.8). They "will be glorified in the kingdom of God" (21.1).

Clement of Rome (First Clement)

The theme of the resurrection of Christ as leading the way for the resurrection of all the faithful, composes an important kernel in Clement of Rome's Letter to the Corinthians, or *First Clement*.[20] Examples of resurrection can be seen through nature: the change of day and night, the decay of seed in the soil, the consequent bearing of fruit.[21] As a sign of resurrection, Clement uses the mythological story of the Phoenix bird,[22] an interesting interaction of developing Christian and existing pagan cultures.[23] These images of transition from darkness to light and from one ontological condition to another, show that the fulfillment of God's will benefits the believer with "life in immortality, splendor in righteousness, truth with boldness, faith with confidence, self-control with holiness! And

---

[20] The epistle is normally dated to the end of the reign of Domitian (95 or 96 CE). In *ca.* 150, Dionysius, bishop of Corinth, wrote to the Roman bishop Soter, that the epistle sent by Clement was still being read periodically during the Christian service (Eusebius, *Hist. Eccl.* 4.23). Eusebius also mentions that Clement's letter was read in the worship services in many churches, in his own time (*Hist. Eccl.* 3.16). Irenaeus speaks very favourably of this letter and summarizes its first chapters in *Haer.* 3.3.3. The epistle is frequently utilized by Clement of Alexandria (*Paedagogus* 1.91.2 and in *Stromata*). The popularity of *First Clement* certainly contributed to assigning to Clement of Rome the anonymous works known as the *Clementines* (Κλημέντια), including *2 Clement,* two epistles *De virginitate,* the *Apostolic Constitutions,* the *Clementine Homilies,* the *Clementine Recognitions,* and *Epitomes.* That Clement of Rome was the author of *1 Clement* was the unanimous opinion of the ancient church (Hermas, *Vis.* 2.4.3; Irenaeus, *Adv. Haer.* 3.3.3; Eusebius, *Hist. Eccl.* 4.22.1, 4.23.11).

[21] *1 Clem.* 24.3–5.

[22] *1 Clem.* 25.

[23] The hypothesis that Clement confuses φοίνιξ as a bird with φοίνιξ as the palm tree seems to be not applicable in this instance. It is not the only occasion when Clement, as many other Christian authors, looks for examples from pagan history or life that could support the Christian cause (see *1 Clem.* 55.1). However, this reference to the ancient mythology seemed to be embarrassing for Clement of Alexandria as he omits reference to the phoenix bird of *1 Clem.* 25 and the virtuous pagans of 55.1. Later Photius directly questioned the orthodoxy of this letter (*Bibliotheca* 126, PG 103:408A).

all these things fall within our comprehension."[24] The comprehensive character of divine salvific knowledge is available to all.[25] This knowledge, revealed through Christ, enlightens our darkened minds, makes us capable of penetrating the "heights of heaven," seeing Christ "as in a mirror, his faultless and transcendent face."[26] Knowledge of Christ makes us capable of seeing God!

Clement lays the groundwork for many important themes of later mystical theology, such as union with God and vision of God. The concept of illuminative light, the source of which is God, shows us the knowledge of everlasting things, bringing us into direct contact with God himself. It is God's will "that we should taste immortal knowledge" and divine glory.[27] Salvation is understood primarily in terms of direct participation in the new life of Christ.

An example of such faithful following of God's will is Enoch, who, through his obedience to God, did not experience death.[28] The scriptural characters of Enoch and Elijah have a prominent place in the development of the concept of deification. The two figures present an exception to the prevailing consequence of sin, which is death. Both are taken directly to heaven, into the presence of God, without experiencing death. At the opposite pole, "any who do anything contrary to the duty imposed by his [God's] will, receive death as penalty."[29] Here again, we see the theology of two ways. However, in Clement, we find a more mystical and epistemological emphasis: "Let us see him in our mind, and let us look with the eyes of the soul."[30] "We have been considered worthy of greater knowledge."[31]

---

[24] *1 Clem.* 35.2.

[25] This could be a response to the elitist notion of knowledge available only to the Gnostic.

[26] *1 Clem.* 36.2.

[27] Again, *1 Clem.* 36.2.

[28] *1 Clem.* 9.3.

[29] *1 Clem.* 41.3.

[30] *1 Clem.* 19.3.

[31] *1 Clem.* 41.4.

Second Clement

The divinity of Christ is firmly confirmed in the opening statement of *Second Clement*,[32] perhaps in reaction to Christian Gnosticism.[33] The document maintains, similar to other writings of the Apostolic Fathers, an eschatological perspective, which runs throughout the entire sermon. Christ's second coming is imminent, but Christians still live in two worlds, which are in conflict. One is the world of "adultery and corruption and greed and deceit,"[34] while the age to come is the kingdom of God.[35] Repentance is necessary in order to obtain the eternal reward.[36] There is a strong emphasis on the bodily resurrection. Salvation of the Christian takes place in the flesh following the example of Christ's incarnation: "If Christ . . . became flesh . . . so also we will receive our reward in this flesh,"[37] and the flesh receives immortality from the Holy Spirit.[38]

In passing, the author affirms the spiritual, not material, pre-existence of Christ prior to incarnation.[39] The pre-existence of Christ is linked to the pre-existence of the church, "created before the sun and moon."[40] The incarnation of Christ is related to the embodiment of the church on earth, "For she [the church] was spiritual, as was also our Jesus, but was revealed in the last days in order that she might save us."[41] This movement from spiritual to material, and the close linear interconnection between the two, are important elements of the sermon.

---

[32] *2 Clem.* 1.1.

[33] Helmut Koester suggests that *2 Clement* could be an anti-Gnostic sermon from mainstream Christianity in Egypt (*Introduction to the New Testament.* Vol. 2, *History and Literature of Early Christianity* [Philadelphia: Fortress, 1984] 233–36). The genre and content of this work supports an assumption that it is rather a sermon of unknown presbyter (*2 Clem.* 17.3) than the epistle (Michael Holmes, *The Apostolic Fathers* 65). This sermon dates approximately from 140–60 CE.

[34] *2 Clem.* 6.4.

[35] Reminiscent of two ways theology of *Epistle of Barnabas* 18.1–2.

[36] *2 Clem.* 6.6–7; 8.1; 9.7; 13.1.

[37] *2 Clem.* 9.5.

[38] *2 Clem.* 14.5.

[39] *2 Clem.* 9.5.

[40] *2 Clem.* 14.1.

[41] *2 Clem.* 14.2.

The plan of salvation that existed in the mind of God from eternity is unfolding now in the created world and does not deny the world's materiality, but rather regenerates it. This process of transformation started with Christ's incarnation (whose divinity is affirmed), continued with the establishment of the church, and culminates in the coming resurrection of the flesh. The human body is "a temple of God"[42] and the vehicle through which spiritual transformation of the soul becomes apparent.[43]

Ignatius of Antioch

The letters of Ignatius of Antioch (perhaps not without later redactions and interpolations) offer the most extensive contribution to the period of the Apostolic Fathers. Seven letters[44] were written by Ignatius early in the second century (traditionally *ca.* 110 CE) on his way to martyrdom in Rome. The concept of martyrdom, therefore, is one of the central themes, and signifies not only his extraordinary heroism and passionate love with a willingness to die for Christ,[45] but this rhetoric provides an interesting insight into Ignatius' understanding of union with Christ. Martyrdom is an opportunity to imitate the passion and death of Christ, to become God's true disciple.[46] Achieving martyrdom, for Ignatius, proves that he could reach not only the full measure of Christian discipleship, but a somewhat sacramental and sacrificial identification with Christ himself. In his passion mysticism, Ignatius identifies himself with the "pure bread of Christ" and a "sacrifice to God."[47] Here, to portray his martyrdom, Ignatius uses language that was traditionally applied to the Eucharist and the salvific ministry of Christ. Martyrdom is the culmination of a new birth[48] into the likeness of Christ, where the believer experiences the process of Christification, and becomes a full replica of Christ.

---

[42] *2 Clem.* 9.3.

[43] *2 Clem.* 12.2–4.

[44] There are three recensions of his letters. The long recension was originated in the fourth century and has six spurious letters. The short recension is a Syriac abridgement of the letters to Ephesians, Romans, and Polycarp. The middle recension, known to Eusebius, is generally accepted as authentic.

[45] *Rom.* 7.2.

[46] *Eph.* 1.2; 3.1; *Rom.* 3.2; 4.2; 5.2.

[47] *Rom.* 4.1–2.

[48] "The pangs of birth are upon me" (*Rom.* 6.1).

The language Ignatius uses is bold and explicit. Death for Christ is the justification of his position as a bishop, the climax of his salvation. This imitation of the Lord is not only christocentric, but also Trinitarian: it is "constant communion with God" (*Eph.* 4.2); it is doing everything "in the Son and the Father and the Spirit" (*Magnesians* 13).

All Christians are called to be imitators and carriers of Christ (χριστοφόροι *christoforoi*), of God (θεοφόροι *theoforoi*), and of holiness (ἁγιφόροι *hagiforoi*).[49] The example of Ignatius himself in this process of imitation earns him the title θεοφόρος *theoforos,* which he does not hesitate to use in the prefacing address of all his letters. The process of salvation is expressed in terms of life and death[50] and is closely related to the incarnation. Christ's incarnation, death, and resurrection are aspects of realized eschatology for Ignatius, though future consummation still awaits.[51]

Christ is "the new man" and the divine plan of salvation includes our "faith in him and love for him, his suffering and resurrection."[52] "There is only one physician, who is both flesh and spirit, born and unborn, God in man, true life in death, both from Mary and from God, first subject to suffering and then beyond it, Jesus Christ our Lord."[53] Ignatius's christological formulas present important elements for the development of the doctrine of Christ and the Trinity in later Patristic thought, like "born and unborn (γεννητός καί ἀγένητος *gennētos kai agenetos*)," which are key terms in the Arian controversy. However, Ignatius' "God in man," under the influence of the Apologists, becomes supplanted by "Logos-sarx (Logos-flesh)"; nevertheless, Ignatius' term played an important role during the Council of Chalcedon.

In *Magn.* 5.1 Ignatius lays out what is standard theology for the Apostolic Fathers: the two ways, "death and life." To believe in Christ's

---

[49] *Eph.* 9.2. See also *Eph.* 1.1; 10.3; *Trall.* 1.2.

[50] *Magn.* 5.

[51] *Eph.* 19.3; *Philad.* 9.2.

[52] *Eph.* 20.1.

[53] *Eph.* 7.2. Ignatius frequently mentions the historicity of Christ's bodily incarnation from Mary, his death and resurrection (*Eph.* 18; 20.2; *Magn.* 11; *Trall.* 9; *Philad.* 9.2; *Smyrn.* 1–3). As God the Father raised Christ from the dead "in the same way [it] will likewise also raise us up in Christ Jesus who believe in him, apart from whom we have no true life" (*Trall.* 9.2).

[54] *Trall.* 2.1.

death is the way to escape death.[54] Christ's suffering "is our resurrection."[55] With its heavy emphasis on the salvation of the faithful, the soteriological perspective in Ignatius has both terrestrial and celestial dimensions; not only humanity, but also celestial beings, are subjects of divine judgment and condemnation based on their belief or disbelief in the efficacy of the blood of Christ.[56]

An important aspect of Ignatius' theology is a concept of "a union of flesh and spirit that comes from Jesus Christ."[57] He even talks about "the blood of God."[58] Flesh and spirit are not only complementary characteristics of the Incarnate God, Jesus Christ, but also significant characteristics of redeemed humanity. Apart from necessary care for bodily needs,[59] this union of flesh and spirit has at least two dimensions: first, the full integrity of human nature that participates in salvation and eternal life; second, conformity between Christian teaching and practice. The salvific unity of flesh and spirit is paralleled by the unity of doctrine and practice.[60] All of human nature is called to be a bearer of God. It is sin, not materiality, that brings separation between humankind and God. Fleshly things become spiritual through Christ when enacted by those who are spiritual.[61]

While the *Epistle of Barnabas* still deals with controversies of the NT period, and attempts to reinterpret Christianity in terms of the OT in a way satisfactory to Christian mentality, Ignatius adopts a stricter dividing line between these religious traditions. In the letter to the Magnesians he writes, "For if we continue to live in accordance with Judaism, we admit that we have not received grace,"[62] and later in the same letter, "It is utterly absurd to profess Jesus Christ and to practice Judaism. For Christianity did not yet believe in Judaism, but Judaism in Christianity."[63] The OT

---

[55] *Smyrn.* 5.3.

[56] *Smyrn.* 6.1.

[57] *Magn.* 1.2; also *Magn.* 13.1; *Rom.* preface; *Smyrn.* 12.2; 13.2; *Polyc.* 1.2; 2.2.

[58] *Eph.* 1.1.

[59] *Polyc.* 1.2.

[60] See J. P. Martin, "La pneumatologia en Ignacio de Antioquia," *Salesianum* 33 (1971): 379–454.

[61] *Eph.* 8.2.

[62] *Magn.* 8.1.

[63] *Magn.* 10.3. See also, *Philad.* 6.1. Some political issues of the time could contribute to such a very negative and aggressive approach to Judaism by Ignatius. He does not want

just pointed to God, but Christ "is the door of the Father" through which everybody, including patriarchs and prophets, have entered "in God's unity"; all the prophets "preached in anticipation of him . . . the gospel is the imperishable finished work."[64] Here again, his motif of realized eschatology plays a decisive part. Christ, who is High Priest, supersedes the priests.[65] This approach, subordinating Judaism, and for that matter Judeo-Christianity, to Christianity, would receive extensive development in the work of Christian Apologists of the second century and later.

This subordination can be seen in his conception of the ecclesiastical structure of the church, possibly a fusing of a Jewish-Christian system of elders with a gentile-Christian system of overseers and deacons.[66] Ignatius' threefold model consists of a bishop (overseer), presbyters (elders), and deacons, with monarchical authority in the bishop's hands. He does not extend the ecclesiastical authority above the level of the local bishop. His strong emphasis on obedience to the bishop is remarkable. This obedience safeguards the church's harmonic unity with God.[67] As Christ "is the mind of the Father, just as the bishops appointed throughout the world represent the mind of Christ."[68] Even more, "the bishop presides in the place of God."[69] The bishop is the representation of God in the church, nothing could be done without the consent of the bishop.[70] The bishop seems to be subject only to God,[71] and even more, this unity "with the bishop and those who lead" in the church has an everlasting effect "as an example and a lesson of incorruptibility."[72] It is the first example in Christian theology of institutional deification.

Christianity to be associated with the Jewish uprisings against Rome in the reign of Trajan. Ignatius wants to be sacrificed as a disciple of Christ, but not as a Jewish rebel. 1 Pet 2:19–21; 4:15 had already said that Christians did not do anything wrong or illegal, but always suffered innocently like Christ, and this would also be highlighted later by the Apologists.

[64] *Philad.* 9.1–2.

[65] *Philad.* 9.1.

[66] cf. Paul's Phil 1:1.

[67] *Eph.* 5.1; 6:1.

[68] *Eph.* 3.2.

[69] *Magn.* 6.1. Ignatius returns to this metaphoric "deification" of the episcopal seat in *Trall.* 3.1.

[70] *Magn.* 7.1; *Smyrn.* 8; *Polyc.* 4.1.

[71] *Polyc.* 4.1.

[72] *Magn.* 6.2.

"Deification" of the episcopal office is directly connected with participation in God. Believers cannot be in union with Christ if they are not in total harmony and unity with the bishop. Later, with the concept of apostolic succession developed by Irenaeus, special institutional grace would be conferred upon certain offices in the ecclesiastic hierarchy. Similarly, the efficacy of the sacrament, the special grace related to this sacrament, would depend on ecclesiastical office. The doctrine of papal infallibility could represent a later development of this institutional deification. However, it should be noted that in Ignatius, the personality of the individual who holds the office is very important; there is no special grace independent of the character of the person. It seems fair to agree with the suggestion made by Schoedel that Ignatius' unrelenting call for unity in the churches, and obedience to the bishop, is simultaneously a call for personal recognition and support for the ratification of his own merit.[73]

The concept of ecclesiastical unity in Ignatius is connected with the theme of sacramental unity. As Ignatius writes to the Philadelphians, "Take care, therefore, to participate in one Eucharist. For there is one flesh of our Lord Jesus Christ, and one cup which leads to unity through his blood; there is one altar, just as there is one bishop, together with the presbytery and the deacons."[74] In the Eucharist we participate in "incorruptible love"[75]; it is "the medicine of immortality."[76] The last phrase, apparently coined by Ignatius, became the key description of the Eucharist in Patristic literature.

The collective unity of believers as the body of Christ, through the unity of the Eucharist and obedience to the bishop, is combined with the personal unity of each individual with God through Christ. The apogee of christo-affiliation is martyrdom, which brings a person to identification with Christ. For Ignatius, the imitation of Christ, as Norman Russell writes, "is not a metaphysical spirituality of the soul's escape and ascent, but an internalized eschatology, a literal assimilation to the resurrected life of Christ."[77]

---

[73] William R. Schoedel, *Ignatius of Antioch: A Commentary on the Letters of Ignatius of Antioch* (Philadelphia: Fortress, 1985) 10–14.

[74] *Philad.* 4.1.

[75] *Rom.* 7.2.

[76] *Eph.* 20.2.

[77] Norman Russell, "The Concept of Deification in the Early Greek Fathers" (Ph.D. diss. Oxford University, 1988) 169.

Polycarp of Smyrna

The figure of Polycarp of Smyrna is noteworthy in the early post-apostolic church. A friend of Bishops Ignatius and Papias, Polycarp was directly appointed bishop by the apostles, according to Irenaeus, who met him personally in his early youth.[78] He died as a martyr, as recounted in the letter written from the church of Smyrna to the church of Philomelium, known as *The Martyrdom of Polycarp (Martyrium Polycarpi)*. Polycarp himself wrote a letter to the Philippians, displaying a caring, pastoral style, but devoting very little attention to deification related themes. He affirms Christ's incarnation, resurrection, and second coming.[79] The faithful will be raised from the dead[80] and will reign with Christ in his kingdom.[81]

Conclusion

As we can observe, in the Apostolic Fathers we do not yet have explicit language of deification; at the same time, this corpus of literature introduces a number of themes that later will be associated with theōsis. With their exhortational rather than dogmatic theology, the Apostolic Fathers offer an "economic" model of deification,[82] closely linked to soteriology. The imitation of Christ plays an important role in the Apostolic Fathers. To be saved is to be like Christ as much as possible. Martyrdom, especially as it is presented in Ignatius, is the culminating point of such imitation; it obtains some form of identification with Christ. However, this identification with Christ, or christification, is not spelled out in an ontological sense. Rather, the goal is to imitate Christ's virtuous, sinless life and suffering. Nevertheless, deification as christification, with its climax in the theology of Ignatius, lays the groundwork for more explicit future discourse of direct participation in God. Eschatological expectations, with

---

[78] *Adv. Haer.* 3.3.4.
[79] *Polyc.* 1.2; 2.1; 6.3; 7.1.
[80] *Polyc.* 2.2.
[81] *Polyc.* 5.2.
[82] Having to do with the *oikonomos*, the "household" of faith, or the relational aspect of spiritual life.

a more holistic approach to anthropology, the meaning of the Eucharist, the role of the bishop, proper knowledge of God: all these aspects, in christocentric contextualization, introduce a number of deification themes to Christian theology. Christ is the revelation of God: "The faithful in love bear the stamp of God [χαρακτῆρα θεου *charaktēra theou*] the Father, through Jesus Christ" (Ignat. Magn. 5.2). "We have been created anew" (Barn. 6.14). From the beginning deification appears as one of the most complex, and at the same time fascinating, issues in Christian theology.

Deification in the Apologists of the Second Century

Vladimir Kharlamov

The work of the second-century apologists reflects a different style of theological discourse from that of the Apostolic Fathers. The expansion of Christianity throughout the Roman Empire and the contact of new Christian communities with Greco-Roman culture challenged the apologists to defend, interpret and reconcile their developing Christian subculture to the surroundings. The significant part of this endeavor was both to explain and to appropriate Christian beliefs in terms understandable for that culture. Instead of the esoteric spiritualism of Gnostic communities, the apologists appealed to philosophic reasoning.

It was a period when Christian theological terminology took its first shape, and in Robert Grant's words "the basic method of traditional Christian theology" was created.[1] As a result of this apologetic work, Christianity began to emerge not simply as a subculture in the Greco-Roman world, but received its intellectual contours suitable to the standards, and expressed in terms of, Hellenistic civilization.

---

[1] Robert M. Grant, *Greek Apologists of the Second Century* (Philadelphia: Westminster, 1988) 11.

Justin sets the stage for this task. His *Apologiae* and *Dialogus cum Tryphone* became foundational treatises that provided focal lines of argument with Greek and Jewish counterparts. His influence by far supersedes not only other writers of the second century, but has far reaching effect on subsequent generations of Christian writers as well. However, in his case, more than with other Apologists of the second century, the key focus of the discourse seems to be oriented more toward Christian communities themselves, rather than to the task of converting new believers. Justin wants to strengthen the followers of Christ in matters of faith by equipping them with arguments that would serve as a manual for reaffirming and deepening their own convictions.

Justin, more than any other apologist, makes use of the soteriological significance of the incarnation, death, and resurrection of Christ. The other apologists prefer not to speak about the incarnation—the most controversial tenet of Christian theology for Hellenistic culture. Some of them do not incorporate the meaning of this event into their discourse at all. All of them, however, would view Christian teaching as deeply rooted in antiquity, preceding all other ancient traditions. The apologetic value of this argument is to refute one of the accusations justifying persecution of Christians, that Christianity presents innovation and does not respect the old ways. Apologists try to turn the tables around and argue to the contrary. Starting with Justin, they argue that if anything good can be found in other religions and in Greek philosophy, it comes from Moses and the Old Testament prophets. Non-Christians just borrowed this truth of the scriptures without acknowledging the source of their wisdom, and often simply distorted it.[2]

The predominantly non-ecclesiastical orientation of the apologists' discourse contributes to their treatment of deification themes, which do not receive significant attention. Nevertheless, the notion of deification occasionally occurs in their discourse. With a few exceptions in Justin[3] and Theophilus,[4] it is embedded within an elaborate philosophical, rather than scriptural, setting.

---

[2] Justin, *1 Apol.* 23, 44, 54, 59–60; *2 Apol.* 13; *Dial.* 7, 69–70; Tatian, *Orat.* 31, 35–41, Theophilus, *Ad Autol.* 2.30, 2.33, 3.26, 3.29; and throughout Athenagoras' *Legatio*, where he vigorously refutes the charge of Christianity with atheism.

[3] *Dial.* 124.

[4] *Ad Autol.* 2.24.

Justin Martyr

In Justin we do not find technical vocabulary for the concept of deification. He, as noted by Norman Russell, "does not use θεοποιέω" [and we can add, other Greek words that communicate this notion] even in his discussion of pagan deification."[5] For him, as for the Apostolic Fathers, the notion of deification is similar to the achievement of immortality, incorruptibility, and eternal life in the presence of God.[6]

Appropriating a term from the discourse of divinization in mythology and in the cult of the Roman emperors, Justin uses ἀπαθανατίζω *apathanatizō*.[7] The process of immortalization for Justin is not ontological, but rather moral: "we have learned that those only are deified [literally, "immortalized"—ἀπαθανατίζεσθαι *apathanatizesthai*] who have lived near to God in holiness and virtue."[8] Every human being is created capable of reasoning and of contemplating God, with free determination to choose to follow divine commandments or not. People are responsible for their actions.[9] Only by imitating the divine goodness may people participate in the incorruption of the Logos and enjoy fellowship with God.[10] Like the Apostolic Fathers before him, Justin is more interested in the moral, than in the ontological, aspects of immortalization. For Justin it is more important to point out what should be done in order to obtain immortality, than what happens with human nature when it becomes immortalized. This can be termed the "economic" (practical) type of deification.

Justin does not see the human soul as immortal by nature. If it were immortal, that would make it unbegotten and equal to God, and we would

---

[5] Norman Russell, "The Concept of Deification in the Early Greek Fathers" (Ph.D. diss. Oxford University, 1988) 170.

[6] *1 Apol.* 8.2; 10.2.

[7] *1 Apol.* 21.3. Even though ἀπαθανατίζω *apathanatizō* first was found in Plato, *Charmides* 156d, the emphasis on virtuous life in order to gain immortality that Justin follows here was introduced by Philo, *Conf. Ling.* 149. See Russell, "Concept of Deification," 171–72.

[8] *1 Apol.* 21.6; Justin, *Apologiae Pro Christianis*, Patristische Texte und Studien, Bd. 38, ed. Miroslav Marcovich (Berlin: de Gruyter, 1994) 64. These two occasions where Justin uses ἀπαθανατίζω *apathanatizō* in *1 Apol.* 21 are translated as "deification" and "to deify" in ANF 1:170.

[9] *1 Apol.* 28.

[10] *1 Apol.* 10; *2 Apol.* 4; 11.7–8. Cf. *1 Apol.* 39, *Dial.* 88.5.

end up with many eternal god-like beings that would contradict the aseity of the only one true God.[11] The soul does not exist on its own, but according to the will of God, who is the life giver and life taker.[12] This leads Justin to make a distinction between the object of participation and the subject that participates. The subject that participates does not become equal or identical with the object of participation. As Norman Russell summarizes, "Participation in Justin implies a unity-with-distinction, a similarity through moral likeness of beings which are dissimilar ontologically."[13] From Justin's interpretation of the soul's participation in the principle of life, which resembles the dialectic of Plato's *Parmenides*, we can draw an analogy that will be very important for a better understanding of the later development of the concept of deification as human participation in God. As the "[soul] lives not as being life, but as the partaker of life; but that which partakes of anything, is different from that of which it does partake";[14] similarly, participation of the human individual in the divine nature[15] never brings this person to the identical status as that with which he or she participates.

However, it would not be correct to conclude that human immortality does not have any ontological implications for Justin. First, such implications can be seen in his epistemology. He does not deny the ontological bridge between uncreated God and created human being. Human nature is originally good and every human being is capable of

---

[11] *Dial.* 5.

[12] *Dial.* 6. *Dial.* 5–6 might imply that Justin believed in the temporality of the soul's existence that would correspond to the temporality of divine punishment. Death of the soul, however, does not coincide with death of the body but is the result of God's will. Only "some which have appeared worthy of God never die" *Dial.* 5.3 (Justin, *Dialogus Cum Tryphone*, Patristische Texte und Studien, Bd. 47, ed. Miroslav Marcovich [Berlin: de Gruyter, 1997] 79–80; ANF 1:197). At the same time, in 1 *Apol.* 21 he speaks about "everlasting fire" of punishment for not repented sinners. Justin's argumentation in *Dial.* 5–6, ambiguous as it might look, does not necessarily give a reason to suggest that Justin denies eternal punishment; rather, he emphasizes that the soul does not exist on its own, but according to God's will. Here he agrees with Ireneaus *Haer.* 2.34 and opposes Plato's concept of the soul's reincarnation. About the eternal character of punishment, Justin also clearly speaks in *1 Apol.* 8, 28 and *Dial.* 130.

[13] Russell, "Concept of Deification," 175.

[14] *Dial.* 6.1; Marcovich, *Dialogus Cum Tryphone*, 81–82, ANF 1:198.

[15] 2 Pet. 1:4.

participating in God through what Justin calls, using the Stoic term, *logos spermatikos*.[16] Because of this seed of the Logos, divinely implanted into every human being, humanity can be edified with knowledge of God. Here Justin sees a fundamental harmony between Christianity and the good of Greek philosophy, "those who lived reasonably [according to the Logos—μετὰ Λόγου *meta Logou*] are Christians."[17] This list would include Socrates, Heraclitus and others like them. "Whatever things were rightly said among all men, are the property of us Christians."[18] The diversity of opinions among pagans is an indication that, in spite of their capacity to receive some divine knowledge through the seed of the Logos, they were not getting full knowledge. The fulfillment of knowledge comes only through Christ, who is the incarnation of the entire Logos, "For the seed and imitation imparted according to capacity is one thing, and quite another is the thing itself, of which there is the participation and imitation according to the grace which is from Him."[19] This wisdom is granted to Christians who try to live in accordance with God's commandments, revealed in Christ. The mind of a person cannot see God, unless instructed by the Holy Spirit.[20]

The significant aspect of knowing God is expressed in the rite of baptism and the Eucharist. Baptism, as the second birth and "regeneration,"[21] is "the water of life" and bath of "repentance and knowledge."[22] In the Eucharist, Christians, by partaking of bread and wine, participate in the body and blood of Jesus Christ. Justin is interesting by presenting the ritual of the Eucharist in the early church;[23] however, theologically, in relation to the notion of deification, except for the element of "transmutation" (μεταβολήν) and the importance of the Eucharist "for our salvation,"[24] he does not elaborate significantly on this aspect of

---

[16] *2 Apol.* 8.3; 13.3. Cf. *1 Apol.* 46.2.

[17] *1 Apol.* 46.3; Marcovich, *Apologiae Pro Christianis*, 97; ANF 1:178.

[18] *2 Apol.* 13.4; Marcovich, *Apologiae Pro Christianis*, 157; ANF 1:193. Even Plato was inspired by Moses (*1 Apol.* 44).

[19] *2 Apol.* 13.6; Marcovich, *Apologiae Pro Christianis*, 157; ANF 1:193.

[20] *Dial.* 4.1.

[21] *1 Apol.* 61.

[22] *Dial.* 14.1.

[23] *1 Apol.*65–67.

[24] *1 Apol.* 66.2.

sacramental theology. The mystical aspect of incorporation into Christ through baptism, or participation in the "medicine of immortality" through the Eucharist is not developed by the apologists to the same extent as by Paul and Ignatius.

Another ontological implication related to human immortality is resurrection of the dead. He explicitly correlates the resurrection of the dead with attainment of incorruptibility and immortality.[25] A propensity toward immortality and freedom from suffering is the *telos* (goal) of human existence that will be realized at eschaton. The human soul is not immortal by nature, but in the resurrection, immortality becomes an ontological property of renewed human nature.[26] Resurrection of the dead is only possible because of Christ, "God will raise us up by his Christ, and will make us incorruptible, and undisturbed (ἀπαθεῖς [free from suffering]), and immortal."[27] As the result of Christ's incarnation, death, resurrection, and ascension, humanity received the gift of salvation and eternal inheritance in the Kingdom of God.[28] Christ's salvific work marked a new beginning for humankind as a symbol of the eighth day, "Christ, being the first-born of every creature, became again the chief of another race regenerated by himself through water, and faith, and wood, containing the mystery of the cross."[29]

Toward the end of *Dialogus cum Tryphone*, Justin offers his only explicit statement on deification. In this passage, to communicate the idea of deification, he uses θεὸς γίγνομαι *theos gignomai* (to become a god), which is the first time in Christian tradition such semantics are used. It is a common phrase in patristic literature henceforward. Justin employs θεὸς γίγνομαι *theos gignomai* in the context of his interpretation of Ps. 81:6 (LXX). In this instance, he is also the first among Christian writers to use this biblical text in relation to deification. For him every human being is responsible for personal sins and was created capable of becoming a god:

---

[25] *1 Apol.* 19.4; 52.3, *Dial.* 45.4.

[26] *1 Apol.* 19.

[27] *Dial.* 46.7, Marcovich, *Dialogus Cum Tryphone*, 146, ANF 1:218. See also *Dial.* 117.3.

[28] Cf. *1 Apol.* 46, *Dial.* 139.5.

[29] *Dial.* 138.2, Marcovich, *Dialogus Cum Tryphone*, 308, ANF 1:268.

The Holy Spirit reproaches men because they were made like [ὁμοίως *homoiōs*] God, free from suffering and death, provided that they kept His commandments, and were deemed deserving of the name of His sons, and yet they, becoming like Adam and Eve, work out death for themselves; let the interpretation of the Psalm [LXX 81:6-7] be held just as you wish, yet thereby it is demonstrated that all men are deemed worthy of becoming gods [ὅτι θεοὶ κατηξίωνται γενέσθαι *hoti theoi katēxiōntai genesthai*], and of having power to become sons of the Highest; and shall be each by himself judged and condemned like Adam and Eve.[30]

Freedom of the will and natural human predisposition to divine grace are important elements in this process. In addition to that, the process of becoming gods is closely connected with adoptive divine filiation. The full realization of this process is accomplished in resurrection, when we "should in God's appointed time rise again and put on incorruption."[31] Blessings for those saved will be enjoyed, according to Justin, in two stages. First, the righteous will participate in the Millennial Kingdom, which will be a prelude to God's final reckoning and retribution.[32] Here, Justin shares the chiliastic expectations of some Christian communities of his time, but he acknowledges that there are others who are of "the pure and pious faith, and are true Christians" who "think otherwise."[33] Aside from chiliastic expectations, that were not universally shared by all Christians, restoration of the universal divine order, reconciliation of humanity with God, and immortal life in the glory of God free of corruption and suffering, are the elements of deification in Justin that apply to every Christian. The whole goal of Christ's voluntary incarnation was to proclaim divine teaching "for the conversion and restoration of the human race."[34] The Logos became man and "a partaker of our sufferings, [that] he might also bring us healing."[35] The world was created for people's sake, that some of

---

[30] *Dial.* 124.4; Marcovich, *Dialogus Cum Tryphone*, 285, ANF 1:262.

[31] *1 Apol.* 19.4; Marcovich, *Apologiae Pro Christianis*, 60; ANF 1:169.

[32] *Dial.* 80–81.

[33] *Dial.* 80.2; Marcovich, *Dialogus Cum Tryphone*, 208; ANF 1:239.

[34] *1 Apol.* 23.2; Marcovich, *Apologiae Pro Christianis*, 66; ANF 1:171.

[35] *2 Apol.* 13.4; Marcovich, *Apologiae Pro Christianis*, 157; ANF 1:193.

them, who through "their works show themselves worthy of this his design, they are deemed worthy, and so we have received—of reigning in company with him, being delivered from corruption and suffering."[36]

Tatian

Tatian was a student of Justin in Rome. As was his teacher, Tatian was a convert to Christianity after searching for truth in Greek philosophy and then in the Christian Scriptures. Whereas Justin was searching for the elements of truth in pre-Christian philosophy, Tatian despises Hellenistic culture. However, he follows Justin's argument that if Greeks had any knowledge whatsoever, they received it from Moses without acknowledging their source.[37] The only time that Tatian speaks of people as gods, is when he criticizes the pagan idea of divinization.[38] He uses *theopoieō* only once, metaphorically, when he argues against those who trust human medicine and "deify the objects of nature," namely drugs, over the healing help that comes from God.[39] Tatian is resistant to the whole idea of any human transformation in the Hellenistic context,[40] although he acknowledges human ability to advance "far beyond his humanity towards God himself."[41] However, this human advancement seems to be more like regaining its original condition than in any sense a transfiguration of human nature.

The incarnation of Christ does not occupy the central position in his discourse. He alludes to it only once, when he attempts to demonstrate that such a notion as to declare, "that God has been born in the form of man," is not uniquely Christian, and then he points to examples from

---

[36] *1 Apol.* 10.2; Marcovich, *Apologiae Pro Christianis*, 45–46; ANF 1:165.

[37] *Orat.* 40.1; this is the *Oration to the Greeks*.

[38] *Orat.* 10.2; 12.4. Also in *Orat.* 3.2 he makes reference to an unfortunate experience of Empedocles who proclaimed himself a god and to prove his divine status jumped into a volcanic crater, which ended his divinity.

[39] *Orat.* 18.2.

[40] *Orat.* 10.1.

[41] *Orat.* 15.2; Tatian, *Oratio Ad Graecos and Fragments, Oxford Early Christian Texts*, ed. Molly Whittaker (Oxford: Clarendon, 1982) 30–31.

Greek mythology to support his premise.[42] He never even uses the word "Christ;" however, he speaks about generation of the Logos and his participation in creation.[43]

Tatian has a peculiar tripartite anthropology. For him, human nature has body/flesh, and two types of spirit. The first spirit is material or created spirit,[44] which corresponds to the human soul,[45] and is not limited only to human beings. It is found in the whole of creation: luminaries, angels, people, animals, plants, and waters. The nature of material spirit is one and the same, although "it possesses differences within itself."[46] This differentiation in each particular thing resembles *entelecheia* (inner substance of the thing) of Aristotle. Material spirit in created entities functions as the ontological principle forming their shape and existence.[47] Therefore, to worship pagan gods is to worship material spirit.[48]

The human soul is the animating principle of the body. It is inseparable from the body and does not have independent existence. The whole idea that the soul can benefit from separation from the body seems ridiculous to Tatian.[49] Therefore, the soul is as mortal as the body; both are born, die and dissolve at the same time, and then at the end of the world resurrect for the final judgment.[50]

The second spirit is called perfect, divine, heavenly, or spiritual spirit. It is higher than the soul, and it functions as the receptacle of the image and likeness of God.[51] The divine spirit both comes from God and is the mode for communication with God.[52] Identifying human spiritual spirit with the image and likeness of God instead of with a human's rational

---

[42] *Orat.* 21.1. Whittaker, *Oratio Ad Graecos and Fragments*, 42–43.

[43] *Orat.* 5. Cf. *Orat.* 7.1.

[44] Tatian is notorious for a semi-materialistic approach to reality. Even heaven in his perspective has boundaries (*Orat.* 20.2). Everything which is created has materiality, nevertheless this materiality, for example in angels, is spiritual (*Orat.* 15.3).

[45] *Orat.* 12.1.

[46] *Orat.* 12.5. Whittaker, *Oratio Ad Graecos and Fragments*, 24–25.

[47] *Orat.* 12, cf. *Orat.* 4.2.

[48] *Orat.* 4.2.

[49] *Orat.* 16.1.

[50] *Orat.* 13.1, 15.1, cf. *Orat.* 6.2.

[51] *Orat.* 12.1.

[52] *Orat.* 13.1–3.

faculty (*nous*) is, in Finch's opinion, "Tatian's most distinctive and influential contribution."[53]

The divine spirit is intimately connected to the soul.[54] It is through this connection of the human soul with the divine spirit, that the human being can participate in God and obtain immortality and incorruptibility.[55] However, this immortality is conditional, not ontological. Neither angels nor humans possess goodness as an ontological characteristic of their nature, but have free predisposition toward both good and evil. The misuse of free will caused separation from God. The concept of the human fall is an important aspect of Tatian's theology, however, it is presumed by him rather than explicitly stated in a biblical context. He never mentions Adam by name nor makes direct allusions to Genesis 3.[56] Throughout *Oratio ad Graecos* emphasis is placed on an angelic rebellion copied by human beings, and on the intervention of demons in the life of humanity.

After the fall, the divine spirit left human beings, and people lost the image and likeness of God. However, it did not abandon humanity entirely, at least the souls of some people still retained sparks of the spirit's power.[57] If the soul chooses to follow the divine wisdom and do just things, it can attract the divine spirit back and regain union with God.[58] This return of spiritual spirit, closely associated with the work of the Holy Spirit, restores our immortality[59] and makes us capable of comprehending the Godhead.[60] Here Tatian follows Justin.

In Tatian, the soteriological problem is to regain the image and likeness of God through the knowledge and wisdom of God, which restores the original incorruptibility, immortality, and union with God. The way of

---

[53] Jeffrey Finch, "Sanctity as Participation in the Divine Nature According to the Ante-Nicene Eastern Fathers, Considered in the Light of Palamism" (Ph.D. diss., Drew University, 2001) 153.

[54] *Orat.* 13.3.

[55] *Orat.* 7.1.

[56] See *Orat.* 7, 20.

[57] *Orat.* 13.2–3, cf. 20. In *Orat.* 15.4 Tatian affirms that everyone has a second chance, is capable of repentance, and can defeat death; and throughout *Oratio ad Graecos* Tatian on several occasions confirms that all ages, nations, and genders are admitted to Christian teaching.

[58] *Orat.* 7.1, 13.3, 15.1–2.

[59] *Orat.* 20.2–3; 19.2.

[60] *Orat.* 16.1–2.

return to God is described in terms of moral and intellectual perfection rather than ontological transformation.[61] It requires effort from human beings, and it is a gift from God. It is the return to humankind's true destiny, which is culminated in the general resurrection.

Theophilus of Antioch

Theophilus of Antioch is less critical of Greek culture than Tatian; his theology is closer to Justin's. However, recognizing some validity of Hellenistic wisdom, or rather some similarities between Christian and pagan cultures that resulted from dependence of pagan authors on biblical sources, he attempts to demonstrate Christian revelation as superior to, and more ancient than, the former.[62] Like other apologists of the second century, Theophilus makes use of Logos theology. However, along with Tatian and Athenagoras, he does not correlate it with the incarnation of Christ. Salvation of the human being is presented, perhaps as the result of extensive study of Hebrew Scripture,[63] as obedience to God's law and commandments. This he combines with the doctrine of bodily resurrection, as a reward for obedience.[64]

Human existence, according to Theophilus, is a very dynamic process from the beginning. A human being, who is the breath of God[65] and "the only work worthy of his own [God's] hands,"[66] was created neither perfect nor imperfect, neither mortal nor immortal, but capable of both states.[67] Theophilus says, "For God made man free, and with power over himself."[68] Here Theophilus points to both a human resemblance to, and difference from, God. If Adam were created immortal, it would make him equal to

---

[61] *Orat.* 20.1.

[62] *Ad Autol.* 2.30, 33; 3.26, 29.

[63] See the introduction to Robert McQueen Grant, *Ad Autolycum, Oxford Early Christian Texts* (Oxford: Clarendon, 1970) xvii–xix.

[64] *Ad Autol.* 2.27.

[65] *Ad Autol.* 1.7.

[66] *Ad Autol.* 2.18; Grant, *Ad Autolycum*, 56–57.

[67] But with intent toward immortality: *Ad Autol.* 2.24, 27.

[68] *Ad Autol.* 2.27. ANF 2:105. This sentence is omitted from Grant's English translation, *Ad Autolycum*, 70–71.

God; if he were mortal, God would be responsible for his death.[69] However, originally humans were sinless.[70] In Theophilus this intermediacy of a human being has even spatial significance. God not only created the human person as an incomplete sketch, but also positioned him in paradise, a place between the earth and heaven.

In connection with this original, human intermediacy, Theophilus offers one of the first explicit early references to human deification in Christian theology:

> God transferred him [human being] out of the earth from which he was made into paradise, giving him an opportunity for progress so that by growing and becoming mature, and furthermore having been declared a god (θεὸς ἀναδειχθείς *theos anadeichtheis*), he might also ascend into heaven . . . possessing immortality.[71]

This intermediacy of the human's condition, with a potentiality of full maturity, becomes a significant element of the soteriology and anthropology of some later patristic writers.

The divine commandment not to eat the fruit of the tree of knowledge, for Theophilus, was due to Adam's infancy, a notion later picked up in patristic tradition only by Irenaeus.[72] As little children are not capable of eating solid food, so was Adam "not yet able to acquire knowledge properly."[73] Adam disobeyed this commandment and caused his own "expulsion from Paradise" and "acquired pain, suffering, and sorrow, and finally fell victim of death."[74] Death by itself was not the final divine judgment against Adam, but rather a divine remedy so that Adam would not stay in a sinful state forever; and at the appointed time, through resurrection, he would become new and perfect, righteous and immortal. God "gave him an occasion for repentance and confession."[75] Together

---

[69] *Ad Autol.* 2.27.

[70] *Ad Autol.* 2.17.

[71] *Ad Autol.* 2.24. Grant, *Ad Autolycum*, 66–67.

[72] *Adv. Haer.* 3.22.4, 3.23.5, 4.38.1–2. On this subject see, M. C. Steenberg, "Children in Paradise: Adam and Eve as 'Infants' in Irenaeus of Lyons," in *Journal of Early Christian Studies* 12, no. 1 (2004): 1–22.

[73] *Ad Autol.* 2.25. Grant, *Ad Autolycum*, 66–67.

[74] *Ad Autol.* 2.25. Grant, *Ad Autolycum*, 68–69.

[75] *Ad Autol.* 2.26. Grant, *Ad Autolycum*, 68–69.

with a human's possibility for restoration, the animal world, that transgresses along with humanity, also receives a chance to be redeemed.[76]

By free will Adam broke the divine law and by the same principle a human being can be restored, as a gift of God's "own philanthropy and mercy," if he chooses to obey the will of God.[77] In the context of this passage, we find another explicit reference to human deification. Theophilus does not use θεοποιέω or other direct designators for deification; like Justin, he employs θεὸς γίγνομαι *theos gignomai*. However, if in Justin θεὸς γίγνομαι *theos gignomai* is mentioned in the context of his exegesis of Ps 81:6 (LXX), in Theophilus it is a free standing statement: if someone "were to turn to the life of immortality by keeping the commandment of God, he would win immortality as a reward from him and would become god (γένηται θεός *genētai theos*)."[78]

It does not look like deification in Theophilus goes beyond achievement of immortality and incorruptibility, which is the prerogative of the whole human being, not only of the soul;[79] it is not an escape from corporeality. Purity, righteousness, and immortality are the fruit of a healthy human condition, which one can obtain through obedience to God's law, and through the therapeutic experience of death and resurrection.[80] This new human condition corresponds with the state of maturity, and transcends the original one in which Adam was created. A human being becomes immortal, attains a vision of God, and will be located in heaven.[81] Here we have a concept of deification as full human maturity.

---

[76] *Ad Autol.* 2.17.

[77] *Ad Autol.* 2.17, 27.

[78] *Ad Autol.* 2.27. Grant, *Ad Autolycum*, 70–71. Norman Russell suggests that reference to Ps. 81:6 (LXX) is contextually present (*The Doctrine of Deification in the Greek Patristic Tradition* [Oxford: Oxford Univeristy Press, 2004] 104). Considering Theophilus' connection to Jewish Christianity this suggestion is very plausible, however, at the same time it is very speculative as Theophilus does not make any direct references to Ps. 81:6 (LXX) in this passage nor throughout *Ad Autolycum*.

[79] *Ad Autol.* 1.7.

[80] *Ad Autol.* 2.26.

[81] *Ad Autol.* 1.7, 2.24–26.

Athenagoras

Athenagoras, who is acknowledged as "unquestionably the most eloquent of the early Christian apologists,"[82] demonstrates significant appreciation for the Hellenistic classical tradition. However, in spite of his eloquence and education, he had practically no influence on patristic tradition.[83]

Athenagoras's two known treatises, *Legatio pro Christianis* and *De resurrectione mortuorum*, argue from the standpoint of rational thinking. If his theology of God is "deeply influenced by the popular Platonism,"[84] his anthropology has a definite Aristotelian stamp, indicating a sophisticated knowledge of philosophical sources. His discourse is philosophic rather than historic/biblical. Athenagoras could be viewed as one of the first Christian philosophic theologians. Christology does not play any significant role in his writing. Except for one obscure remark in *Res.* 21.4, he avoids speaking about the incarnation. He does demonstrate for us how elements of Hellenistic culture and Greek philosophy could be appropriated to a new context of Christian discourse and have a different meaning.

Authorship of his second treatise, *De resurrectione*, was recently disputed.[85] However, even if this work does not belong to Athenagoras, as William Schoedel points out, in addition to other similarities, "there is apparently no fundamental difference between the vocabulary and style of the two treatises and the fact that near the end of the *Plea* (37.1) Athenagoras sets aside the problem of resurrection—presumably for some other occasion."[86] Nevertheless, when we try to trace evidence for the

---

[82] Johannes Quasten, *Patrology* (Westminster, Md.: Christian Classics, 1993 [1950]) 1:229.

[83] See the introduction to Athenagoras, *Legatio and De Resurrectione, Oxford Early Christian Texts*, ed. William R. Schoedel (Oxford: Clarendon, 1972) ix–xi.

[84] Grant, *Greek Apologists of the Second*, 106.

[85] See, R. M. Grant, "Athenagoras or pseudo-Athenagoras," *Harvard Theological Review* 47 (1954): 121–29. However, some other scholars find Grant's arguments not conclusive. See, J. L. Rauch, *Greek Logic and Philosophy and the Problem of Authorship in Athenagoras* (Ph. D. diss., University of Chicago, 1968); B. Pouderon, "L'authenticité du traité sur la résurrection attribué à l'apologiste Athénagore," *Vigiliae Christianae* 40 (1986): 226–44. See also, Schoedel, *Legatio and De Resurrectione*, xxv–xxxii.

[86] Schoedel, *Legatio and De Resurrectione*, xxv–xxvi.

Christian concept of deification in the two works, we run into peculiar incongruities, both stylistic and conceptual.

In *Legatio*, Athenagoras consistently draws a distinction between the eternal and uncreated God[87] and "created and perishable" matter.[88] Here, Middle Platonic ontological dualism between material and spiritual, is presented as the dualism between created and uncreated. Everything that is created is non-being.[89] Not only matter, but also a human being "is created and perishable."[90] This disposition underlines his main argument in discourse about gods in paganism. Therefore, to speak about a human being in terms of god is inconceivable.[91] Even such vocabulary as θεὸς γίγνομαι *theos gignomai*[92] and θεοποιέω,[93] that we can find in *Legatio*, is always used in the context of pagan criticism.

However, in spite of the substantial ontological difference that exists between God and the created realm, a human being does have the capability to know God through mind and thought, through mind and thought *alone* (νῷ μόνῳ καὶ λόγῳ *nō monō kai logō*).[94] A human being has some "affinity with the divine,"[95] the human soul is naturally immortal,[96] and in the divine design a human being is destined to another heavenly life where "we may then abide with God and with his help remain changeless and impassible in soul as though we were not body, even if we have one, but heavenly spirit."[97] This heavenly life in bodily form is depicted in rather Platonic spiritualistic terms, contrary to a strong emphasis in *De resurrectione,* his other treatise, on anthropological unity of the soul and the body, and virtual silence about the spirit and human heavenly destiny. In *De resurrectione,* we not only have a more holistic approach to the structure of the human being, who is always, in order to be human, both

---

[87] *Leg.* 30.3.

[88] *Leg.* 4.1.

[89] *Leg.* 4.2.

[90] *Leg.* 8.3.

[91] *Leg.* 20.5–21.1, 22.6–12, 28.8, 29.4.

[92] *Leg.* 20.1. Cf. 18.3, 29.4.

[93] *Leg.* 22.9, 10, 12.

[94] *Leg.* 4.1.

[95] *Leg.* 4.1; 25.3.

[96] *Leg.* 27.2. Cf. *Res.* 13.1, 15.2–8.

[97] *Leg.* 31.4. Schoedel, *Legatio and De Resurrectione,* 76–77.

soul and body,[98] but the resurrected body itself obtains characteristics of immortality akin to the soul.[99]

The human being as a rational creature, invested with intelligence,[100] and a carrier of the image of God,[101] was not created for the sake of God himself, who needs nothing, but for the human's own sake, for never ending life in eternal contemplation of God.[102] Thus, the τέλος *telos* (goal) of human destiny is perpetual existence,[103] which can only be achieved through the resurrection of the body.[104]

With these two premises—natural immortality of the soul and perpetual existence of the entire human being, who consists of soul and body—Athenagoras links together the Greek notion of natural immortality of the soul with the Christian doctrine of bodily resurrection. Both properties of human composite nature should perpetually exist, according to their form. Human "survival guarantees his resurrection, without which he could not survive as man."[105] Both the soul and the body are subjects of the moral order. They both carry the responsibility for what was performed by them in cooperation. Therefore, they both should be rewarded or punished.[106]

In Athenagoras, as in other apologists before him, the soteriological goal is realized in immortality and incorruptibility, which are the attributes of God himself. However, Athenagoras is very clear that any god-language is inappropriate to a human being. Immortality and incorruptibility of the soul are innate and ontological attributes of human nature; however as created being they only resemble, but do not parallel, God's qualities. Unlike Justin, in Athenagoras the human soul never loses immortality. Immortality of the body is the result of the transformation of human nature through resurrection, by the creative power of God. The christological context of this transformation is absent in his writings. From the beginning, a human being was created with some autonomy from God, and with natural ability

---

[98] *Res.* 10.5, 13.1, 15.2, 15.8, 18.4, 21.5.

[99] *Res.* 3.2, 10.5–6.

[100] *Res.* 12.6, 13.1.

[101] *Res.* 12.6.

[102] *Res.* 13.2; 25.4.

[103] *Res.* 12.

[104] *Res.* 16.2.

[105] *Res.* 13.2. Schoedel, *Legatio and De Resurrectione*, 120–21. Cf. *Res.* 25.3.

[106] *Res.* 18–23.

to turn toward, or away from, God. The achievement of perpetual duration is the result of moral obedience. A human being is capable of making rational moral decisions. Rationality, another ontological human quality, has some affinity to the divine, but nevertheless is a human attribute. Athenagoras, unlike other apologists, does not correlate human ability to reason with the Logos theology. By making "God's majesty and universal wisdom" the objects of "eternal contemplation," a human being is guaranteed "eternal survival."[107] The rationality realized in eternal contemplation of God constitutes ultimate union with God.[108] This language of contemplative union with God represents more definitively an early foundation for speculative mysticism than it promotes the Christian idea of deification.

Epistle to Diognetus

In *Epistula ad Diognetum* we do not find the technical language of deification, however, this elegant piece of Christian literature introduces several theological themes that will be important in later development of theōsis. Christians in this apology are introduced as citizens of heaven waiting for incorruptible life. They collectively constitute the soul of the world.[109] The soul as an entity is already understood in Platonic terms as immortal and encased in the captivity of the body.[110] At the same time, as the result of transgression, human nature is not capable of obtaining eternal life outside of the grace and mercy of God.[111] The incarnation of God in Christ not only reveals proper knowledge of God himself, but also, through faith, makes a human being capable of seeing God.[112] True life and true knowledge are essentially connected. One is impossible without the other. This was already depicted in the story of two trees in Paradise, the tree of knowledge and the tree of life.[113] Imitation of the life of Christ constitutes the proper ground for the imitation of God. As we read,

---

[107] *Res.* 13.2.
[108] *Res.* 25.4.
[109] *Diogn.* 5–6.
[110] *Diogn.* 6.
[111] *Diogn.* 9.
[112] *Diogn.* 8, 10.
[113] *Diogn.* 12.

When you love him, you will be an imitator of his goodness. And do not be surprised to hear that a man can become an imitator of God. He can, because God wills it. To be happy does not, indeed, consist in lording it over one's neighbors, or in longing to have some advantage over the weaker ones, or in being rich and ordering one's inferiors about. It is not in this way that any man can imitate God, for such things are alien to his majesty. But if a man takes his neighbor's burden on himself, and is willing to help his inferior in some respect in which he himself is better off, and, by providing the needy with what he himself possesses because he has received it from God, becomes a god to those who receive it—then this man is an imitator of God.[114]

It is the imitation of God that makes us act similarly to God, however, there is not even any implicit indication in the letter that this similarity is ontological in any sense. Here, we have a combination of Christian care for the poor, with the Hellenistic view that benefactors are gods to their beneficiaries.[115] It is a christocentric imitation of God in everyday life that corresponds to moral and virtuous living.

Conclusion

Theological discourse in the apologists, with the exception of Justin, is less christocentric and ecclesiastic compared to the Apostolic Fathers. They have more emphasis on speculative reasoning, that lays the groundwork for what would become traditional methodology of Christian theology. The prominence of philosophic argumentation, along with the appeal to historic antiquity, serve to legitimize Christian truth in the eyes of Hellenist culture. It also introduces several theological themes that would play a more significant role in later developments in the concept of deification. Deification in the Apologists only occasionally goes any further than the attainment of immortality and incorruptibility. In Justin, deification is

---

[114] *Diogn.* 10.4–6 (*Early Christian Fathers*, tr. Cyril C. Richardson. Library of Christian Classics 1 [Philadelphia: Westminster, 1953] 221).
[115] Russell, *Doctrine of Deification*, 101.

paralleled with divine filiation; in Theophilus, with full maturity that supersedes a human's original state.

The apologists do stress contemplation and the vision of God as natural human ability to know God. They do not directly associate contemplation of God with deification, but their contribution is important for the founding of speculative mysticism, which itself becomes an integral part of the notion of deification. Similar to the Apostolic Fathers, the apologists have a holistic approach to human nature; however, they incline toward a Platonically oriented view of the natural immortality of the human soul. Eschatological expectations are not as significant as for the Apostolic Fathers; nevertheless, spiritual other-world-ness is more prominent, especially in *Epistula ad Diognetum*.

Deification is really a cluster of related concepts present in Christian theology from the beginning. It grows out of practical soteriological aspects of Christian spirituality. It is implicitly present in the background of most of the theological controversies. However, it does not get significant treatment as an independent theological issue in the early patristic writers, and yet it is never entirely absent. It exists in early patristic theology predominantly in a contextualized form.

Irenaeus on the Christological Basis of Human Divinization

Jeffrey Finch

Irenaeus' acclamation of "our Lord Jesus Christ, who did, through His transcendent love, become what we are, that He might bring us to be even what He is Himself"[1] provided the most compelling and often-repeated form of the perennial *cur Deus homo*[2] question for generations to come, even until today. Although he never employed the language of theopoiēsis or theōsis,[3] already present in the theology of Irenaeus are all the essential elements of what would come to be regarded as the characteristically patristic understanding of sanctification as divinization: restoration of prelapsarian[4] likeness to God and incorruptibility, initiated

---

[1] *Adversus Haeresis* (hereafter *AH*) 5.pref. (All translations, unless otherwise noted, are taken from ANF 1. Greek and Latin texts of *AH* are from PG 7 and that of *Epideixis* is from SC 406.) Of this dictum, Hastings Rashdall, *The Idea of the Atonement in Christian Theology* (London: Macmillan, 1925) 240, writes: "Here we have the characteristic thought of almost all subsequent Greek theology."

[2] "Why did God become human?"

[3] Gustaf Wingren, *Man and the Incarnation: A Study in the Biblical Theology of Irenaeus*, trans. Ross Mackenzie (Philadelphia: Muhlenberg, 1959) 209 n. 78.

[4] "Before the Fall."

by the union of human nature with divine nature through the incarnation, life, death, and resurrection of the Eternal Son, appropriated existentially as adoption by God and infusion by the Holy Spirit, and finally perfected eternally through the face to face vision of God.

Harnack and Bousset, among others, find in this soteriology the Hellenistic subversion and corruption of the Gospel.[5] Martin George,[6] while acknowledging that Irenaean formulations can bear a rhetorical similarity to the apotheosis of pagan antiquity, believes it is more reasonable to conclude that the idea of Christian divinization implicit in the passage quoted above is most appropriately and accurately attributed to several distinctively biblical themes.[7]

Theological Anthropology: Image and Likeness Recapitulated

Given that Irenaeus "organized his synthesis around the theme of the image and likeness,"[8] it is significant that he was somewhat conflicted on what, precisely, constituted the original image and likeness of God in Adam and on whether or not there was a meaningful distinction between the two.[9] On a number of occasions, Irenaeus seems to presuppose a perfect synonymity between image and likeness.[10] Frequently, when writing of the redemptive recovery of the image and likeness, Irenaeus implies that

---

[5] Harnack, *History of Dogma*, 2:10–11, 240; Wilhelm Bousset, *Kyrios Christos* (trans. John E. Steely; 1913; repr., Nashville: Abingdon, 1970) 432.

[6] Martin George, "Vergöttlichung des Menschen. Von der platonischen Philosophie zur Soteriologie der griechischen Kirchenvater," in *Die Weltlichkeit des Glaubens in der Alten Kirche: Festschrift für Ulrich Wickert zum siebzigsten Geburtstag*, ed. Dietmar Wyrwa et al. (Berlin: de Gruyter, 1997) 135–37.

[7] For instance, creation of humanity in the image and likeness of God (Gen 1:26-27); adoption to divine sonship (Gal 3:26, 4:5; John 1:12-13); the vocation of the Christian to perfection by imitating the perfections of God revealed in Christ (Matt 5:44-48; 2 Cor 3:18; Phil 2:5-11); and a vision of God in the future life, in which the resurrected will be made incorruptible (1 Cor 13:12; 15:53; 1 John 3:2).

[8] I. H. Dalmais, et al, "Divinisation," in *Dictionnaire de spiritualité ascétique et mystique*, eds., M. Viller, et al. Vol. 3 (Paris: Beauchesne, 1957) 1377.

[9] Jacques Fantino, *L'homme, image de Dieu, chez saint Irénée de Lyon* (Paris: Cerf, 1986) 106.

[10] *AH* 3.18.1; 5.12.4. Cf. *AH* 3.21.10; 4.pref.4; 4.20.1; 5.1.1.

Adam's likeness was lost as a consequence of sin, resulting in the departure of the indwelling Spirit. Through Christ's incarnation, however, "He both showed forth the image truly, since He became Himself what was His image; and He re-established the similitude after a sure manner, by assimilating (*synexomoiōsas*) man to the invisible Father through means of the visible Word."[11] In another context, Irenaeus contends (against the Gnostics) that the human body and soul inseparably together constitute the *image* of God, whereas the infused Spirit establishes the *likeness*.[12]

On the basis of *AH* 5.6.1; 5.16.2, it has become something of a scholarly convention to assume that Irenaeus clearly distinguished between the image and likeness of God in the human person.[13] But his interchangeable use of "image" and "likeness" as well as his concept that the only true and full Image of God is the Son, "after whose image man was made,"[14] would seem to weigh against finding in Irenaeus any decisive differentiation between a *natural* image and a *supernatural* likeness. In any case, Irenaeus stressed salvific human participation in God. Thus, it was not in Adam's aspiring to live a divine life, to be God-like, that he sinned, but in his succumbing to the temptation of egoism, that is, in attempting to acquire the glory of immortality and incorruptibility as his own autonomous possession rather than as a gift received from Another.[15] The divinely imposed sentence of death, Irenaeus avers, was a remedial rather than retributive punishment, intended so that the opportunity for sin would die with the body.[16]

A closely related ambiguity in Irenaeus' theological anthropology is whether he understood the indwelling presence of the Holy Spirit to be the third component of the fully human person or whether humans are in

---

[11] *AH* 5.16.2.

[12] *AH* 5.6.1.

[13] See E. Klebba, *Die Anthropologie des hl. Irenaeus* (Munster-en-Westphalie, 1894) 34ff; John Lawson, *The Biblical Theology of St. Irenaeus* (London: Epworth, 1948) 209ff.

[14] *Epid.* 22 (trans. J. A. Robinson in *St. Irenaeus* [London: SPCK, 1920] 90). This distinction between the Image Himself and those only created according to the Image (*kat' eikona*) will be utterly crucial in the Christology and soteriology of Athanasius, but is not of great moment for Irenaeus.

[15] *AH* 3.23.1. See M. Aubineau, "Incorruptibilité et divinisation selon Irénée," *Recherches de Science Religieuse* 44 (1956): 37.

[16] *AH* 3.23.6.

possession of their own created spirits. Gustaf Wingren considers this to be the "central point at issue" with respect to whether or not Irenaeus had adopted a Hellenistic (interior divine spark) view of deification, arguing that within Irenaeus' tripartite anthropology of body, soul, and spirit, "the Spirit throughout is God's own Spirit, not some kind of 'gift' of the Spirit, but the Spirit itself, i.e., God or Christ Himself."[17] Hence, if the Spirit departs, as he did as a consequence of the fall, "man's 'manliness' is thereby incomplete."[18] The acquisition of the Spirit in the Christian economy, then, does not make the redeemed other than human or supra-human, but truly and fully human, because "it is part of man's nature to be divine, and also little by little to become that which he rightly is, namely, God."[19] The sole text upon which Wingren founds his thesis is one in which Irenaeus expands on his rather enigmatic assertion that the innate capacity of human flesh for incorruption is "given by the Spirit," whereas its equal capacity for death and corruption is given "by the breath."

> For the breath of life, which also rendered man an animated being, is one thing, and the vivifying Spirit another, which also caused him to become Spiritual. . . . telling us that breath is indeed given in common to all people upon earth, but that the Spirit is theirs alone who tread down earthly desires. . . . Thus does he[20] attribute the Spirit as peculiar to God, which in the last times He pours forth upon the human race by the adoption of sons; but he shows that breath was common throughout the creation, and points it out as something created.[21]

Klebba and Meyendorff understand Irenaeus to have thought the indwelling Holy Spirit a natural component of the first humans.[22] Gross,

---

[17] *Man and the Incarnation*, 208.

[18] *Man and the Incarnation*, 208.

[19] *Man and the Incarnation*, 209. On p. 211, Wingren contrasts Irenaeus' soteriological humanism to the idea of deification found in Methodius and Athanasius. The latter, he claims, by holding out virginity to be the "highest expression of the Christian life," have sounded the characteristically Hellenistic note on deification by implying that participation in the divine annihilates what is most truly human.

[20] Isa 57:16.

[21] *AH* 5.12.2.

[22] Cf. Klebba, *Die Anthropologie des hl. Irenaeus*, 181 ff; Meyendorff, *Byzantine Theology*, 138.

on the other hand, points to a number of passages in which Irenaeus seems to have in mind a created human spirit which, once purified by its participation in the Holy Spirit, renders the person spiritual. For example, *contra* the Gnostic doctrine of the transmigration of souls, Irenaeus writes of the resurrected as "having their own bodies and having also their own souls and their own spirits."[23] Gross concludes that Irenaeus has anticipated the much later scholastic distinction between uncreated and created grace by finding in our prelapsarian archetypes "a 'spirit of man,' which is to say a spiritual gift, distinct from the divine Holy Spirit, but produced by Him and inseparable from Him."[24]

Created, ordered, and equipped though they were to be children of God, participants in the divine nature, and temples of the Holy Spirit, the creatureliness of the first humans already connoted an inherent weakness to Irenaeus and meant that they were necessarily in possession of only a dependent, relative, and dynamic perfection. Against the Gnostics' determinism, Irenaeus vigorously affirms free will as one aspect of Adam's having been created after the image and likeness of God,[25] a fact which exonerates the Creator for the sin and disorder of the world. Irenaeus anticipates another Gnostic assault on the goodness and competence of the Creator when he asks rhetorically: "What, then? Could not God have exhibited man as perfect from the beginning?"[26] His answer is an unequivocal 'no,' not because of any weakness, aloofness, or selfishness attributable to the Creator, but from the finitude of creatures who "must be inferior to Him who created them, from the very fact of their later origin."[27] As a mother is prudent not to make full use of her power to give solid food to her infant, "so, in like manner, God had power at the beginning to grant perfection to man; but as the latter was only recently created, he could not possibly have received it."[28] The instability which permitted Adam to sin, then, is not due to any deficit in the Creator's beneficence, but attaches to the dynamism of the finite creature, whose

---

[23] *AH* 2.33.5. See also *AH* 3.17.3; 4.39.2; 5.6.1.

[24] Jules Gross, *La divinisation du chrétien d'après les pères grecs: Contribution historique à la doctrine de la grâce* (Paris: J. Gabalda, 1938) 156.

[25] *AH* 4.37.4. Cf. *AH* 4.4.4; 4.38.4.

[26] *AH* 4.38.1.

[27] *AH* 4.38.1.

[28] *AH* 4.38.1. Cf. 1 Cor 3:12.

nature was aboriginally endowed with the capacity for change, improvement, and promotion to adopted divine sonship.

God Partakable

Although Irenaeus understood the human person to have been ordered by the economy of creation toward sharing God's own life and to have been endowed with the created capacity to do so, he was careful to insist at the same time, against the connatural theological anthropology of his Valentinian Gnostic nemesis, that "man should never . . . suppose that the incorruptibility which belongs to him is his own naturally and by thus not holding the truth, should boast with empty superciliousness, as if he were naturally like to God."[29] So Irenaeus' bold affirmations of the heights to which Christian salvation transports the human person must be read in light of his frequent reminders that there always remains a much more foundational, unbreachable, ontological gulf between the Creator and His creatures.[30]

As an alternative to the spirit-matter dualism of the Gnostics, therefore, Irenaeus advanced a Creator-creature duality. God alone, he repeats frequently, is uncreated, incomprehensible, invisible, eternal, unbegotten, inscrutable, ineffable, perfect, and incorruptible by His very nature, which seems to be a circuitous way of saying that God alone is infinite.[31] The Gnostic theory of emanations from the unknowable One, Irenaeus complains, is logically nonsensical at least in part because, in their solicitude to "guard against attributing want of power to Him" by protecting Him from involvement with the created (dis)order, they have constructed an anthropomorphized God whose mutability, "affections and passion," are the distinctive earmarks of creatureliness. If they had only consulted the Scriptures, they would have learned that "God is not as men are; and that His thoughts are not like the thoughts of men. For the Father of all is at a

---

[29] *AH* 3.20.1. Cf. *AH* 2.34.2., 5.3.1. See Aubineau, "Incorruptibilité et divinisation selon Irénée," 28, who reminds us that Irenaeus cannot be understood without reference to the Valentinian Gnostics against whom *AH* was directed.

[30] *AH* 3.8.3.

[31] *AH* 2.24.2; 2.34.2; 3.8.3; 4.38.3. See Aubineau, "Incorruptibilité et divinisation selon Irénée," 32–33; Gross, 157; Dalmais, "Divinisation," 1377.

vast difference from those affections and passions which operate among men."[32] God alone is known to be the immutable ground of the entire world of becoming not merely in spite of His involvement with it, but precisely *because* He is its eternal Creator: "He who makes is always the same; but that which is made must receive both beginning, and middle, and addition and increase."[33]

I used the phrase "Creator-creature duality" advisedly, for Irenaeus would not have the Uncreated as opposed to the created as the corporeal is to the spiritual or as the unknowable Pleroma is to the Demiurge in the strict dualism of the Gnostics. What Irenaeus adds is a keen sense of the Father's constitutive self-donating love. And that love is expressed by Irenaeus in terms of gratuitous human participation in the God who is by nature radically other and inaccessible. Ysabel de Andia goes so far as to suggest that what separates the Christian soteriology of Irenaeus most clearly and decisively from that of the Gnostics is Irenaeus' constant affirmation that salvation entails the creature's participation in God.[34] The metaphysics of the Gnostics, wherein "the only relation which can exist between substances or natures is a relation of consubstantiality,"[35] foreclosed the possibility of the participation of our own created, corporeal nature in the incorporeal or spiritual nature of God. The Gnostics understood the spiritual to be the one and only salutary nature, they also thought salvation to require that all psychic and corporeal natures be vanquished and supplanted. For Irenaeus, however, the alienation and corruption of fallen creatures is resolved neither by annihilation nor by pantheistic absorption, but by assimilation and participation.

For instance, in an analogy redolent of the Johannine eternal life motif, Irenaeus reasons that just as the human body is differentiated from and dependent upon the soul because it "has fellowship (*participatur*) with the soul as long as God pleases," so also "the soul herself is not life, but partakes in that life bestowed on her by God."[36] In addition to this Johannine theme

---

[32] *AH* 2.13.3.

[33] *AH* 4.11.2.

[34] Ysabel de Andia, *Homo vivens: Incorruptibilité et divinisation de l'homme selon Irénée de Lyon* (Paris: Études Augustiniennes, 1986) 325.

[35] de Andia, 169. Cf. de Andia, 223.

[36] *AH* 2.34.4; PG 7:837.

of divine life or eternal life,[37] Irenaeus also customarily uses incorruptibility (*aphtharsia*) as shorthand for the whole gamut of divine virtues or perfections which creatures may possess by gratuitous participation. Butterworth's protestations notwithstanding, at least *aphtharsia* certainly means much more to Irenaeus than mere survival of the soul after death.[38] Indeed, Irenaeus affirmed in opposition to the Gnostic doctrine of the transmigration of souls, that the soul of the rich man who had neglected the beggar Lazarus retained its individuation in "the form of a man" after the death of his body, but was not among the redeemed and did not, therefore, enjoy a share in the divine incorruptibility.[39]

How, if at all, did Irenaeus understand God's life and incorruptibility to be partakable by creatures while at the same time remaining singularly His own? Are they somehow external to His "totally inaccessible" essence, as the neo-Palamite school of thought insists?[40] Such a solution is insupportable from the textual evidence, at least in part because Irenaeus writes just as readily of human participation in God Himself[41] and in the Holy Spirit[42] and in the Son[43] as he does of human participation in God's perfections, such as incorruptibility, freedom, light, glory, life, salvation, and wisdom.[44] As appears to be the case with Paul,[45] Irenaeus understood what de Andia identifies as God's "five divine attributes: power, life, eternity, light, glory," along with each of His other virtues, to be "perfections of the divine essence";[46] the Basilidean Gnostics were wrong, for instance, to

---

[37] See also *AH* 1.10.1; 5.3.3; 5.12.6; 5.13.3. See Aubineau, "Incorruptibilité et divinisation selon Irénée," 50.

[38] *Contra* G. W. Butterworth, "The Deification of Man in Clement of Alexandria," 162.

[39] Luke 16:19–26; *AH* 2.34.1.

[40] Vladimir Lossky, *The Mystical Theology of the Eastern Church* (London: James Clarke, 1957; reprint, Crestwood, N.Y.: St. Vladimir's Seminary Press, 1998) 67.

[41] e.g.: *AH* 4.28.2, "*participes Dei*"; *AH* 4.20.5, "*tou Theou metechontes.*"

[42] *AH* 5.7.1.

[43] *AH* 3.17.2.

[44] Incorruptibility: *AH* 3.18.7; 3.19.1; 5.3.3; 5.7.2; *Epid.* 31, 40; Freedom: *AH* 3.19.1; 4.18.2; 4.34.1; Light: *AH* 4.14.1; Glory: *AH* 4.14.1; 4.16.4; 4.39.2; Life: *AH* 3.2.1; 4.18.5; 4.20.5; 5.3.2; 5.4.2; 5.5.1; Salvation: *AH* 3.18.2; 4.33.5; 5.6.2; 5.14.1; 5.19.2; Wisdom: *AH* 5.3.2. See de Andia, *Homo vivens*, 169–70.

[45] See 1 Tim 6:16, where he writes that God "alone has immortality (*monos echōn athanasian*)." Cf. Rom 1:23; 1 Corinthians 15.

[46] *Homo vivens*, 29.

conceptualize life (*zoē*) as an emanation subsequent to or derivative of the divine essence because

> God *is* life and incorruption and truth. And these and such like attributes have not been produced according to a gradual scale of descent, but they are names of those perfections which always exist in God. . . . For with the name of God the following words will harmonize: intelligence, word, life, incorruption, truth, wisdom, goodness, and such like.[47]

Unlike the Nous, Aletheia, Ennoea, and the other hypostasized properties of the Gnostic Bythos that lie outside the latter's reductively transcendent essence, the Father of Jesus Christ, according to Irenaeus, "is a simple uncompounded Being, without diverse members, and altogether like and equal to Himself."[48]

Irenaeus rather forcefully denies, then, that God's activities, perfections, or attributes are external to His essence and therefore somehow more communicable or participable to creatures than is God Himself in His essence. God doesn't merely possess His virtue; He is his virtue. God is what He has. Therefore, as Irenaeus understands salvific human participation in God, the life and light and incorruptibility that are internal to the divine Being must be differentiated clearly from those corresponding perfections which are the gifts of God. As de Andia contends: "The terms 'immortality' and 'eternity,' like 'incorruptibility,' in so far as they are the gifts of God, designate human participation in divine life, eternity, and incorruptibility, but not the divine eternity or incorruptibility as such."[49]

Yet it is clear that Irenaeus believed those essentially divine virtues of which *zoē* and *aphtharsia* are frequently emblematic in his lexicon truly to be communicated through the self-donating generosity with which God grants His adopted children a created share in His own uncreated virtues, for, as he says, "it is not possible to live apart from life, and the means of life is found in participation in God; but to participate in God is to know God and to enjoy His goodness."[50] God commands obedience not because

---

[47] *AH* 2.13.9, emphasis added. Cf. 2.28.4, 2.34.2, 4.11.2.

[48] *AH* 2.13.3.

[49] de Andia, *Homo vivens*, 30.

[50] *AH* 4.20.5: *Subsistentia autem vitae de Dei participatione* (= *metochēs*, Gk) *evenit; participatio autem Dei* (= *metochē de Theou*, Gk) *est videre Deum et frui benignitate eius.*

His vanity needs to be fed by our subservience, but because "man stands in need of communion with God," therefore His purpose for sending the Son was that "His disciples should share in His glory."[51]

Here Irenaeus has turned Hellenistic emanationism on its head by insisting on the immediacy of God's presence to His creation, even though this immediacy does not render Him comprehensible or vulnerable to be "measure or handled," which seems to be the point of his foreclosing the possibility of human knowledge "with regard to His greatness, or with regard to His essence."[52] In other words, it does not appear that Irenaeus was here suggesting that God has withheld a distinct mode of Himself— His essence—from His otherwise immediate presence and generous self-disclosure to the world. It is precisely the Christian God's ubiquitous presence to, and active providence over, the world that demonstrate and prove His transcendence:

> As regards His greatness (*secundum magnitudinem*), therefore, it is not possible to know God, for it is impossible that the Father can be measured (*mensurari*); but as regards His love (*secundum autem dilectionem eius*)— for this it is which leads us to God by His Word—when we obey Him we do always learn that there is so great a God.[53]

Irenaeus refuses to designate a distinct part or mode of God as intrinsically, eternally unknowable, for God is unknowable only insofar as "no man has searched out His height."[54] His point seems to be that the God who has given Himself in an act of love to be known and participated in, because He is infinite, cannot be participated in exhaustively or known comprehensively. The Gnostic error which Irenaeus was addressing in all this, as he sees it, was to have thought the Creator, by virtue of His involvement with the material world of change, to have been entirely immanent and comprehensible, from which misconception they made the further mistake of imagining a reductively transcendent and intrinsically unknowable Pleroma beyond the Creator.[55] Such a bifurcated

---

[51] *AH* 4.14.1. Cf. *AH* 3.20.2.
[52] *AH* 3.24.2. Cf. *AH* 4.19.2.
[53] *AH* 4.20.1. See also *AH* 2.6.1.
[54] *AH* 4.20.4
[55] *AH* 4.19.3.

view of God is incompatible with the Christian faith because it wants to collapse the uniquely Christian theandric (divine-human) mystery into transcendent and immanent components. In other words, the Gnostic solution is unacceptable because it attempts to ground the transcendence/immanence dialectic in a real, ontological distinction or differentiation within the divine realm rather than in the eternal difference between the immeasurable Uncreated and finite creatures. According to Irenaeus, therefore, the opposition between Exod 33:20 ("no man shall see God and live") and Matt 5:8 ("Blessed are the pure in heart, for they shall see God") is not resolvable by attributing the former reference to God's eternally invisible essence and the latter to His visible energies. Instead, Irenaeus attempts to reconcile this apparent contradiction by making appeal to Luke 18:27: "For those things that are impossible with men are possible with God."[56]

Irenaeus established the metaphysical possibility of human participation in an ever transcendent God on the christological distinction between the uncreated, eternal Son and the created humanity to which He was united by the Holy Spirit through the flesh assumed at the incarnation.[57] Jesus Christ is at once Himself the union between God and creation and also our own way to union with God.[58] What distinguishes the New Covenant from the Old, therefore, is not a different, now immanent God, as the Gnostics want to believe, but a different kind of human relation to God, one in which "the faith of men in God has been increased, receiving in addition the Son of God, that man too might be a partaker of God."[59]

As will be the case for Athanasius and Augustine, then, Irenaeus' christocentric doctrine of divinization is virtually coextensive with his understanding of adoptive divine filiation.[60] And the grace of "receiving

---

[56] *AH* 4.20.5.

[57] See de Andia, *Homo vivens*, 164–68. By insisting that this is the sole basis on which Irenaeus establishes the possibility of human union with God, she correctly excludes an essence-energies differentiation of the Palamite type in Irenaeus.

[58] *AH* 4.13.1.

[59] *AH* 4.28.2.

[60] Bousset, *Kyrios Christos*, 423, citing *AH* 3.6.1; 3.19.1; 4.38.4. Lawson, *The Biblical Theology of St. Irenaeus*, 158–59, citing *AH* 4.33.4. Cf. Wingren, *Man and the Incarnation*, 161; Harnack, *History of Dogma*, 2:241, 273 n.1.

through the Son that adoption which is by Himself" is equivalent in Irenaeus' mind to receiving "from Him the greater glory of promotion . . . that He might call man forth into His own likeness, assigning him as imitator to God and imposing on him His Father's law, in order that he may see God, and granting him power to receive the Father (*capere Patrem*)."[61] To be made a participant in the divine nature is to be united to the Father by configuration to the created humanity which His divine Son assumed from the Virgin, took to the cross, raised from the dead, glorified in Heaven, and now feeds to His disciples. Already implicit in Irenaeus' correlation of adoptive sonship with participation in divine incorruptibility is the trinitarian dimension of human salvation.[62]

Christ the Head

As I have begun to show above, the principal redemptive-economic act by which Irenaeus understood our primordial likeness to God and native capacity for sharing His life to have been restored was the incarnation of the Logos, in which a "communion of union"[63] was forged between God and the human race. Perhaps the basic structure of this conception is best captured in the sentence with which Irenaeus concludes *Adversus Haeresis* and which Normann calls "a synopsis of Irenaeus' theology."[64] Therein, Irenaeus writes of the Father's will

> that His offspring, the First-begotten Word, should descend to the creature (*facturam*), that is, to what had been molded (*plasma*), and that it should be contained (*capiatur*) by Him; and, on the other hand, the creature should contain (*capiat*) the Word, and ascend to Him, passing beyond the angels, and be made after the image and likeness of God.[65]

---

[61] *AH* 3.20.2.

[62] *AH* 5.16.2.

[63] See *Epid.* 31 (Robinson, *St. Irenaeus*, 97–98), SC 406:126.Cf. *Epid.* 6; *AH* 4.34.4. Torrance, *The Doctrine of Grace in the Apostolic Fathers*, 76 n. 4, suggests that this phrase recalls Ignatius of Antioch.

[64] Friedrich Normann, *Teilhabe, ein Schlüsselwort der Vätertheologie* (Münster: Aschendorff, 1978) 95.

[65] *AH* 5.36.3.

It is within this descending and ascending movement that the participatory exchange between God and man is perfected, but in such a way that man may only receive (*capere*) what he cannot take to himself at his own initiative nor under his own strength.

In refuting the Gnostics' docetic denial of the incarnation, Irenaeus proffers a nascent two-natures Christology, grounding his *commercium* soteriology entirely in the freedom and mercy of God:

> Therefore, as I have already said, He caused human nature to cleave to and to become one with God . . . . And again, unless it had been God who had freely given salvation, we could never have possessed it securely. And unless man had been joined to God, he never could have become a partaker of incorruptibility (*metaschein tēs aphtharsias*). For it was incumbent upon the Mediator between God and men, by His relationship to both, to bring both to friendship and concord, and present man to God, while He revealed God to man. For in what way could we be partakers of the adoption of sons, unless we had received from Him through the Son that fellowship which refers to Himself, unless His word, having been made flesh, had entered into communion with us?[66]

Against those proto-Arians (Ebionites) who, on the other hand, "assert that He was simply a mere man, begotten by Joseph,"[67] Irenaeus marshals the text of Ps 82:6-7 ("I said, You are all the sons of the Highest, and gods; but you shall die like men"), claiming that when Jesus quotes it to those who accused him of blasphemy, as recorded in John 10:34, he

> speaks undoubtedly these words to those who have not received the gift of adoption, but who despise the incarnation of the pure generation of the Word of God (and) defraud human nature of promotion into God. . . . For it was for this end that the Word of God was made man, and He who was the Son of God became the Son of man, that man, having been taken into the Word (*ton Logon chōrēsas*), and receiving the adoption, might become the son of God. For by no other means could we have attained to incorruptibility and immortality, unless we had

---

[66] *AH* 3.18.7, PG 7:937. See Gross, 151.
[67] *AH* 3.19.1.

been united to incorruptibility and immortality. But how could we be joined to incorruptibility and immortality unless, first, incorruptibility and immortality had become that which we also are, so that the corruptible might be swallowed up by incorruptibility and the mortal by immortality, that we might receive the adoption of sons?[68]

It is worth noting at this juncture that in both of these lengthy quotations, long before Arius appeared on the scene to propose a created savior, it is evident that Irenaeus has already seen and identified the exigency which both Athanasius and the Cappadocians will exploit in developing their cases against Arius and Eunomius respectively, to wit, that for the final beatitude of human salvation to be secure eternally (unlike Adam's "infantile" and capricious possession of the same), it must involve a participation in or union with the immutable, eternal God. Again in response to the Ebionites, Irenaeus asks rhetorically:

Or how shall man pass into God (*chōrēsei eis Theon*) unless God has first passed (*echōrēthē*) into man? And how shall he escape from the generation subject to death if not by means of a new generation. . . . Or how shall they receive adoption from God if they remain in this kind of generation which is naturally possessed by man in this world?[69]

Irenaeus does not specify how human nature has been united with the divine nature of the Logos in the person of Jesus Christ, nor does he address the manner in which the hypostatic divinization of Christ's human nature is extended to humanity as a whole,[70] except to say that the Logos

---

[68] *AH* 3.19.1, PG 7:939. Cf. *AH* 3.6.1, where Irenaeus attempts to demonstrate with Ps 82:1 that the Psalmist refers to the Son as well as to the Father as God.

[69] *AH* 4.33.4.

[70] Emile Mersch, *Le corps mystique du Christ* (2nd ed.; Paris: Desclée de Brouwer, 1936), 1:340 (E.T. *The Whole Christ: The Historical Development of the Doctrine of the Mystical Body in Scripture and Tradition* [London: Dennis Dobson, 1938]), finds the most vulnerable weakness of Irenaeus' theory of recapitulation in its failure to distinguish "what pertains to the humanity of Christ and what is proper to His divinity in the work of our incorporation in Him," as does Bousset, *Kyrios Christos*, 433–34, who concludes that Irenaeus' Christology was developed entirely in service to his soteriology: Christ was the manifested God (*epiphanēs Theos*) who made immortality visible so that the human race could share in it.

"commenced afresh (*in seipso recapitulavit*) the long line of human beings, and furnished us, in a brief, comprehensive manner, with salvation; so that what we had lost in Adam—namely, to be according to the image and likeness of God—we might recover in Christ Jesus."[71] Correlated with the recapitulation concept, but, alas, not much more enlightening as to the precise mode of divine-human union, is his often repeated idea in *Adversus Haeresis* that the purpose and effect of the incarnation was at least in part to habituate human nature for supernatural participation in God. The eternal Logos "dwelt in man and became the Son of man that He might accustom (*assuesceret*) man to receive God, and God to dwell in man, according to the good pleasure of the Father."[72] The Holy Spirit descended on the man Jesus for the purpose of "becoming accustomed (*assuescens*) in fellowship with Him to dwell in the human race, to rest with human beings, and to dwell in the workmanship of God."[73] So also in baptism "we do now receive a certain portion of His Spirit, tending towards perfection, and preparing us for incorruption, being little by little accustomed (*assuescentes*) to receive and bear God."[74]

Bousset only slightly overstates the case when he writes that "the whole doctrine of recapitulation in Irenaeus is thoroughly anti-Gnostic in orientation."[75] Against the Gnostic despisers of the material order, Irenaeus repeatedly returns to the affirmation that the God of creation and the God of redemption are one and the same; Christ is able to effect the *anakephalaiōsis*, that is, to recreate a human nature which was corrupted and disordered by sin.[76] Similarly, a constant theme running throughout the work of Irenaeus is that the end (redemption) is like the beginning (creation); the Word of God "was made a man among men that He might join the end to the beginning, that is, man to God."[77] As Adam came from the virgin earth, so did Christ come from the virgin Mary;[78] as sin was wrought by a tree, so also redemption;[79]

---

[71] *AH* 3.18.1.

[72] *AH* 3.20.2.

[73] *AH* 3.17.1.

[74] *AH* 5.8.1.

[75] Bousset, *Kyrios Christos*, 437.

[76] *AH* 3.16.6; 3.18.1; 4.6.2.

[77] *AH* 4.20.4.

[78] *Epid.* 32, 33; *AH* 3.22.4.

[79] *AH* 5.16.3; *Epid.* 34.

as the devil defeated Adam, so did Christ assume Adam's particular body[80] ("Summing up all things in Himself")[81] in order to defeat Satan.[82] Although Irenaeus first makes allusion to recapitulation with reference to Eph 1:10, writing that Christ will return at the end of history "to gather all things in one (*anakephalaiōsasthai ta panta*),"[83] more often he places the event of recapitulation not at the parousia, but at the incarnation.[84]

The christological or incarnational basis Irenaeus finds for human participation in God, however, is at once pneumatological. The redeemed are incorporated into the Son's economic relation to the Father only through the Son's economic relation to the Holy Spirit. However ambiguous may be Irenaeus' pneumatological Adamic anthropology, he clearly sees human assimilation to and participation in God, or the recovery and perfection of that divine image and likeness according to which we were created, to be effected primarily by the infused presence of the Holy Spirit, which is dependent upon our union with the God-man: "Christ recapitulated everything in Himself; uniting man to the Spirit and causing the Spirit to dwell in man, He is Himself made the head of the Spirit, and gives the Spirit to be the head of man, for it is by the Spirit that we see, hear, and speak."[85]

If the basis for our participation in God does not lie in a partitioning of God, it can be found in the "bodily consubstantiality of Christ with humanity"[86] largely because his flesh, which Irenaeus insists is not "different from ours" or "from another substance" than our own,[87] was perfused by the Holy Spirit. "The flesh of Christ is the means by which the divine life is given to man precisely because the divinization of man begins with the glorification of the flesh of Christ."[88] In contrast to the Gnostic false

---

[80] *AH* 5.1.3, PG 7:1123.

[81] *AH* 3.18.6, and see Harnack, *History of Dogma*, 2:273.

[82] *AH* 3.18.6; 3.23.3; 5.21.1; *Epid.* 31. Methodius (*Symp.* 3.4) also holds the first Adam to have been assumed by the Logos at the incarnation.

[83] *AH* 1.10.1.

[84] *AH* 3.16.6. See also *AH* 4.6.2; 4.38.1; 5.19.1.

[85] *AH* 5.20.2. See J.-M. Garrigues, *L'énergie divine et la grâce chez Maxime le Confesseur* (Paris: Beauchesne, 1976) 288, who finds here in Irenaeus a precursor to Maximus' doctrine of the created *habitus* or *hexis* of grace; Christ gives us the uncreated Spirit only through his own created humanity.

[86] de Andia, 336.

[87] *AH* 5.14.3.

[88] de Andia, *Homo vivens*, 336.

alternative between connaturality and annihilation, Irenaeus proposed a relationship of communion between the flesh and the Spirit of God, a relationship in which they are united while remaining distinct from one another, yet united effectively and securely enough so that the flesh comes to possess created attributes which are essential to the uncreated God.[89] Irenaeus understands 1 Cor 15:49 to consist of configuration to the Son by the operation of the indwelling Holy Spirit, consequent upon the Spirit's operation in the incarnate body of the Word.[90]

Finally, a glance back at Irenaeus' attempted demonstration of the merely relative or dynamic perfection given to human nature by God through the economy of creation reveals that he understood this face-to-face vision of God whereby the redeemed are made participants in His life, incorruptibility, and immortality to have been fully attainable only after the death and glorification of the body in the general resurrection. Just as Adam was not in possession of a fixed perfection, so also the redeemed in this life progress only gradually toward the fullness of likeness to God: "But we do now receive a certain portion of His Spirit, tending towards perfection, and preparing us for incorruption . . . which also the apostle terms 'an earnest.'"[91] God's "super-eminent kindness" is revealed in His chosen destiny for His creatures to "reflect the glory of the uncreated One," for even though they are now and will forever remain mere creatures, "they shall receive a faculty of the Uncreated (*virtutem infecti* = *dynamin agenētou*), through the gratuitous bestowal of eternal existence upon them by God."[92] It was necessary that the human race pass through the stages of creation, growth, strengthening, and healing whereby it is "rendered after the image and likeness of the uncreated God"[93] in the course of "ascending towards the perfect, that is, approximating to the uncreated One (*proximum infecto fieri* = *plēsion tou agennētou ginomenou*),"[94] toward the final end that one "should be glorified; and being glorified, should see his Lord. For God is He who is yet to be seen, and the beholding of God is productive of immortality (*efficax incorruptelae*)."[95]

---

[89] *AH* 5.12.4.
[90] *AH* 5.9.3.
[91] *AH* 5.8.1, quoting Ephesians 1:13.
[92] *AH* 4.38.3, PG 7:1107.
[93] *AH* 4.38.3.
[94] *AH* 4.38.3.
[95] *AH* 4.38.3. Cf. *AH* 4.14.1.

It is evident, therefore, that the writings of Irenaeus cannot be marshaled to support the neo-Palamite position that the fathers of the Church grounded the possibility of sanctifying participation in God upon a real distinction between an intrinsically incommunicable divine essence and God's communicable energies. Irenaeus assumes and implies that the divine persons of the Holy Spirit and the Son are no less communicable than are the divine perfections which Irenaeus clearly locates within what he repeatedly insists is God's entirely simple essence. The divine essence is unknowable, according to Irenaeus, only in the specific sense that the fullness of who and what God is remains incomprehensible, inexhaustible, and immeasurable. To participate in the divine nature, as he understood the concept, is to receive adoptive sonship to God the Father, which is to be assimilated to God the Son through incorporation to the humanity He assumed, recapitulated, sanctified, and suffused with the Holy Spirit at the incarnation. It is to attain one's divinely ordained created perfection through the noetic and obediential reception of God's uncreated self-gift.

Athanasius on the Deifying
Work of the Redeemer

Jeffrey Finch

Introduction

Athanasius marks a watershed in the development of the Christian soteriology because, as Jules Gross could say with the prohibitive weight of scholarly consensus in his corner, "for the Alexandrian doctor, the divinization of the Christian is not just a more or less secondary or casual element, as it was for most of the Fathers before him, but is the central idea of his theology."[1] The divinization of the Christian is the central idea of his theology largely because Athanasius founded his argument against the Arians for the fully divine identity of Jesus Christ on the soteriological

---

[1] Jules Gross, *La divinisation du chrétien d'après les pères grecs: Contribution historique à la doctrine de la grâce* (Paris: Librairie Lecoffre, 1938) 202. For concurring views, see I. H. Dalmais, "Divinisation," in *Dictionnaire de spiritualité, ascétique et mystique* (Paris: Beauchesne, 1954) vol. 3, col. 1380; A. G. Hamman, *L'homme image de Dieu* (Paris: Descleé 1987) 153; Keith Edward Norman, "Deification: The Content of Athanasian Soteriology" (Ph.D. diss., Duke Univ., 1980) 77ff; Basil Studer, *Gott und unsere Erlosung im Glauben des Alten Kirche* (Dusseldorf, 1985) 147–48.

grounds that the redeemed cannot be made participants in the divine life of the Holy Trinity through incorporation into the Son if the Son himself had been divine only by gratuitous participation:

> And again, if, as we have said before, the Son is not such by participation (*ek metousias*), but, while all things originated have by participation (*ek metousias*) the grace of God, He is the Father's Wisdom and Word of which all things partake (*metechei*), it follows that He, being the deifying and enlightening power of the Father, in which all things are deified and quickened (*ōn to theopoion kai phōtistikon tou Patros en hōta panta theopoieitai kai zōopoieitai*), is not alien (*allotrioousios*) in essence from the Father, but coessential (*homoousios*). For by partaking of Him, we partake of the Father (*toutou gar metalambanontes, tou Patros metechomen*); because that the Word is the Father's own. Whence, if He was Himself too from participation (*ek metousias*), and not from the Father His essential Godhead and Image, He would not deify (*etheopoiēse*), being deified Himself (*theopoioumenos*). For it is not possible that He, who merely possesses from participation (*ek metousias*), should impart of that partaking to others, since what He has is not His own, but the Giver's.[2]

A similar line of reasoning is found as the prelude to his most explicit statement on the deifying effect of the incarnation in his *Orationes contra Arianos*: "Again, if the Son were a creature, man had remained mortal as before, not being joined to God (*synaptomenos tō theō*); for a creature had not joined (*synōpte*) creatures to God, as seeking itself one to join (*synaptonta*) it; nor would a portion of the creation have been the creation's salvation, as needing salvation itself."[3] Then, after lauding the Word's assumption of the flesh and his conquest of the Serpent on our behalf through the cross and resurrection, Athanasius proceeds immediately to suggest that the union of God and humanity in the person of Jesus Christ

---

[2] *De synod.* 51, PG 26:784b (*Patrologiae cursus completus. Series Graeca, vol. 26, Opera Omnia*, ed. J.-P. Migne [Paris: Migne, 1887]). All quoted translations of the writings of Athanasius are taken from NPNF 2, vol. 4 (*Nicene and Post-Nicene Fathers*, Second series, vol. 4, eds. Philip Schaff and Henry Wace [Peabody, Mass.: Hendrickson, 1994]) unless otherwise indicated.

[3] *Contra Arianos* (*CA*) 2.69, PG 26:293.

itself, prior to and logically apart from his self-oblation of the cross, effected a restoration of our prelapsarian likeness to God and, indeed, the deification of human nature:

> For therefore did He assume the body originate and human, that having renewed it as its Framer, he might deify it in Himself (*en heautō theopoiēse*) and thus might introduce us all into the kingdom of heaven after His likeness (*kath' homoiotōta ekeinou*). For man had not been deified if joined to a creature (*ouk an de palin etheopoiēthē ktismati synaphtheis*), or unless the Son were very God, nor had man been brought into the Father's presence unless He had been His natural and true Word who had put on the body. And as we had not been delivered from sin and the curse, unless it had been by nature human flesh, which the Word put on (for we should have had nothing common with what was foreign), so also the man had not been deified (*etheopoiēthē*), unless the Word who became flesh had been by nature from the Father and true and proper (*idios*) to Him. For therefore the union (*synaphē*) was of this kind, that He might unite (*synapsē*) what is man by nature to Him who is in the nature of the Godhead (*kata physin tēs theotētos*), and his salvation and deification (*theopoiēsis*) might be sure.[4]

Such formulations have led one school of historians, apparently initiated early in the twentieth century by Adolph von Harnack, but including contemporary scholars as well, to complain that Athanasius held to a "physical theory of redemption," which contaminated the Gospel with an Hellenistic and excessively realistic metaphysic whereby the human flesh which had become enslaved to corruption and death through sin was thought to be healed and immortalized through mere contact with divinity through the incarnation of the Logos, thus evacuating the need for Christ's atoning death.[5] Hence, what one could call the Harnack

---

[4] *CA* 2.70, PG 26:296ab. See J. Riviere, *Le dogme de la Rédemption*. 3d ed. (Paris: Étude théologique, 1931) 147.

[5] Cf. Adolph von Harnack, *History of Dogma,* 7 vols. (New York: Dover, 1961) 3:165; J. Tixeront, *History of Dogma,* 3 vols. (St. Louis: Herder, 1910–16) 2:148; M. Werner, *The Formation of Christian Dogma: A Historical Study of its Problem* (London, 1957) 168; M. F. Wiles, "In Defense of Arius," *Journal of Theological Studies* 13 (1962) 346; Aloys Grillmeier, *Christ in Christian Tradition* (New York: Sheed and Ward, 1965) 313–14; R.

critique of Athanasian soteriology can be summarized in three distinct, though interrelated, assertions. First, Athanasius' metaphysical realism fails to distinguish adequately between the humanity that the Logos adopted or assumed through the Virgin Mary and the humanity of those innumerable individual persons who preceded and followed Christ. Secondly, divinization is therefore thought by Athanasius to extend mechanically or automatically to all of humanity, not respecting individual freedom and responsibility. Thirdly, Athanasius is alleged to have taught that the incarnation itself, apart from Christ's life and sacrificial death, was responsible for effecting our salvation and deification, thus failing to account for a substantial portion of the Pauline corpus.

What I propose to do here is to examine each of these allegations in the light of Athanasius' writings and to demonstrate that, though legitimate in some ways, they fail to account fully or adequately for the breadth of his vision.

The One and the Many

In response to those who complain that Athanasius' rhetoric of union with God through the coessential Son's assumption of our humanity is "an abuse of Platonic language," Gross proposes that Athanasius should be understood to have conceived human nature "as a concrete reality, as a kind of 'generic man'—to employ an expression from Philo—in which every individual participates, but in a way in which the accidental properties—'habits and qualities'[6]—play the role of that which we would call the principle of individuation."[7] Athanasius posits the consubstantiality of all humans when he inveighs against those who say "that the Son is a creature" with the retort that the sayings of Christ "I and the Father are one" (John 10:30) and "he who has seen me has seen the Father" (John 14:9) would necessarily mean that the Father is a creature also, according to the following rationale:

P. C. Hanson, *The Search for the Christian Doctrine of God: The Arian Controversy, 318–81* (Edinburgh: T. & T. Clark, 1988) 450.

[6] *De synod.* 53.

[7] Gross, 208–9.

Those to whom we are alike (*homoioi*) and whose identical nature we share (*tēn tautotēta echomen toutōn*), with these we are one in essence (*homoousioi*). For example, we men, because we are alike (*homoioi*) and share the same identical nature (*tautotēta echontes*), are one in essence (*homoousioi*) with each other. For it belongs to us all to be mortal, corruptible, capable of change, originating from nothing.[8]

But Gross also joins Harnack's critique, in this respect, when he opines that because Athanasius never drew a fully adequate distinction between *ousia* and *hypostasis*, he was unable to see as clearly as those who followed him that the divinization of human nature accomplished by the incarnation "does not automatically extend to that of human persons."[9] Martin George proposes similarly that Athanasius failed to distinguish sufficiently between the two stages of Christ's adoption of our humanity, which also correspond to the difference between *physis* and *hypostasis*. It was not until John of Damascus that the distinction was explicated between the Son's adoption of our human nature considered as a whole at the Annunciation and the adoption of individual persons or hypostases through baptism and the cooperation of faith.[10] Yet, George also believes that the most recent historical research has revealed the Harnack school's critique to be a shortsighted "reduction" of the patristic doctrine of divinization to the acquisition of incorruptibility (*aphtharsia*) only. He further objects to the false dichotomy between the ontological and the moral dimensions of salvation which Harnack's epithet "physical redemption" assumes and implies, observing that Athanasius in particular, along with all the Eastern fathers, refused to separate the two, but strove to include every aspect of the human person in the transforming work of redemption, not only the will or behavior.[11]

---

[8] *Ad Serap.* 2.3, tr. Shapland, *The Letters of Saint Athanasius Concerning the Holy Spirit* (New York: The Philosophical Library, 1951) 154–55; PG 26:612b.

[9] Gross, 210.

[10] Martin George, "Vergöttlichung des Menschen. Von der platonischen Philosophie zur Soteriologie der griechischen Kirchenvater," in *Die Weltlichkeit des Glaubens in der Alten Kirche: Festschrift für Ulrich Wickert zum siebzigsten Geburtstag*, ed. Dietmar Wyrwa et al. (Berlin: de Gruyter, 1997) 145, citing John Damas., *De fide orth.* 61.3.17; 86.4.13.

[11] George, "Vergöttlichung," 119.

Others are equally quick to Athanasius' defense. Dietrich Ritschl maintains that Athanasius' "theory of deification is not a Greek speculation, but the decisive element in the salvific work of Christ, which, through his true humanity, is very different from a mechanical restoration."[12] E. P. Meijering appeals to Athanasius' understanding that the redeemed person may become a son of God only by participation, which implies that far from being mechanical or automatic, the sonship of the redeemed is contingent and mutable: "From this it clearly appears that men can lose their sonship which they have by participation, and what one can lose one cannot be by nature."[13] Kolp also takes exception to what he views as a sloppy and misleading interpretation of Athanasius' realism: "Because the Son was incarnate does not mean that each and every man automatically is deified in due process. The link between the two concepts is much more complex—and even ambiguous—than that."[14] Along these lines, Dalmais notes that by juxtaposing the *admirabile commercium* theme with that of revelation, Athanasius forges something of a middle way between Clement's and Origen's noetic emphasis and the Irenaean preference for the physical theory; the divinization of the human race is brought about both by a communion of natures in the divine person of the Logos and by His revelation of the Father.[15] Norman gets even more textually specific;[16] in one of the many instances on which he quotes 2 Pet 1:4, Athanasius asserts: "For He has become man that He might deify (*theopoiēsē*) us in Himself, and He has been born of a woman and begotten of a Virgin in order to transfer (*metenegkē*) to Himself our erring generation, and that we may become (*genōmetha*) henceforth a holy race and 'partakers of the divine nature (*koinōnoi theias physeōs*).'"[17] By his use of the present middle subjunctive (*genōmetha*) in a purpose clause, Norman thinks that

---

[12] *Athanasius: Versuch eine Interpretation* (Zurich: EVZ, 1964) 43.

[13] *Orthodoxy and Platonism in Athanasius: Synthesis or Antithesis?* (Leiden: Brill, 1974) 144–45, citing *De synod.* 53.

[14] Alan Lee Kolp, "Participation: A Unifying Concept in the Theology of Athanasius" (Ph.D. diss., Harvard University, 1976) 251.

[15] Dalmais, "Divinisation," 1381, citing the thought that follows immediately upon the *enēnthrōpēsen/theopoiēthōmen* phrase from *DI* 54 quoted above: "and He manifested Himself by a body that we might receive the idea of the unseen Father."

[16] "Deification," 104.

[17] *Ep. ad Adelph.* 4.

Athanasius betrays his tacit understanding that the incarnation did not automatically or mechanically divinize the human nature of which every individual is an instantiation, but gave to every member of the human race only the potential to be divinized, as Athanasius more explicitly indicates elsewhere when he writes that God prepared for the Logos a created body "that in Him we might be capable of being renewed and deified (*hin' en autō anakainisthēna kai theopoïēthēnai dynēthōmen*)."[18] P. Galtier also considers and rejects the proposal that Athanasius believed the Logos to have assumed the collective human race at the incarnation, this on the grounds that Athanasius repeatedly affirmed that only baptized believers are joined to God through Christ.[19]

Human Cooperation and Appropriation

Athanasius is not nakedly vulnerable to the aforementioned allegations that his soteriology is another instance of the so-called physical theory of the atonement and is a mechanical, magical, or "automatic and passive" process whereby mere contact with the divine nature of the Logos suffices to divinize the whole of human nature also because he insisted at every turn that the divine-human exchange of the incarnation must be appropriated to each individual through the obedient imitation of Christ, ascetical practices, and reception of the sacraments.[20]

First of all, Athanasius clearly believes and teaches that the grace of divinization must be acquired by an intentional human effort at reproducing the life and virtues of God Himself through discipleship and imitation. It is well known and documented how central a role the imitation of God played in Plato's soteriology and in that of the Middle Platonists and Neoplatonists who followed in his wake, as well as in the Greek mystery religions. "According to the Hellenistic philosophies," one author aptly summarizes, "it was an act of man's own virtue to become god-like and be the god's perfect imitator; it was an act of purely human effort and human

---

[18] *CA (Contra Arianos)* 2.47.

[19] P. Galtier, "Saint Athanase et l'âme humaine du Christ," *Gregorianum* 36 (1955) 557–63.

[20] Kolp, "Participation," 272–73. Cf. Gross, 213; *CA* 3.19–22.

industry."[21] Although the same certainly cannot be said of Athanasius, a firm resolve on the part of believers to live their lives after the pattern of their theandric exemplar is essential if they are to have a share in the sonship He gained for them. Above all, it is by the patient and merciful manner of His suffering that Christ has provided a model for believers to follow in order to become virtuous with the virtue which is Him: "That not only should we bear His image, but should receive from Him an example and pattern (*formam exemplumque*) of heavenly living; that as He has begun, we should go on, that suffering we should not threaten, being reviled, we should not revile again. . . . For those who are thus disposed and fashion themselves according to the Gospel, will be partakers of Christ (*particeps Christi*)."[22] Whereas the essential Son possesses these virtues from the Father *kath ousian*, the Father's adopted sons must strive to acquire them by co-operating with God's operations through the exercise of the will; the Son's "likeness (*homoiōsin*) and unalterableness (*atrepsion*) was different from such copy (*mimēsin*) of the same as is ascribed to us, which we acquire from virtue on the grounds of observance of the commandments."[23] From the Gospel parable of the talents (Matt 25:23) Athanasius draws the following conclusion: "our will ought to keep pace with the grace of God, and not fall short; lest while our will remains idle, the grace given us should begin to depart."[24]

Yet, it must be emphasized that Athanasius was not flirting with a latent form of Pelagianism here. In the *CA* 3:19-23 discourse treated above and in similar passages where Athanasius disputes the Arian account of how creatures may come to be merciful like God,[25] Athanasius is not "attempting to prove that men can earn their condition as sons," as J. Roldanus reads it, for "adoption remains a grace, but, for man, faith and virtue are the indispensable conditions for the continuation of the

---

[21] E. Kantorowicz, "*Deus per naturem, deus per gratiam*," *Harvard Theological Review* 45 (1952) 276.

[22] *Ep. fest.* 2.5; cf. 10.7.

[23] *De decret.* 20.

[24] *Ep. fest.* 3.3. See also *Ep. fest.* 10.4: "For through virtue a man enters in unto God . . . but through vice a man goes out from the presence of the Lord." Cf. *Ep. fest.* 13.2: because God "is good and philanthropic, He distributes to each a due reward according to his actions."

[25] *Ep. fest.* 2.2; 10.7–8.

inhabitation of the Holy Spirit in him."[26] Indeed, much like Augustine's dispute with the Pelagians, one of the central issues in contention between Athanasius and Arius is whether or not the salvation and deification of persons could be accomplished on the strength of obedience, imitation, and willful effort alone. In the case of Antony, for example, Athanasius is at pains to demonstrate that "Antony's holiness is not achieved, it is received" and that "the monk's deeds are not, strictly speaking, his own."[27] When Athanasius begins to speak of "Antony's first struggle against the devil," as though to forestall whatever Pelagian-like conclusions the reader might be tempted to draw from the coming discourse on Antony's ascetical heroism, he quickly adds "or rather this victory was the Savior's work in Antony."[28] Antony was able to overcome the temptations of the flesh only because "the Lord was working with (*synērgei*) Antony—the Lord who for our sake took flesh."[29]

In another context, Athanasius exhorts his flock to "imitate the deeds of the saints," but warns immediately thereafter that "when we render a recompense to the Lord to the utmost of our power . . . we give nothing of our own, but those things which we have before received (*accepimus*) from Him, this being especially of His grace, that He should require, as from us, His own gifts."[30] What we have received by grace is necessary for our salvation, but not is such a way as to obviate the equally critical necessity of human response. Athanasius even views Christ's exhortations to the imitation of God as acts of grace themselves: "For we too, albeit we cannot become like God in essence (*homoioi kat' ousian*), yet by progress in virtue imitate God (*ex aretēs beltioumenoi mimoumetha ton Theon*), the Lord granting us this grace in the words 'Be ye merciful as your Father is merciful' and 'Be ye perfect as your heavenly Father is perfect.'"[31] Far from being incorporated into the Logos automatically or mechanically, then, believers must be vigilant over the conduct of their lives by cooperating with this

---

[26] *Le Christ et l'homme dans la théologie d'Athanase d'Alexandrie* (Leiden: Brill 1968) 151.
[27] Robert C. Gregg and Dennis E. Groh, *Early Arianism: A View of Salvation* (Philadelphia: Fortress, 1981) 147–48.
[28] *VA* 7.
[29] *VA* 5.
[30] *Ep. fest.* 5.4.
[31] *Ad Afros* 7.

didactic grace of Christ if they hope to have a divinizing share in Him: "Let us keep our whole mind from guile . . . so that, being altogether pure, we may be able to partake of the Logos (*possimus fieri Verbi participes*)."[32]

Secondly, in addition to the obedient imitation of Christ, believers must cooperate with the grace of divinization by mortifying their flesh through asceticism. The ascetical practices which Athanasius enjoined for the purification of the soul from its aboriginal idolatry of creation in Adam, although possibly still tainted with a certain measure of Hellenistic spirit-matter dualism,[33] are entirely ordered toward this end of preferring God to all created things.[34] Just as the first humans fell into sin by spurning their utter dependency on participation in the uncreated Logos in favor of a virtual apotheosis of the sensible, created world, so likewise "our increase is no other than the renouncing things sensible (*aesthētōn*) and coming to the Word Himself."[35] This ascetical elixir to the first humans' idolatrous turning away from the contemplation of God toward creatures as ends in themselves is exemplified most fully in Antony, whose life Athanasius regards as corresponding with and, in some sense, recapitulating that of the pre-lapsarian Adam. Far from being elevated to some ethereal, supra-human mystical ecstasy, Antony "was altogether even as being guided by reason, and abiding in a natural state."[36] Indeed, Athanasius is obviously intent here upon emphasizing the genuinely human character of true virtue:

> But fear not to hear of virtue (*aretē*), nor be astonished at the name. For it is not far from us, nor is it without (*exōthen*) ourselves, but it is within us and is easy if only we are willing. . . . For the Lord said, 'The Kingdom of heaven is within you' (Luke 17:21). Wherefore virtue has need at our hands of willingness (*thelein*) alone, since it is in us and is formed from us. For when the soul (*psychēs*) has its spiritual faculty (*noeron*) in a natural state, virtue is formed. And it is in a natural state when it remains as it came into existence.[37]

---

[32] *Ep. fest.* 5.5. Cf. *CA* 1.45; 2.70; 3.38; *DI* 57.

[33] Roldanus, 258.

[34] Roldanus, 300.

[35] *CA* 3.52, PG 26:432.

[36] *VA* 14, PG 26:865.

[37] *VA* 20, PG 26:873. Cf. *VA* 34.

Yet, even in *Vita Antoni*, his most sustained treatment of the ascetical life, Athanasius is careful to subsume all human striving under the omnipotent grace of God; at the end of the day, Antony was enabled to defeat the wiles of the devil not on the strength of his own powers of obedience, but only also because Christ "took flesh and gave the body victory over the devil, so that all who truly fight can say, 'not I but the grace of God which was with me.'"[38]

Thirdly, salvific participation in God's nature is appropriated to the individual by the grace of God conferred through the sacraments, especially those of baptism and the Eucharist. Baptism is regenerative and recreating for Athanasius because it is the sacrament through which the indwelling Holy Spirit is initially given:[39] "For He has bid us to be baptized . . . into the name of Father, Son, and Holy Spirit, for with such an initiation we are made sons (*huiopoioumetha*) verily."[40] By being "regenerated from above of water and the Spirit (*anōthen ex hydatos kai pneumatos anagennēthentes*)," we are "made Word (*logōtheistēs*)."[41] Recalling that the Son is invoked during the rite of baptism, Athanasius argues against his Arian interlocutors that it would be futile for us to be baptized "into a creature," since the purpose of baptism is "that we might be joined to the Godhead (*synaphthōmen tē theotēti*)." The assistance of a created son would be superfluous because "God who made Him a Son is able to make us sons (*huiopoiēsai*) also."[42]

The Eucharist receives far less attention from Athanasius than his so-called "physical theory of redemption" might lead one to expect.[43] Even in his *Festal Letters*, Athanasius writes more often of the Eucharist as "an earnest of that heavenly feast" than in accordance with the realistic tones of his Logos-sarx christology.[44] Lest this language of promise be interpreted

---

[38] *VA* 5, quoting 1 Cor 15:20.

[39] Roldanus, 151. See also Gross, 214, who cites *CA* 1.34; 2.41; *DI* 14; and *Ad Serap.* 1.22 as instances in which Athanasius links baptism with divinization.

[40] *De decretis* 31.

[41] *CA* 3.33, PG 26:383.

[42] *CA* 2.41. Cf. 1.34, where Athanasius writes that through baptism in the name of the Father, Son, and Holy Spirit, "we too, being numbered among works, are made sons."

[43] Harnack, *History of Dogma*, 4:291. See also Gross, 214, n. 7: "Saint Athanasius seems to have seen in the Eucharist a means for preserving and strengthening the grace of deification. But, as the passages where he speaks of it are very obscure, it is preferable not to rely on it."

[44] *Ep. fest.* 6.1.

in a strictly typological sense, however, he is careful to admonish: "we, my beloved, the shadow having received its fulfillment and the types being accomplished, should no longer consider the feast typical," for Christ was "changing the typical for the spiritual" and therefore "promised them that they should no longer eat the flesh of a lamb, but His own, saying 'Take, eat and drink; this is My body and My blood.'"[45] In another Eucharistic allusion, Athanasius concludes one movement of his argument for the divinity of Christ addressed to the philosopher Maximus by stating: "And we are deified not by partaking (*metechontes*) of the body of some man, but by receiving (*lambanontes*) the Body of the Word Himself."[46] It is through communion with His sacramental body and blood, among the other means we have been discussing, that the redeemed are "able to partake of the Logos (*fieri Verbi participes*),"[47] but only on the condition that they are "prepared to draw near to the divine Lamb and to touch heavenly food" by the purification of their bodies and minds from "lusts" and false doctrines.[48] Hence, the Eucharist seems for Athanasius not to be a means by which our participation in God is effected in the first place, but rather strengthened and made more stable.[49]

By the Incarnation Alone?

Yet, it is when Athanasius speaks of divinization or human participation in God outside the context of the incarnation that the imputations to him of a mechanical or automatic conception of salvation fall most decisively short. The *admirabile commercium* did not end simply with the hypostatic union of the God-man forged at the incarnation, but extended to the entirety of Christ's life and, especially, to the events of his cross and resurrection.

Although Athanasius may not have integrated the atoning death of Christ on the cross with his doctrine of divinization as fully as he could

---

[45] *Ep. fest.* 4.4.
[46] *Ad Maximum* 2, PG 26:1088.
[47] *Ep. fest.* 5.5.
[48] *Ep. fest.* 5.5.
[49] Cf. Norman, "Deification," 126.

have done,[50] he does repeatedly aver that the cross was both necessary to fulfill the sentence of death imposed on humanity in the persons of Adam and Eve and efficacious to deliver the whole of the human race from it.[51] Because death and corruption had gained a strangle hold on both the human race and the whole of creation through Adam's sin and because he was "unable to bear that death should have the mastery—lest the creature should perish and His Father's handiwork in men be spent for nought," Christ was not content "merely to appear," but fashioned for himself a human body in the virgin Mary and

> makes it his own (*idiopoioumenou*) as an instrument (*organon*). . . . And thus taking from our bodies one of like nature, because all were under penalty of the corruption of death, He gave it over to death in the stead of all (*anti pantōn*) and offered it to the Father (*prosēge tō Patri*) . . . to the end that, firstly, all being held to have died in Him, the law involving the ruin of men might be undone (inasmuch as its power was fully spent in the Lord's body, and had no longer holding-ground against men, his peers), and that, secondly, whereas men had turned toward corruption, He might turn them again toward incorruption and quicken them from death by the appropriation of His body and by the grace of the Resurrection.[52]

The cross was required for the salvation of the human race, Athanasius continues, because "no otherwise could the corruption of men be undone save by death as a necessary condition."[53] So, in order to suffer the consequences intrinsic to Adam's sin, the Logos, who is by nature impassible and incorruptible, freely "takes (*lambanei*) to Himself a body capable of death, that it, by partaking (*metalabon*) of the Word Who is above all, might be worthy to die in the stead of all (*anti pantō*), and might, because of the Word which was come to dwell in it, remain incorruptible."[54]

---

[50] Gross, 213.

[51] Cf. J. Riviere, *Le dogme de la Rédemption*, 151.

[52] *DI* 8, PG 25:109. Cf. *CA* 3.33.

[53] *DI* 9.

[54] *DI* 9. Here, as whenever Athanasius discusses the incarnation, the word translated with "participation" (*metalabon*) cannot have a merely analogical meaning; the human body of Jesus could be rendered "worthy to die in the stead of all" only by becoming the body of the Logos or, at the very least, by receiving the Logos into itself.

The indispensability of the cross and resurrection to his soteriology of divinization is made most explicit perhaps when Athanasius addresses the *cur Deus homo* question forthrightly in *De decretis*, answering that "the Word was made flesh in order to offer up (*prosenegke*) this body for all and that we, partaking (*metalabontes*) of His Spirit, might be deified (*theopoiēthēnai dunēthōmen*), a gift which we could not otherwise have gained than by His clothing Himself in our created body."[55] The incarnation here does not stand aloof as though everything else in the life, death, and resurrection of the incarnate Word were a mere artifact of the initial act of redemption by hypostatic union, but is internally ordered to self-oblation of the Son on the cross by virtue of the death-bound condition of the flesh He took. Indeed, Gustaf Aulén notes that although Athanasius "makes less mention of the devil than almost any of the Fathers," and at times seems to downplay the significance of sin (in *DI* 7, he suggests that if death and corruption had not been consequent upon sin, mere repentance would have sufficed to save humanity), the fact is that in contrast to Anselm's "isolation of the death of Christ," Athanasius saw sin and death as an integrated whole, the power of which could be broken only by both the incarnation and the sacrificial atonement together: for Athanasius, as for all of the fathers, "The work of Christ . . . is a victory over death because it is a victory over sin."[56]

As with the whole of his soteriology, Athanasius' *theologia crucis* turns on the difference between the divine person of the Word of God and the humanity he assumed, which is not other than our own. The "exalted" of Phil 2:6, Athanasius inveighs against the Arians, refers not to the person of the Logos, but to the resurrected human nature he adopted and offered to the Father on the cross:

> Since, then, the Word, being the Image of the Father and immortal, took the form of the servant and as man underwent for us death in his flesh, that thereby He might offer (*prosenegke*) Himself for us through death to the Father; therefore also as man He is said because of us and

---

[55] *De decretis* 14.

[56] Gustaf Aulén, *Christus Victor: An Historical Study of the Three Main Types of the Idea of the Atonement*, tr. A. G. Herbert (New York: Macmillan, 1969) 43–44. Cf. Roldanus, 168ff.

for us to be highly exalted, that as by His death we all died in Christ, so again in the Christ Himself we might be highly exalted.[57]

Likewise, by way of reaffirming the irreducible mystery that the Word suffered in the flesh and yet remained impassible, Athanasius does not take recourse to anything like a distinction between the impassible essence and the passible hypostatic energies. Instead, he writes:

> For what the human body of the Word suffered, this the Word, dwelling in the body, ascribed to Himself (*synōn autō*), in order that we might be enabled to be partakers of the Godhead of the Word (*tēs tou Logou theotētos metaschein dynēthōmen*). And verily it is strange (*paradoxon*) that He it was Who suffered and yet suffered not. . . . But this He did, and so it was, in order that Himself taking (*dechomenos*) what was ours and offering it as a sacrifice (*prosenegkōn eis thysian*), He might do away with it, and conversely might invest us with what was His.[58]

In these several representative passages,[59] Athanasius quite clearly gives the very explanation for which Hanson claims to be at a loss: the cross is a necessary and integral part of the salvific *commercium* of the Word because the humanity he assumed at the incarnation for the purpose of saving it by uniting it to himself was "under the penalty of the corruption of death." It was specifically and only because the human race had become "wanting through the transgression and dead by sin" that "the perfect Word of God puts around Him an imperfect body and is said to be created 'for the works,' that, paying the debt in our stead (*opheilēn apodidous*), He might, by Himself, perfect what was wanting to man."[60] All of his treatises, even those in which his primary concern is to define the essential divinity of the Son both prior to and after the incarnation, are imbued with references to the substitutionary theory of the atonement, which Athanasius treats with as much matter-of-fact, sanguine assurance as he does the principle that salvation entails participation in God's nature. For this reason,

---

[57] *CA* 1.41.
[58] *Ad Epictetum* 6, citing 1 Cor 15:53.
[59] See also *CA* 1.43, 48, 51, 60; 2.7, 13, 65; 3.57–58.
[60] *CA* 2.66.

then, because the sacrifice of the cross is an integral element in the salvific *commercium* of the Word's mission, Athanasius is able to call the death of Christ "the first cause (*aitia prōtē*) of the Savior's being made man"[61] and "the sum (*kephalion*) of our faith."[62]

Neither is it only the incarnation and Passion of the cross by which this marvelous exchange has been effected, but also by the entire human life of Christ, most especially by the essentially impassible Word's adoption of human Passion. Jesus underwent anxiety and sorrow at the betrayal and death of his friends not because he was a mere creature and was therefore *necessarily* subject to the vagaries of human emotion, but "that in the flesh He might suffer and thenceforth the flesh might be made impassible and immortal (*apathēs kai athanatos*)."[63] Athanasius understands 1 Pet 4:1 ("Since, therefore, Christ suffered in the flesh") to apply to hunger, thirst, fear, exhaustion, and every other properly human passion, as well as to the cross.

And while He Himself, being impassible in nature (*apathēs tēn physin*), remains

> as He is, not harmed by these affections, but rather obliterating and destroying them, men, their passions as if changed (*metabantōn*) and abolished (*apēleimmenōn*) in the Impassible, henceforth become themselves also impassible and free from them forever. . . . For as the Lord, putting on the body, became man, so we men are deified (*theopoioumetha*) by the Word as being taken to Him (*proslēphthentes*) through His flesh, and henceforth inherit life everlasting.[64]

---

[61] *DI* 10, citing 2 Cor 5:14; Heb 2:9, 14; Gal 6:17; 1 Cor 15:21; 1 Tim 6:15.

[62] *DI* 19.

[63] *CA* 3.58.

[64] *CA* 3.34. Cf. *CA* 3.53, where Athanasius reasons that because it was the second Person of the impassible Godhead who was raised from childhood as Jesus of Nazareth, he "advanced in the flesh" strictly according to his "manhood" which was "deified," that is, progressively assimilated to the divine Person who inhabited it. This growth was undertaken so that "man's advance might abide and fail not, because of the Word which is with it." See also Gross, 213.

Beyond what Christ accomplished for us and without us, Athanasius also finds an exemplary and didactic dimension to the divinizing effects of the Word's incarnation, one which cannot be dismissively attributed to a naively realistic Platonism: "by the works of His body (*sōmatos ergōn*) He teaches them" who failed to learn of God "from His Providence and rule over all things."[65] Here Athanasius reveals the works of the Word's body, which we might call God's *created* energies, to be most decisive in reversing the stultifying consequences of the sin of concupiscence by restoring the possibility of human knowledge of God. Like "a kind teacher" who condescends to the epistemic level of his students, the Logos, seeing that the human race "were seeking for God in nature and in the world of sense . . . takes to Himself (*lambanei*) a body" so that "they who think that God is corporeal may from what the Lord effects by His body (*ho Kyrios ergazetai dia tōn sōmatos ergōn*) perceive the truth, and through Him recognize the Father."[66] Thus it was primarily through the created works of the essential energy rather than through manifold uncreated energies of God that He made Himself known in Christ: "the Word disguised Himself by appearing in a body, that He might . . . persuade them by the works (*ergōn*) He did that He is not Man only, but also God."[67] The two "works of love" accomplished by the incarnation were "putting away death from us and renewing us again" and "secondly, being unseen and invisible, in manifesting and making Himself known by His works (*ergōn*) to be the Word of the Father."[68] Athanasius also writes that one of the two purposes of the incarnation (the first being "putting away death from us and renewing us again") consists in the "unseen and invisible" Logos "manifesting and making Himself known by His works (*dia tōn ergōn*), to be the Word of the Father, and the Ruler and King of the universe."[69] Moreover, immediately following the *DI* 17 definition in question, Athanasius returns to the principle theme of this particular movement of the treatise and clarifies that the Logos is "known from the body by His

---

[65] *DI* 14.
[66] *DI* 15.
[67] *DI* 16.
[68] *DI* 16.
[69] *DI* 16.

works," which the context makes clear are the created works of the created flesh He assumed.[70]

We can conclude, then, that although Athanasius was less precise than he could have been about the nature of the incarnation, as was true of every Church father prior to the Council of Chalcedon, his soteriology of deification, or participation in the divine nature, was no crudely physical or mechanical theory as Harnack et al. dismissively characterized it, but was a development and explication of the Pauline and Johannine emphasis on salvation as adoptive sonship to God the Father through incorporation by grace into God the incarnate Son. For, at the end of the age our humanity will be "perfected in Him and restored, as it was made at the beginning, nay, with greater grace. For, on rising from the dead, we shall no longer fear death, but shall ever reign in Christ in the heavens."[71]

---

[70] *DI* 17.
[71] *CA* 2.67.

Augustine's Conception of Deification, Revisited

Robert Puchniak

The theology of Augustine of Hippo, a veritable font for religious thought in the Latin West for the past 1600 years, rarely dwells on the subject of deification. Certainly in comparison to its prominent place in Eastern Christian thought, the language of deification scarcely enters Augustine's mind (if we take the surviving literary works as evidence). The careful evaluation of Augustine's limited use of this concept has been undertaken by Gerald Bonner; his is the definitive statement.[1] Since the publication of Bonner's article in 1986, however, we have been privy to the unexpected discovery of new sermons of Augustine.[2] Thanks to these new findings, we can now supply a modest addendum to Bonner's work, given that deification is the key idea in one of these letters, the one known as *Dolbeau*

---

[1] Gerald Bonner, "Augustine's Conception of Deification," *Journal of Theological Studies*, n.s. 37 (1986) 369–86.

[2] See Francois Dolbeau, "Nouveau sermons de saint Augustin pour la conversion des paiens et des donatistes (V)," *Revue des Etudes Augustiniennes* 39 (1993) 57–108; and also *The Works of Saint Augustine: Newly Discovered Sermons*, tr. Edmund Hill, O.P. (Hyde Park, N.Y.: New City, 1990).

6 or *Mainz* 13. Augustine supplies an extended meditation in *Dolbeau* 6 on a subject so seldom mentioned elsewhere. In what is a homiletic exposition of Psalm 81, he gives voice to a rich theological anthropology. In so doing, he connects the concept of a "deifying God" *(deificatorem deum)* to the soul's spiritual warfare, the biblical vision of salvation history, and the gathering of members of the ecclesial "Body of Christ."

The Principal Passages

Bonner cites only fifteen examples of the words DEIFICARI and DEIFICATUS (and seven of these, he argues, are "irrelevant" to the theology of deification). Among the "relevant" passages he includes:

Ep. **10.2:** Augustine laments to his close childhood friend, Nebridius, that "amid uproar and restless comings and goings" a person cannot "achieve the familiarity with death that we are seeking. For in leisure . . . [one] would be permitted to become godlike" [in contemplation].[3] This letter, written ca. 388–91, dates to the period after his conversion and baptism, but before his ordination as a priest in Hippo. An echo of the youthful Augustine's Neoplatonic yearning for the fulfillment of the philosophical life can be heard here.

Enarrat. In Ps. **49.2:** Here we find multiple references clustered together: (i) In reference to Psalm 81, he says, "It is quite obvious that God called human beings "gods" in the sense that they were *deified by his grace*,[4] not because they were born of his own substance." (ii) ". . . . He alone deifies who is God of himself, not by participation in any other."[5] (iii) "Moreover he who justifies is the same as he who deifies, because by justifying us he made us sons and daughters of God . . ." (iv) "If we have been made children of God, we have been made into gods; but we are such by the grace of him who adopts us."[6] This *enarratio* (explanation)

---

[3] *Letters 1–99. The Works of Saint Augustine: A Translation for the 21st Century,* vol. II/1, tr. Roland Teske, S.J. (Hyde Park, N.Y.: New City, 2001) 34.

[4] My italics.

[5] Bonner, "Augustine's Conception," 384.

[6] *Expositions of the Psalms (33–50). The Works of Saint Augustine* (same series), vol. III/16, tr. Maria Boulding, O.S.B. (Hyde Park, N.Y.: New City, 2000) 381.

exhibits special affinity with our sermon in question, *Dolbeau* 6; the use of *deificatio* is sustained and is applied to the Christian mysteries.

Enarrat. in Ps. 117.11: Commenting on "The Lord's right hand has proved its might," Augustine writes, "Great might is needed to raise up the lowly, to deify a mere mortal, to make the weak perfect, to grant glory through abasement and victory through suffering."[7]

Serm. 126.14: "And there he stood, in front of the eyes of a servant, in the form of a servant, saving the form of God for deified eyes, and he said to him, *Am I with you all this time, and you do not know me?*"[8] (dated to 417 AD).

Serm. 166.4: "God, you see, wants to make you a god; not by nature, of course, like the one whom he begot; but by his gift and by adoption"[9] (dated to after 410 AD).

From the limited evidence, Bonner drew several astute conclusions:

(1) Augustine "believed his teaching on deification was based on Scripture"[10] and he rejected the Plotinian idea that deification could be achieved by the independent efforts of a philosopher, unaided by grace; deification was possible only "from a participation in God made possible by divine initiative."[11]

(2) The "christocentricity" of Augustine's thought was integrated into his understanding of deification; Augustine says clearly that "adoption by grace" is impossible without the mediation of the God-man. Augustine does, like the Greek Fathers, use the language of "participation" in God,[12] and he was in agreement with the theologies of both Irenaeus and Athanasius[13] (Bonner cites *Serm.* 192.1: "To make gods those who were men, He was made man who is God").

---

[7] *Expositions of the Psalms* (99–120). *The Works*, vol. III/19, tr. Maria Boulding (2003) 337.

[8] *Sermons (94A–147A) On The New Testament. The Works*, vol. III/4, tr. Edmund Hill, O.P. (1992) 278.

[9] *Sermons (148–183) On The New Testament. The Works*, vol. III/5, tr. Edmund Hill (1992) 209.

[10] Bonner, "Augustine's Conception," 371.

[11] Ibid., 372.

[12] Ibid., 373–74.

[13] Ibid., 376.

(3) Augustine's understanding of the unity of Christ and His church is closely associated with his use of deification: the elevation of humanity as adopted sons and daughters involves not only individual believers, but the whole church.[14] Moreover, deification is, in Augustine's thought, "a state which will be attained only in the life to come." There can be no claims to final perfection in this life; deification in its fullness is eschatological.

(4) Though the use of the term, *deificatio*, is scarce, "Augustine was apparently prepared to equate justification and deification, regarding both as the consequence of man's adoption." Bonner refers to the same *Enarrat. In Ps.* 49, cited above: "For He justifies, who is just of Himself and not of another; and He deifies, who is God of Himself and not by participation in another. Now He who justifies, Himself deifies, because by justifying He makes sons of God."

(5) Further, Bonner argues that deification is a matter for consideration within "dogmatic" theology rather than "contemplative" theology, because "it describes the consequences of the saving work of Christ rather than a mystical state enjoyed by a contemplative." In response to this assertion, one may reasonably question, however, whether such a distinction between "dogmatic" and "contemplative" types of theology would have been made by Augustine himself. It can be argued, moreover, that when Augustine spoke, in either catechetical or polemical tones, his threefold aim was to teach, to persuade and to delight (and the first of these was paramount). All of his work he wished to be edifying, for his teaching "with the help of the divine testimonies" aimed to "induce belief" by garnering obedience to their authority.[15] The delineation between dogmatic and contemplative tasks is ours, and not Augustine's. For him, all theology ought to be *both* dogmatic (insofar as it is sound in its articulation) *and* contemplative (insofar as it coaxes the deepening of faith).

Bonner's understanding of deification in Augustine's thought does indeed ring true in light of our "new" sermon of Augustine. *Dolbeau 6* has for its focus Psalm 81: "God has stood up in the synagogue of gods," and it begins with a remarkably dense catechetical passage (6.1) on the dynamics

---

[14] Ibid., 375–76.

[15] *On Christian Teaching*, IV.146; tr. R. P. H. Green (Oxford: Oxford University Press, 1997).

of deification. "We carry mortality about with us, we endure infirmity, we look forward to divinity. For God wishes not only to vivify, but also to deify us." *(Gerimus mortalitatem, toleramus infirmitatem, exspectamus diuinitatem. Vult enim deus non solum uiuificare, sed etiam deificare nos.)* Augustine reassures his audience that it is "God's promise" that persons will be made gods. In true Athanasian fashion, he repeats the age-old axiom of Christian hope: "The Son of God became a son of man, in order to make sons of men into sons of God." *(Filius dei factus est filius hominis, ut filios hominum faceret filios dei.)* Augustine tells of a forward-looking vision: what has begun with the incarnation will be completed in the future, will be made manifest at a definite time *(certo tempore apparebit)*. The promise of God is that He will make human persons "gods not by nature but by adoption, by grace." The "true God," he proclaims, is a "deifying God" *(deificatorem deum)*, a "god-making God" *(deificum deum)*.

There is abundant optimism in this opening section, wherein Augustine accentuates the end and goal of Christian hope.

Augustinian Polemic

On this day, however, we find Augustine in a fighting mood. His catechesis and spiritual guidance were laced with polemical concern. He set the stage for an argument with his initial comments: the gods that are made by the hand of a craftsman are not like the gods made by the "true" God. "Our God," he says, makes us into gods, but "*they* worship gods they make" *(Vos adoratis deum, qui uos facit deos; illi autem adorant deos, quos faciendo et adorando perdunt ut ipsi dii fiant)*, thus criticizing pagan practices of idol worship, which must have been, given his attention to the matter, still very prevalent in the North Africa of 404, when this sermon was delivered.[16]

---

[16] Francois Dolbeau has argued, regarding the circumstances of the delivery of this sermon, for the likelihood that Augustine was not in a rural township but in a town or city where some people in his audience understood Greek (see para. 2). He further places the sermon, along with *Mainz* 12, in Carthage in the winter of 403–404. Augustine was engaged in an ongoing refutation of the pagan religious practices alive in North Africa, a region that had received many lavish imperial monuments to the gods, dating back to the Severan dynasty. But now, legal interdiction against the pagan cults, which took force in the late fourth century, was blamed for the multiplication of civil troubles and for natural

When one worships the product of one's own hand, he warns, one loses the chance to become a god; the crafting of idols amounts to a "falling away" and lost opportunity (6.3).

Augustine asks, so what do people want: to become gods, or to make gods? (*Quid ergo uolunt homines: dii fieri, an deos facere?*) (6.3). One can sense the word play of a master rhetorician coming to the fore. He calls upon his audience to worship not "what you have made" but instead "the one who made you." The "godless" fashion an image "and slap a name on it" (*imponere illi nomen*). He makes an appeal to the self-respect of those in the crowd: "It is an insult to you (*iniuria tibi est*) that you should be like the one you have made" (6.5). The creation of the human person as *imago Dei* bestows dignity on all individuals. That someone would hope to be like an idol should arouse an indignant response, he insists. Why? Because an idol cannot do justice to the depth of "your inner self" (*interiorem hominem tuum*). Augustine calls upon people to use their intelligence "to see the truth" (*uis uidere ueritatem*). The inner self, he tells them, was bestowed with "all the senses," and these ought to be used to recognize the dignity of the human person, not to "become like the caricature, the idol" (*simulacro*).

> If the inner self becomes somehow or other insensitive, stupid, he becomes in a certain manner like an idol, and having ruined in himself the image of the one by whom he was made, he wishes to take on the image of the one which he has made [*si fiat insensatus quodammodo homo interior, fit ad quendam modum similis simulacro et, perdita in se imagine eius a quo factus est, eius quem fecit uult capere imaginem*]. (6.5)[17]

---

catastrophes. Pagan complaints during the 'tempora christiana' abounded. Amidst the provocation and counter-provocation, we find Augustine appealing to unusual language, "un terme inhabituel," as Dolbeau says, *deificatio* (*Revue des Etudes Augustiniennes*, 39 [1993] 57–108).

[17] Would some of the people in his audience be familiar with Augustine's own story of how he had long sullied the image of the one who made him? It had been six years or more since the writing of his *Confessions*. Augustine had admitted that he remained 'ignorant' of what it meant to be created in God's image, and that he even 'insulted and opposed' the idea, being 'deceived with promises of certainty' by the Manichees as well as his own 'childish error and rashness' (*Confessions*, VI.iv [5], trans. Henry Chadwick [Oxford: Oxford University Press, 1991]).

With the aid of the "spirit of God," he continues, it is possible to discern properly, and to see one's unlikeness to the simulacrum of the idol. He laments those who lack such discernment, but their lack of discernment, he reassures, is no loss of "God's work in themselves," which can never be killed (6.7). Augustine further chides those who trust in the impotency of idols, and he warns of the power of "our God" to cast demon worshippers "into the eternal fire" (6.9). (He equates the *numina* of the idols with demons.) He cautions his audience against the temptation to seek counsel from diviners or soothsayers (6.10). He equates such superstitious action with "seeking the society of demons" (*socius daemoniorum*) and the forfeiture of a divine inheritance as an "associate of Christ" (*socius Christi*). Those who heard him, he assumes, were "under enormous pressures" (6.11), affected by illness and strife, and thus vulnerable to the balm of the diviners. Augustine, as bishop, appears keenly aware of the quoditian tribulations of the *parvuli* (little ones), whose faith he cared for.

After this excursus into condemning idolatry, he returns to the matter of deification. He reminds his listeners that Christians were not called to lives of comfort and luxury, and that they must endure their hardships (*ferto condicionem tuam*). Such suffering is part and parcel of life after the Fall: "Indeed, it was our very nature that first sinned, and we derive from there what we are born with" (6.11) (*Etenim ipsa natura nostra prima peccauit, et ducimus inde quod nascimur*). The endurance of suffering will lead to the immortal possession of deification, he assures. The divine initiative is directed at sufferers who will be "recreated" into blessed immortals (*Dicit creator: "Recreabo uos"*). Deification does not occur in the isolated peace of the quiet, contemplative life, or in the seclusion of retreat, but rather it begins in the "craftsman's furnace" (*fornax artificis*), in this "world full of scandals, iniquities, corruption, oppression" (6.12). He tells his flock that they find themselves in the age of the "oil press" and the screws are being tightened so as to separate the oil from the dregs (6.15). He speaks not to a spiritual elite who have chosen Mary's "better part," but instead to many Martha's who cannot but help find themselves engaged in worldly toil.

This sermon, *Dolbeau* 6, offers us a concrete example of Augustine *the theologian* translating core ideas of more detailed and targeted doctrinal works into the pastoral concerns of Augustine *the bishop*. In appealing to the inherent dignity of persons created in the image of God, Augustine echoes some of the concerns of *The Trinity*, which he had begun in 400 and would not complete until 416, thus placing *Dolbeau* 6 (dated to 404) in the midst of his meditations on the three Persons of the Godhead. In *The Trinity*, he implores his reader: "With the example of the Image [Christ] before us, let us also not depart from God. For we are, likewise, the image of God, not indeed an equal image, since it was made by the Father through the Son, not born of the Father as that is" (VII.3.5).[18] (Hence Augustine's distinction in *Dolbeau* 6 that one is made a "son of God" not in substance or by nature, but rather by grace.) The human person is an image of the Image, and is called to imitate the Image by "striving." Further, he writes, "For the true honor of man is to be the image and the likeness of God which is preserved only in relation to Him by whom it is impressed" (XII.11.16). Contrariwise, man's "likeness to the beasts is his disgrace" (XII.11.16). The best possession of the immortal soul is the "image of God its Creator," something that will not cease to be (XIV.2.4). We look into a mirror to see an image, he writes, and by looking *through* our own image we may catch a glimpse of "Him by whom we have been made." Augustine cites 2 Cor 3.18: "But we, with face unveiled, beholding the glory of God, are transformed into the same image . . . " Human persons, as the *imago Dei*, share in God's glory (XV. 8.14). Being the image of the blessed Trinity, human persons are endowed with memory, understanding, and will, which are themselves intended for remembering, seeing, and loving God (XV.20.39). In *Dolbeau* 6, Augustine is especially keen on insisting that the sacred image of God within the human person not be defiled by the worship of corrupt idols. That which is worshipped ought to glorify and not debase the image of God within. The intimate relationship between worship and theological anthropology seems never far from Augustine's mind, as he implores his audience to remember their created dignity.

Many of the above theological ruminations were made audible in the living church addressed by Augustine in 404. The concerns voiced in *Dolbeau* 6 fit a particular historical context; they reveal Augustine engaged in battle, yet again. As Peter Brown has remarked, in a new addition to his

---

[18] *The Trinity*, tr. Stephen McKenna, C.S.S.R. (Washington: Catholic University of America Press, 1963).

classic work, *Augustine of Hippo: A Biography,* we find "an Augustine [in 404] struggling with all the rhetorical and didactic resources at his disposal to keep the Christian congregation from being absorbed back into a world in which Christianity had by no means yet captured the cultural high ground."[19] The "triumph" of Christianity was in no way complete at this point in North Africa's history. Another sermon from earlier in the same year (*Dolbeau* 198; *Mainz* 62), delivered on the *Kalends* feast of January 1, 404, serves to illustrate this point and merits brief comparison, given its many common themes. Augustine faced his audience then on the "festival of the nations," when people indulged in "the joys of the world and the flesh, with the din of silly and disgraceful songs" (198.1). He warned that mixing with non-Christians was "not safe and sound" (198.2), if it led to the corruption of virtue: "Are you going to join today in the celebration of good luck presents [on the feast of Fortuna] with a pagan, going to play at dice with a pagan, going to get drunk with a pagan?" (198.2) Augustine called upon his people instead to fast, as they wrestled (he would hope) with their consciences. He knew there was great temptation for Christians to join in the "frivolities," "extravagant pleasures," "unrestrained drunkenness," and gambling—it was a time of great excess (198.8). Augustine was aware that engaging in such activity was morally reprehensible, and further, defiled one's interior life. He urged people to protect the "temple of prayer" which is the heart; to keep one's "inner room" guarded against "bodily allurements" (198.1).[20] It is curious,

---

[19] Peter Brown, *Augustine of Hippo: A Biography*, new ed. (London: Faber and Faber, 2000) 457. Brown adds, "The sermons preached by Augustine in 404 were nothing less than a series of master classes on the nature of true relations between God and man" (458).

[20] Regarding the veneration of idols (a subject closely associated with an inability to discern the image of God in humanity and the Christian hope of deification), Augustine's problem was not merely that Christians had bowed down to pagan idols, but also that Christians had engaged in unacceptable "adoration of columns or the stones of buildings in holy places, or even of pictures" in their own churches (*Serm.* 198.16). Some 'educated pagans' had, it seems, begun to challenge Christians who criticized their (pagan) image veneration—Christians too were venerating icons and physical holy places. Augustine was at pains to clarify that what ought to be worshipped is not the thing itself, but what it signifies. He wanted Christians to search for the image of the divine craftsman with the eyes of the mind (198.31), though the mind itself, wrapped up in sin, "stands in need of purification" (198.37).

however, that while Augustine's preoccupation during the *Kalends* festival was with the spiritual dangers of paganism, he did not elect to incorporate the "*deificatio*" logic of *Dolbeau* 6.

Infrequency of Deification Imagery

It is worth asking why Augustine so rarely turned to the use of the concept of deification. One clue to an answer may be found in his "magnum opus," *The City of God*, wherein deification is discussed in its pagan context, and with unfavorable criticism. Here Augustine voices his intense displeasure with the practice of deifying—and then worshiping—men; one such example being that of Diomede, who was turned into a god after being credited with founding various towns and spreading Greek culture into Italy.[21] This sort of deification is a deception, Augustine argued, and amounts to the worship of false gods. In so doing, the "living God" is neglected; "temples, altars, sacrifices and priests" become devoted to "dead men" (XVIII.18) instead of their rightful recipient. One cannot escape from "the city of this world" and advance in faith, he warns, if one is captive to the practices of "Babylon." Given the eagerness of the ancient Greeks and Romans to deify and worship their own, we can suppose that Augustine was especially cautious in using the language of deification in the Christian church, lest he mislead some into imagining that Christians themselves become equals of God Almighty. Moreover, Augustine was always wary to state unambiguously that the deified faithful do not become "God by nature" but rather "gods by grace." Augustine achieves in *Dolbeau* 6 a remarkable homiletic move: he can, on the one hand, deconstruct the pagan use of idols and, on the other, provide his own congregants food for thought on the interior life of the soul.

Henry Chadwick, in his comments on the newly discovered sermons, has remarked, "two themes appear to be recurrent [in these sermons of 404]. The first is that true religion is inward and a matter of the heart . . . A second prominent theme is that true faith will issue in a reformed moral life."[22] Augustine was first and foremost a bishop, a teacher and caretaker

---

[21] *The City of God*, XVIII.16ff.
[22] "New Sermons of Augustine," *Journal of Theological Studies*, n.s. 47 (1996) 69–91.

of souls, who would consistently remind those in his care of the loftiest aspirations, for adoption by the hand of the divine architect, which, he would also declare, is not fully knowable in the present life for human persons tainted by sin. He spoke instead of the *possibilities* of human life, while not forgetting the present human condition of alienation from God.[23] As a champion of a theological view that wholly rejected the immodest Pelagian confidence in human ability to achieve perfection in this life, Augustine was loathe to overemphasize human striving independent of divine assistance; deification was not an accomplishment but a gift. All mention of deification in *Dolbeau 6* is careful to underscore God's providential action: the divine agent acts upon the human recipient, and does so within the protective confines of the church. The faithful together await, with restless longing, the consummation of history which finds the members of the "body of Christ" transfigured into "gods." Augustine reminded people that deification was a divinely granted *possibility*, ecclesial in its dimensions, and the *telos* of present aspirations.

Lastly, it is essential to be reminded that the proper location for the language of deification was the *sacramental* life of the church community. It is no mistake that we find Augustine delivering the message of deification within a liturgical setting. He did not understand the transfiguration of humanity into "gods" to be a private affair. The piety of every individual was, Augustine believed, nurtured within the "cultus," within sacred liturgical celebrations.[24] The community was bonded together by the sacraments and unifying participation was most often felt in the shared Eucharist—itself a constant reminder of the Christian mysteries, of God's active presence in their midst, working a transformation among them. Augustine, as spiritual father, sought to communicate an understanding that "our present passage from death to life, which takes place through faith, is accomplished in the hope of the future resurrection and glory in the end."[25] A foretaste of the eschatological deification was offered in and

---

[23] On the subject of Augustine communicating 'possibilities,' see Eugene TeSelle, *Augustine the Theologian* (New York: Herder and Herder, 1970) 68.

[24] See Frederick Van der Meer's classic work, *Augustine the Bishop: Church and Society at the Dawn of the Middle Ages*, trans. Brain Battershaw and G. R. Lamb (New York: Harper, 1961) 277ff.

[25] *Ep.* 55, trans. Roland Teske, S. J., in *The Works of Saint Augustine: Letters 1–99*, vol. II/1 (Hyde Park, N.Y.: New City, 2001).

through the church's sacramental life. Only there could one find a haven against the many snares that populated Augustine's spiritual imagination.[26]

---

[26] A debt of gratitude is owed to Rev. Gabriel Coless, O.S.B. for his illuminating remarks offered in response to early drafts of this work.

Divinization and Spiritual Progress in Maximus the Confessor

Elena Vishnevskaya

The intellectual output of Byzantium's Maximus the Confessor (588–620) presents an unparalleled balance of theology and philosophy, with faith as the moving force of all reflection. The Confessor's spiritual experience leads him to extraordinary heights of mystical knowledge, which is the guiding light for all his intellectual endeavors. This mysticism is brought to prominence in his doctrine of divinization.

The Fundamentals of Divinization

For the Confessor, the essential conditions for fulfilling the divinizing process are the magnanimous divine initiative and willing human cooperation. Maximus unceasingly glorifies divine love expressed through grace, which "out of human beings makes us gods. . . . Nothing is more truly Godlike than divine love, nothing more mysterious, nothing more apt to raise up human beings to deification."[1] The greatest testament to love of God for humankind is the incarnation, whereby

---

[1] *Epist.* 2 (PG 91:393BC; *MC* 85). See the list of abbreviations at end of article.

the Creator of nature himself . . . has clothed himself with our nature, without change uniting it hypostatically to himself, in order to check what has been borne away, and gather it to himself, so that, gathered to himself, our nature may no longer have any difference from him in its inclination. In this way he clearly establishes the all-glorious way of love, which is truly divine and deifying and leads to God.[2]

Thus, the Confessor rejoices in the incarnation as the opening up of previously hidden ways by which the human being may finally arrive at the fullness of God, Himself. Maximus is acutely aware, nonetheless, of the reciprocal responsibility on the part of the human being. He avers with confidence that "our salvation is contingent upon our will,"[3] and "the mystery of salvation belongs to those who desire it, not to those who are forced to submit to it."[4] The Confessor's deepest conviction has "God provid[ing] equally to all the power that naturally leads to salvation, so that each one who wishes can be transformed by divine grace."[5] The appropriation of divinization is in direct correlation with one's degree of spiritual appreciation and discernment. By realizing his or her natural freedom, the human being

> might become [a child] of God and divine by grace through the Spirit. For a created [human] could not be revealed as [a child] of God through deification by grace without first being born by the Spirit in the exercise of free choice, because of the power of self-movement and self-determination inherent in human nature.[6]

Hence, in Maximus's view, God will recognize and divinize His own, that is, those who willfully employ their true nature. An intense yearning for relationship with the Creator, as well as an ability to fulfill it, was

---

[2] *Epist.* 2 (PG 91:404BC; *MC* 91).

[3] *Liber ascetic.* 42 (PG 90:953B).

[4] *Orat. Dom.* (PG 90:880B; CWS 104). Maximus may be seen as proposing universal salvation in *Amb.* 7,10 (PG 91:1084D, 1165D); *Ad Thal.* 47 (PG 90:429C); *Expositio in Psalmum* 59 (PG 90:857A); *Mystag.* 7 (PG 91:685BC).

[5] *Amb.* 10 (PG 91:1144A; *MC* 118).

[6] *Amb.* 42 (PG 91:1345D; PPS 93).

bestowed upon the human race by God Himself, who ever moves His creation toward its end in Himself: "He sets in movement in us an insatiable desire for himself who is the Bread of Life, wisdom, knowledge, and justice."[7] Unceasingly, God transposes willing humanity "from the lower to the greater," "from glory to glory,"[8] to divinization:

> He leads us finally in the supreme ascent in divine realities to the Father of lights wherein he makes us sharers in the divine nature by participating in the grace of the Spirit, through which we receive the title of God's children and become clothed entirely with the complete person who is the author of this grace, without limiting or defiling him who is Son of God by nature.[9]

Accordingly, to know God is to seek His face without ceasing, to attain progressively to the divine vision which penetrates the luminous darkness. Still, Maximus does make an ontological distinction between Christ and creature: in the former, "there dwells in bodily form the complete fullness of deity by essence," while "in us the fullness of deity dwells by grace whenever we have formed in ourselves every virtue and wisdom . . . in faithful reproduction of the archetype."[10] For the Confessor, the union of God and the believer is fulfilled while preserving the differences between the two distinct natures,[11] analogous to the sustained integrity of the two natures—and the energies issuing from them—in the person of Christ. Hence, although created in the image of God, human nature has yet to be fulfilled through the hypostatic union (union of natures) realized in the Logos incarnate:[12]

---

[7] *Orat. Dom.* (CCSG 23:70, 769–71; CWS 118).

[8] *Amb.* 48 (PG 91:1364A). Here, Gregory of Nyssa's influence can be noted.

[9] *Orat. Dom.*
(CCSG 23:70, 774–80; CWS 118).

[10] *CT* 2.21 (PG 90:1133D; CWS 152). Cf. "Participated divine existence can only be a free gift from God . . . . This God-giving-Himself is the divine 'energy'" (John Meyendorff, *Byzantine Theology: Historical Trends and Doctrinal Themes,* rev. 2d ed. [New York: Fordham University Press, 1983] 187).

[11] *Opusc.* 8 (PG 91:97A).

[12] *Amb.* 36 (PG 91:1289BC).

For he did not come to debase the nature which he himself, as God and Word, had made, but he came that the nature might be thoroughly deified which, with the good pleasure of the Father and the co-operation of the Spirit, he willed to unite to himself in one and the same *hypostasis*.[13]

Divine essence remains inaccessible,[14] but humanity is able to rise "above nature," into a new mode of existence,[15] that is, the human being inherits by grace that which belongs to God by nature:

We shall become that which in no way results from our natural ability, since our human nature has no faculty for grasping what transcends nature. For nothing created is by its nature capable of inducing deification, since it is incapable of comprehending God. Intrinsically it is only by the grace of God that deification is bestowed proportionately on created being. Grace alone illuminates human nature with supernatural light, and, by the superiority of its glory, elevates our nature above its proper limits.[16]

Hence, divinization involves the mode of nature, or *tropos,* rather than its governing principle, or *logos.* Human nature is taken to extraordinary heights through a new, divine, mode of being which sustains the *logos* proper to created nature:[17]

God becomes to the soul (and through the soul to the body) what the soul is to the body, . . . so that the soul receives changelessness and the body immortality; hence, the whole man . . . is divinized . . . . He remains wholly man in soul and body by nature, and becomes wholly God in body and soul by grace and by the unparalleled divine radiance of blessed glory.[18]

---

[13] *Opusc.* 7 (PG 91:77C; *MC* 185).

[14] *Amb.* 34 (PG 91:1288B).

[15] Lars Thunberg, *Man and the Cosmos: The Vision of St. Maximus the Confessor* (Crestwood, N.Y.: St. Vladimir's Seminary Press, 1985) 88.

[16] *Ad Thal.* 22 (CCSG 7:141, 90–98; PPS 118).

[17] *Amb.* 36 (PG 91:1289CD).

[18] *Amb.* 7 (PG 91:1088C; PPS 63).

Maximus understands divinization as involving the human constitution in its entirety.[19] In the final act of homecoming, both soul and body will be granted resurrection, that is, the psychosomatic whole of the human being will be reinstated in its relationship with God. Meyendorff says Maximus does not pose "an absorption into God's essence,"[20] nor even "contemplation of divine essence (which is inaccessible), but communion in divine energy, transfiguration, and transparency to divine action in the world"; humanity's own energy, when in tune with the divine, propels it toward life in the Logos, that is, realization of God's primordial design in divinization.[21]

Faith is instrumental to divinization, for it enables one's filial adoption as a child of God, which is a spiritual birth,[22] but "faith without love does not bring about the illumination of knowledge in the soul."[23] Maximus brings faith and love together in his allegorical interpretation of Peter and John. The character of Peter represents unshakable faith and a life of *praxis,* or practical life; John stands for perfect love and a life of *theōria,* or contemplation. Both men, who are portrayed rushing to the tomb of Christ, symbolize two different yet converging spiritual modes of existence.[24]

Ascetic Practice and Contemplation

Maximus is drawing on his experience of monasticism, whose tradition of *praxis* and *theōria* is a paradigm of divinization or "life in Christ,"[25] which is also relevant for the entire Body of Christ. *Praxis* and *theōria* are mutually interdependent, and, in their correlation, represent the fruition of spiritual life. *Praxis* acquires, in the Confessor, a double perspective, including both purification from passions and attainment of virtues.

---

[19] While still preserving the legacy of his ascetic teacher, Evagrius, Maximus seeks to correct his Origenistic proclivity; Evagrius was concerned, above all, with the mind's state of pure prayer.

[20] Meyendorff, *Byzantine Theology,* 72.

[21] Meyendorff, *Byzantine Theology,* 133.

[22] *Amb.* 42 (PG 91:1348C; PPS 94).

[23] *CC* 1.31 (PG 90:968A; CWS 38).

[24] *Amb.* 57 (PG 91:1380D).

[25] Thunberg, *Man and the Cosmos,* 22.

Maximus defines passions "as a movement of the soul contrary to nature either toward irrational love or senseless hate of something."[26] Passions spring up as a result of the disoriented will that chooses the sensible over the spiritual; "and precisely in the quality of being falsely preferred the sensual or visible becomes sinful, dangerous, venomous, evil."[27] Passions have to be eradicated at the root level, that is, in the domain of the will, whereby sin has entered the human arena. Human will needs to be reoriented toward divine will, for "only God is good by nature, and only the one who imitates God is good by his will."[28] The Spirit is able to convert those who are willing to cooperate with the plan of deification.[29]

In addressing the problem posed by passions, Maximus relies on *apatheia,*[30] or detachment, that is, "a peaceful state of the soul in which it becomes resistant to vice."[31] Unassisted by *apatheia,* the mind—which the Confessor identifies with "the inner man"[32]—easily loses its spiritual focus, like "a little sparrow whose foot is tied tries to fly but is pulled to earth by the cord to which it is bound."[33] Along with Evagrius, who praises detachment as "the flower of practical activity" and credits it with "engendering love,"[34] the Confessor espouses *apatheia* as spiritual liberation that opens one up to a direct divinizing relationship with God.

Apatheia is effective only when coupled with an active doing of good, the practice of virtues.[35] Love is really the bedrock of the edifice of divinizing virtues.[36] Humans are called to practice the virtues, particularly love—

---

[26] *CC* 2.16 (PG 90:988D–989A; CWS 48).

[27] Georges Florovsky, *Collected Works,* vol. 9, *The Byzantine Fathers of the Sixth to Eighth Century,* ed. Richard S. Haugh, trs. Raymond Miller, et al. (Vaduz: Büchervertriebsanstalt, 1987) 239.

[28] *CC* 4.90 (PG 90:1069C; CWS 85).

[29] *Ad Thal.* 6 (CCSG 7:69, 21–23; PPS 103–4).

[30] Originally a Stoic concept, it was introduced into the Christian milieu by Clement of Alexandria.

[31] *CC* 1.36 (PG 90:968AB; CWS 39).

[32] *CC* 4.50 (PG 90:1060AB; CWS 80–81).

[33] *CC* 1.85 (PG 90:980C; CWS 44–45).

[34] *Capita praktika ad Anatolium* (PG 40:1221B)

[35] Maximus's exposition of virtues bears a strong resemblance to that of Evagrius, who presents it in his *Capita praktika ad Anatolium* (PG 40:1221BC). Note Evagrius's dependence on Clement of Alexandria, *Strom.* 2.6.

[36] *Epist.* 2 (PG 91:396B; *MC* 86).

"one and the same universal: owed to God and attaching human beings to one another."[37] While passions and vices fracture the unity of human nature,[38] love and other virtues restore being and, thus, prove salvific: "Nothing is either so fitting for justification or so apt for divinization . . . as mercy offered with pleasure and joy from the soul to those who stand in need." Christ Himself walked the path of forbearance and suffering; hence, "the one who can do good and who does it is truly God by grace and participation."[39] To partake of the virtues is to partake of God Himself, who is the most perfect embodiment of them all:

> Whoever by his choices cultivates the good natural seed shows the end to be the same as the beginning and the beginning to be the same as the end. . . . The goal of everything is given in its beginning and the end of everything is given in its ultimate goal. As to the beginning, in addition to receiving being itself, one receives the natural good by participation: as to the end, one zealously traverses one's course toward the beginning and source without deviation by means of one's good will and choice. And through this course one becomes God, being made God by God.[40]

For Maximus, the work of salvation needs to be deliberately internalized—in imitation of Christ—by every human being; this divinizing process takes place within the context of the Church. Lossky understands the Confessor to be saying that the union that begins in this life, "will be consummated in the age to come, after the resurrection of the dead."[41] Epifanovich observes that "the internal grace-giving content of church life . . . is hidden behind symbols but in such a way that even they convey the grace which corresponds to the mystical connotation of each of them."[42] Maximus, himself, avers: "Holy Church bears the imprint and image of God since it has the same activity as he does by imitation

---

[37] *Epist.* 2 (PG 91:401D; *MC* 90).

[38] *Epist.* 2 (PG 91:400D; *MC* 89).

[39] *Mystag.* 24 (PG 91:713AB; CWS 211–12).

[40] *Amb.* 7 (PG 91:1081D–1084A; PPS 58–59).

[41] Vladimir Lossky, *The Mystical Theology of the Eastern Church* (Cambridge: James Clarke, 1968) 179.

[42] S. L. Epifanovich, *Prepodobnyi Maksim Ispovednik i vizantiiskoe bogoslovie (Saint Maximus the Confessor and Byzantine Theology)* (Kiev, 1915) 82.

and in figure."[43] Thus, for the Confessor, "liturgy reflects the exalted moments of divinization which belong to future life," offering a preview of the longed-for beatitude, here and now.[44]

The Confessor views the sacraments of the Eucharist and baptism as divinizing media which impart divine grace to those who are immersed in the life of the Church. He identifies the Eucharist as "holy communion of the spotless and life-giving mysteries," whereby "we are given fellowship and identity with [God] by participation in likeness, by which man is deemed worthy from man to become God."[45] The Eucharist, as the center of liturgy, discloses that Christ will take away "the marks of corruption and will bestow on us the original mysteries which have been represented for us through symbols here below."[46] God also inhabits the believer and communicates His righteousness "through the grace of holy baptism."[47] "Baptized in Christ by the Spirit, we have received the first incorruptibility of the flesh; we await the final incorruptibility of Christ in the Sprit."[48]

While highly esteeming the value of practical life, and its ecclesiastic realizations, Maximus acknowledges the limited and transitory value of the first stage of spiritual life. The experience of "an ascetic in the practice of virtues" is indispensable yet incomplete without the experience of "a contemplative in the hidden place of wisdom which can exist only in the habit of the virtues."[49] Thus, Maximus passes on to natural contemplation of the *logoi* of the created order, which render the world as "God's mirror."[50] Contemplation helps the believer see the world as sustained by its partaking of the divine energies; the Logos creates and relates to the cosmic order through these energies. Maximus's idea of natural contemplation "as an experience of a merely symbolical reflection of the divine realities" reinforces his stress on apophaticism and betrays an influence of Pseudo-Dionysius.[51]

---

[43] *Mystag.* 1 (PG 91:664D; CWS 186).

[44] Epifanovich, 82.

[45] *Mystag.* 24 (PG 91:704D; CWS 207).

[46] *Mystag.* 24 (PG 91:705A; CWS 208).

[47] *CC* 4.73 (PG 90:1065C; CWS 83).

[48] *CT* 1.87 (PG 90:1120B; CWS 145).

[49] *CT* 2.74 (PG 90:1160AB; CWS 163).

[50] Hans Urs von Balthasar, *Cosmic Liturgy: The Universe According to Maximus the Confessor*, 3d ed., tr. Brian E. Daley (San Francisco: Ignatius, 2003) 176.

By practicing asceticism and contemplation, believers exalt God,[52] who is "knowable in ideas about him" and "unknowable in himself."[53] In his turn, God provides in contemplation "a growing nourishment of the intellectual through the sensible and a transformation of the sensible into the world of the mind."[54]

Further, in the act of divine condescension, God leads the human being toward Himself, guiding the creature along the path of spiritual maturity, for one's earthly action and contemplation are still in need of perfection.[55] Therefore, the "most hidden knowledge of [God]" is granted to the human being at the third, or final, stage of Christian life, that is, *theologia,* or theology proper, whereby believers contemplate God, Himself, by acquiring a "simple understanding according to which they no longer pursue the divine and ineffable Word by sensation or anything that appears."[56]

Purification in Love

Maximus envisages *theologia* as a "relationship" with the God who transcends all knowledge.[57] For the Confessor, the whole Christian pilgrimage culminates in the intimate divine-human union of purification in love and ensuing divinization: "The mind is deemed worthy of the grace of theology when on the wings of love it has passed beyond all the preceding realities, and being in God it will consider the essence of himself through the Spirit, insofar as it is possible to the human mind."[58] While the first two stages of spiritual life are the "Sabbaths," *theologia* is the "Sabbath of Sabbaths," crowning all that had led to it.[59]

---

[51] Lars Thunberg, *Microcosm and Mediator: The Theological Anthropology of Maximus the Confessor,* Acta Seminarii Neotestamentici Upsaliensis, no. 25 (Lund: C.W.K. Gleerup, 1965) 376.
[52] *CT* 2.32 (PG 90:1140B; CWS 154).
[53] *CC* 4.7 (PG 90:1149AB; CWS 76).
[54] Von Balthasar, *Cosmic Liturgy,* 304–5.
[55] *CT* 2.87 (PG 90:1165BC; CWS 166).
[56] *Mystag.* 24 (PG 91:709A; CWS 210).
[57] Thunberg, *Microcosm,* 379.
[58] *CC* 2.26 (PG 90:992C; CWS 50).
[59] *CT* 1.37–39 (PG 90:1097C; CWS 135). Cf. ibid. 2.64–65.

It is at the stage of *theologia,* or purification in love, that the final mediation between God and the created order is fulfilled. Perfect love heals divisions, unifies being, and leads to a life "lived naturally in accordance with the perfect natural *logos.*"[60] Having reached "the blessed end for which all things are ordained," the faithful enjoy unimpeded union with God.

The ultimate beatitude of divine-human union subsumes, for Maximus, the return of "our entire self," or image, to God, the archetype.[61] This is a union "of limit and the unlimited, of measure and the unmeasurable, of circumscription and the uncircumscribed, of the Creator with the creature, of rest with movement."[62] Speaking of the end as "perfect fulfillment"[63] of the soul's journey, Maximus espouses "the direct experience . . . of God,"[64] available now to those who have arrived at "an ever-moving rest" in God.[65] The "experience of God" is a type of "knowledge, based on active engagement, which surpasses all reason"; the "rest in God" is a type of "participation in the known object which manifests itself beyond all conceptualization."[66]

In union with God, the faithful finally "possess not just a part of the fullness but rather acquire through participation the entire fullness of grace."[67] Maximus celebrates the end, whereby the redeemed are "now divinized by love and made like him by participation in an indivisible identity to the extent that this is possible."[68] In "the union that is beyond nature,"[69] the human being's energies are no longer driven by nature or sense, but by God's grace.[70]

---

[60] *Epist.* 2 (PG 91:400C; *MC* 89).

[61] *Amb.* 7 (PG 91:1088A; PPS 63). Cf. Gregory of Nazianzus, *Orat.* 28.17, cited in Maximus, *Amb.* 7 (PG 91:1077B; 1085C).

[62] *Ad Thal.* 60 (PG 90:621B) quoted in von Balthasar, *Cosmic Liturgy,* 272.

[63] *Amb.* 7 (PG 91:1072B; PPS 48).

[64] *Ad Thal.* 60 (CCSG 22:77, 67, 69; PPS 126).

[65] *Ad Thal.* 59 (CCSG 22:53, 131); *Ad Thal.* 65 (CCSG 22:285, 543); *Amb.* 67 (PG 91:1401).

[66] *Ad Thal.* 60 (CCSG 22:77, 87–90; PPS 12627).

[67] *CT* 2.87 (PG 90:1165C; CWS 166).

[68] *Mystag.* 13 (PG 91:692CD; CWS 200).

[69] *Opusc.* 7 (PG 91:76B; *MC* 183).

[70] *Amb.* 10 (PG 91:1153C; *MC* 125).

In this supra-logical communion, believers "terminate [their] proper faculties along with everything in [their] nature that has reached completion."[71] Maximus writes: "For what is more desirable to God's precious one than to be divinized, that is for God to be united with those who have become god and by his goodness to make everything his own."[72] Indeed, God's *skopos*, as well as Maximus's aspiration of capturing the spirit of divine intent,[73] is realized in the divinization of the human being and transfiguration of the whole cosmos.

Abbreviations

Maximus's Texts

Ad Thal	*Quaestiones ad Thalassium*
Amb.	*Ambiguorum liber*
CC	*Capita de charitate*
CT	*Capita theologiae et oeconomiae*
Epist.	*Epistula*
Liber ascetic.	*Liber asceticus*
Mystag.	*Mystagogia*
Opusc.	*Opuscula theologica et polemica*
Orat. Dom.	*Expositio orationis Dominicae*

Editions, Series, and Collections

CCSG	Corpus Christianorum, Series Graeca
CWS	Classics of Western Spirituality
MC	*Maximus the Confessor* (Andrew Louth 1996)
PG	Patrologia Graeca (ed. J.-P. Migne)
PPS	Popular Patristic Series (ed. John Behr)

---

[71] *Ad Thal.* 22 (CCSG 7:141, 89–90; PPS 117–18).

[72] *Amb.* 7 (PG 91:1088C; PPS 63–64).

[73] See *Epist.* 24 (PG 91:609C) where Maximus cites 2 Pet 1:4, a biblical passage commonly construed to envisage the goal of God's creation as participation in divine nature.

Selected Bibliography

Balthasar, Hans Urs von. *Cosmic Liturgy: The Universe According to Maximus the Confessor.* 3d ed. Translated by Brian E. Daley. San Francisco: Ignatius, 2003.

Epifanovich, S. L. *Prepodobnyi Maksim Ispovednik i vizantiiskoe bogoslovie (Saint Maximus the Confessor and Byzantine Theology).* Kiev, 1915.

Florovsky, Georges. *Collected Works.* Vol. 9, *The Byzantine Fathers of the Sixth to Eighth Century.* Edited by Richard S. Haugh. Translated by Raymond Miller et al. Vaduz: Büchervertriebsanstalt, 1987.

Lossky, Vladimir. *The Mystical Theology of the Eastern Church.* Cambridge: James Clarke, 1968.

Meyendorff, John. *Byzantine Theology: Historical Trends and Doctrinal Themes.* Rev. 2d ed. N.p., 1983. Reprint, New York: Fordham University Press, n.d.

Thunberg, Lars. *Man and the Cosmos: The Vision of St. Maximus the Confessor.* Crestwood, N.Y.: St. Vladimir's Seminary Press, 1985.

———. *Microcosm and Mediator: The Theological Anthropology of Maximus the Confessor.* Acta Seminarii Neotestamentici Upsaliensis 25. Lund: Gleerup, 1965.

Reforming Theōsis

Myk Habets

Worlds Apart

The doctrine of theōsis is clearly established within the Eastern branch of Christendom and to this day remains the central motif uniting various aspects of Byzantine theology, from theology proper to anthropology.[1] But what of the Latin West? The West has historically given far more attention to moral holiness and so has focused on the elimination of sin as *culpa* rather than on salvation as liberation from moral corruption. While the theme of theōsis is not a dominant one in the West, it is not without its supporters. As one recent author reminds us: "although the West does not embrace the explicit notion of theosis in any major way, deification is not entirely absent from its tradition."[2] Theōsis—the deification of the human person—can and indeed must be seen to be

[1] Two works are considered to be more or less authoritative on the subject: J. Gross, *La divinisation du chrétien d'après les pères grecs: Contribution historique à la doctrine de la grâce* (Paris: Gabalda, 1938); E.T.: *The Divinization of the Christian According to the Greek Fathers*, tr. P. A. Onica (Anaheim, Calif.: A & C, 2002); and M. Lot-Borodine, *La Déification de l'homme selon la doctrine des Pères grecs* (Paris: Cerf, 1970).

[2] D. B. Clendenin, *Eastern Orthodox Christianity: A Western Perspective* (Grand Rapids: Baker, 1994) 124.

compatible with Reformed theology, itself a member of the Great Tradition to which all three streams of Christendom ultimately appeal.

According to Reformed scholars, union with Christ is at the heart of Reformed theology. While various theologians debate where exactly union with Christ "fits" into the *ordo salutis*, it is certain that it is an integral component.[3] While union with God and theōsis are not identical they are closely related. In her study of the patristic use of theōsis Anna Williams concludes that

> there is a firm core that distinguishes this doctrine from some other models of sanctification. First, we can safely say that where we find references to human participation in divine life, there we assuredly have a claim specifically of theosis. This kind of claim regarding participation in divine life is carefully to be distinguished, however, from the idea of divine indwelling in the human person . . . A second infallible marker of the doctrine, then, is the union of God and humanity, when this union is conceived as humanity's incorporation into God, rather than God's into humanity.[4]

According to this well-reasoned definition, a Reformed doctrine of union with Christ (*unio mystica*) is compatible with a doctrine of theōsis.

Theōsis and the West

It is important to highlight that not only did the early church and Eastern Orthodoxy adopt the language of theōsis, so did the Protestant Reformers. Since the mid-seventies a new interpretation of Luther known as the "Finnish School" has arisen under the influence of Tuomo Mannermaa. The central thesis of this school is that for Luther, salvation is conceived as union with Christ, based on Luther's phrase "*in ipsa fide Christus adest*" ("in faith itself Christ is really present").[5] The Finnish School argues that

---

[3] See R. Letham, *The Work of Christ* (Leicester: IVP, 1993) 55–56.

[4] A. N. Williams, *The Ground of Union: Deification in Aquinas and Palamas* (New York: Oxford University Press, 1999) 32.

[5] Tuomo Mannermaa, "Why is Luther So Fascinating? Modern Finnish Luther Research," in *Union With Christ: The New Finnish Interpretation of Luther,* eds. C. E. Braaten and R. W. Jensen (Grand Rapids: Eerdmans, 1998) 4, 19–20.

for Luther faith is a real participation in Christ: in faith a believer receives the righteousness of God in Christ, not only in a nominal and external way, but genuinely and inwardly. This insight radically challenges traditional Luther scholarship. If the forensic model of justification argues that through faith we are *declared* righteous, while in actuality we are not *made* righteous, this new reading of Luther argues that through faith we participate in the whole Christ, who in his divine person communicates the righteousness of God. Herein lies the bridge from Reformation thought to the Orthodox idea of salvation, understood as theōsis.[6]

Theōsis is present not only in Luther but also in Calvin.[7] For Calvin, the concept of theōsis comes closest to what is more commonly in the West termed "union with Christ."[8] It has been argued that the *unio mystica* is central to Calvin's theology.[9] If this is true, then logically the doctrine of theōsis is also of importance to Calvin's theology.[10] In one of his rare uses of the word "deification" Calvin writes, "We should notice that it is the purpose of the Gospel to make us sooner or later like God; indeed it is, so to speak, a kind of deification."[11] Echoing Eastern Orthodox writers, Calvin

[6] For comprehensive essays from Finnish theologians and responses from American Lutherans, see *Union With Christ*. On post-reformation Lutheran theology of theōsis see R. Hauke, *Gott-Haben – um Gottes Willen. Andreas Osanders Theosisgedanke und die Diskussion um die Grundlagen der evangelisch verstandenen Rechtfertigung. Versuch einer Neubewertung eines umstrittenen Gedankens,* (Frankfurt: Lang, 1999).

[7] Despite the contrary opinion of Norris; F. W. Norris, "Deification: Consensual and Cogent," *Scottish Journal of Theology* 49 (1996) 420. See C. Mosser, "The Greatest Possible Blessing: Calvin and Deification," in *Scottish Journal of Theology* 55 (2002) 36–57 for a solid refutation of Norris' contention.

[8] See D. E. Tamburello, *Union With Christ: John Calvin and the Mysticism of St. Bernard.* Columbia Series in Reformed Theology (Louisville: Westminster John Knox, 1994). Bray is incorrect when he writes, "Deification corresponds most closely to the Western understanding of the imitation of Christ in Orthodox theology," G. Bray, "Deification," in *New Dictionary of Theology*, eds. S. B. Ferguson and D. F. Wright (Downers Grove, Ill.: IVP, 1988; electronic edition, 2000).

[9] See, for instance, W. Kolfhaus, *Christusgemeinschaft bei Calvin* (Neukirchen: Moers, 1939); Tamburello, *Union with Christ*; and C. Partee, "Calvin's Central Dogma Again," *Sixteenth Century Journal* 18 (1987) 191–99.

[10] *Calvin's New Testament Commentaries,* Vol. 12: *Hebrews and 1 and 2 Peter,* tr. W. B. Johnston, eds. D. W. and T. F. Torrance (Grand Rapids: Eerdmans, 1963) 330; *The Institutes of the Christian Religion,* tr. H. Beveridge (London: Clarke & Co, 1953) 1.13.14; 2.7.1; 3.2.24; 3.11.10; 3.25.10; 4.17.2, 4, 11.

[11] Referring to 2 Pet 1:4: *Calvin's New Testament Commentaries,* Vol. 12, 330.

makes it plain that this does not mean we partake of the divine *essence* but of the divine *likeness*: "The apostles were simply concerned to say that when we have put off all the vices of the flesh we shall be partakers of divine immortality and the glory of blessedness, and thus we shall be in a way with God so far as our capacity allows."[12]

For Calvin, the process of theōsis is initiated in our election for salvation, is effected in our union with Christ, and is made possible in two interrelated ways, the first of which is by the incarnation of the Son, which represents a divinizing of humanity through the humanizing of divinity. In his *Institutes* Calvin speaks of partaking of the divine nature in terms of the *mirifica commutatio* or "wonderful exchange" whereby

> having become with us the Son of Man, he has made us with himself sons of God. By his own descent to the earth he has prepared our ascent to heaven. Having received our mortality, he has bestowed on us his immortality. Having undertaken our weakness, he has made us strong in his strength. Having submitted to our poverty, he has transferred to us his riches. Having taken upon himself the burden of unrighteousness with which we were oppressed, he has clothed us with his righteousness.[13]

The second way that union with Christ is effected is through the work of the Holy Spirit. This partaking of the divine nature, or more specifically of Christ, is then experienced and further developed through the sacraments and the life of piety lived out in the Spirit's power. From the preceding quotation of Calvin we see the direct parallels between what he considers to be theōsis with what Eastern Orthodoxy advocates in its doctrine of theōsis.

Behind Calvin's treatment of theōsis the doctrine of the Trinity provides a foundation and context by which we can understand the deification of humans. Calvin's doctrine of theōsis, like its classical antecedents, is built around the hypostatic union. Theōsis is only possible because human nature has been deified in the theandric person of the Mediator. As men and women are united to Christ, his divinity deifies them.[14] Our divinization is only

---

[12] Ibid.

[13] *Institutes* 4.17.2.

[14] See D. Willis-Watkins, "The Unio Mystica and the Assurance of Faith According to Calvin," in *Calvin: Erbe und Auftrag*, ed. W. van't Spijker (Kampen: Kok Pharos, 1991) 78.

made possible by the unique work of the incarnate Son who unites us to himself so that through the Holy Spirit we may know and worship the Father. As Mosser puts it: "The believer's union with Christ and the Father, the indwelling presence of the Spirit in our hearts, restoration of the divine image, being made like Jesus and our eventual glorification are each important themes in Calvin's soteriology and eschatology."[15] This provides a suitable overview and summary of the place of theōsis within Calvin's theology.

Moving beyond the Reformation we can trace a continued usage of the doctrine of theōsis within later Reformed theology. One important post-Reformation theologian to adopt the language of theōsis is Jonathan Edwards. From his reflections on the Trinity Edwards presents a brief articulation of theōsis as human participation in the Triune God of love.[16] According to Edwards, God created humans to participate in the Triune communion which could only be achieved through union with Christ. The saints are "exalted to glorious dignity" and "to fellowship" and even "union" with God Himself, but "care is taken" that this is not their own glory, but that it comes from God.[17] By means of the analogy of marriage, Edwards shows his express commitment to the doctrine of theōsis.

> The end of the creation of God was to provide a spouse for his Son Jesus Christ that might enjoy him and on whom he might pour fourth his love, . . . the end of all things in providence are to make way for the exceeding expressions of Christ's love to his spouse & for her exceeding close & intimate union with & high & glorious enjoyment of him.[18]

---

[15] Mosser, "The Greatest Possible Blessing: Calvin and Deification," 55.

[16] See J. Edwards, "An Unpublished Essay on the Trinity," www.truthinheart.com/EarlyOberlinCD/CD/ Edwards/Trinity.htm; D. L. Weddle, "Jonathan Edwards on Men and Trees, and the Problem of Solidarity," *Harvard Theological Review* 67 (1974) 155–75; and F. W. Youngs, "The Place of Spiritual Union in Jonathan Edwards's Conception of the Church," *Fides et Historia* 28 (1996) 27–47.

[17] S. R. Holmes, *God of Grace and God of Glory: An Account of the Theology of Jonathan Edwards* (Grand Rapids: Eerdmans, 2000) 43. Holmes is commenting on the *Miscellanies* of Edwards, personal theological notes he made throughout his life. Holmes notes how the Church is central to Edwards' view of theōsis in the treatise, *Concerning the End for Which God Created the World* (44–49).

[18] Edwards, *Miscellanies* 710, cited in Holmes, *God of Grace and God of Glory,* 58.

Such language leads Holmes to state that "In common with Eastern Orthodox thought, Edwards was prepared to see salvation as theosis, being made one with God."[19] Holmes states the position of Edwards in the simplest terms possible: "God regards the believer as one with Christ and so, ontologically, the believer is one with Christ. Under the metaphysical positions with which Edwards was working, it really is that simple."[20] By asserting an ontological union Edwards clearly goes beyond the Palamite theology by which one may participate in God's *energies,* which are strictly economic, but not in God's *essence,* which is ontological.

The doctrine of theōsis was not neglected in the Western tradition, not least within Reformed theology. It has been there all along, if underdeveloped. With the republication of many contemporary Eastern Orthodox texts on theōsis in English,[21] the re-examination of the theology of the Reformers, especially Luther and Calvin, and recent calls from a number of contemporary Protestant theologians to reintroduce theōsis onto the Western soteriological agenda,[22] the doctrine of theōsis is one of a number of patristic themes being appealed to today to recall the Church to its theological sources and to aid the church in confronting the post-modern era. It is also being used by a number of theologians as a possible way of ecumenical advancement. It is this context that the contribution of T. F. Torrance has much to offer.

---

[19] Holmes, *God of Grace*, 58.

[20] Holmes, *God of Grace*, 149; cf. 184, 242.

[21] Some of which include: V. Lossky, *The Vision of God.* Tr. A. Moorhouse (Crestwood, N.Y.: St. Vladimir's Seminary Press, 1963, 1973²); idem, *Orthodox Theology: An Introduction,* trs. I. and I. Kasarcodi-Watson (Crestwood, N.Y.: St. Vladimir's Press, 1978, 2001); idem, *The Mystical Theology of the Eastern Church* (Crestwood, N.Y.: St. Vladimir's Seminary Press, 1944, 1998); Mantzaridis, *The Deification of Man*; P. Nellas, *Deification in Christ,* tr. N. Russell (Crestwood, N.Y.: St. Vladimir's Seminary Press, 1979, 1987); D. Staniloae, *The Experience of God: Orthodox Dogmatic Theology:* Vol 2: *The World: Creation and Deification,* trs., eds. I. Ionita and R. Barringer (Brookline, Mass.: Holy Cross Orthodox, 1978, 2000).

[22] C. H. Pinnock, *Flame of Love: A Theology of the Holy Spirit* (Downers Grove, Ill.: IVP, 1996); G. D. Badcock, *Light of Truth and Fire of Love: A Theology of the Holy Spirit* (Grand Rapids: Eerdmans, 1997); R. V. Rakestraw, "Becoming Like God: An Evangelical Doctrine of Theosis," *Journal of the Evangelical Theological Society* 40 (1997) 257–69; Clendenin, *Eastern Orthodox Christianity*; and "Partakers of Divinity: The Orthodox Doctrine of Theosis," *Journal of the Evangelical Theological Society* 37 (1994) 365–79.

T. F. Torrance: A Case Study

Commonly regarded as one of the foremost Reformed theologians of the second half of the twentieth century, Thomas Forsyth Torrance provides us with a model of soteriology that is at the same time orthodox and creative.[23] Drawing heavily on the work of the Fathers, in particular Athanasius, Epiphanius, and Cyril of Alexandria, in addition to such Reformed mentors as John Calvin and Karl Barth, the soteriology of Torrance presents us with an opportunity to observe how a modern-day Reformed doctrine of theōsis may be constructed. While his work does not provide a fully systematized doctrine of theōsis, and thus much work remains to be done, it does provide a starting point for Reformed thought to engage with an Eastern Orthodox doctrine of theōsis.

In an address delivered to the World Alliance of Reformed Churches, in Frankfurt on August 5, 1964, Torrance pleaded for "a reconsideration by the Reformed Churches of what the Greek fathers called theosis."[24]

---

[23] Torrance is uniquely qualified to act as a representative of the Reformed tradition in this discussion for several reasons. An ordained Minister of the Church of Scotland, he held the position of Professor of Christian Dogmatics at New College, Edinburgh, for 29 years (1952–79). Torrance founded the *Scottish Journal of Theology*, which he edited for over thirty years, founded the Scottish Church Theology Society, and served as moderator of the General Assembly of the Church of Scotland 1976–77. Throughout his career Torrance has formed theological bridges between the World Alliance of Reformed Churches and the Eastern Orthodox Churches. Torrance was invited to Addis Ababa by Methodius the Greek Archbishop of Axum, and was consecrated as a Presbyter of the Greek Orthodox Church and given the honorary title of Protopresbyter. In 1970, at a session of the General Assembly in Edinburgh, the Patriarch of Alexandria conferred on Torrance the Cross of St. Mark, which was followed in 1977 by his being given the Cross of Thyateira by the Greek Orthodox Archbishop in London. Instigating further talks between these two traditions, Torrance sought theological consensus on the doctrine of the Trinity, for agreement in this area would influence all further discussions. Between 1986 and 1990 discussions took place, resulting in the "Agreed Statement on the Doctrine of the Holy Trinity," reached at Geneva on 13 March 1991. See *Theological Dialogue Between Orthodox and Reformed Churches*, vols. 1 & 2, ed. T. F. Torrance (Edinburgh: Scottish Academic, 1985, 1993). Torrance considers this historic agreement to be one of the supreme achievements of his career. For Torrance's most important writings on his relation to Reformed theology see "The Deposit of Faith," *Scottish Journal of Theology* 36/1 (1983) 1–28; "'The Substance of the Faith': A Clarification of the Concept in the Church of Scotland," *Scottish Journal of Theology* 36/3 (1983) 327–38; "The Distinctive Character of the Reformed Tradition," in *Incarnational Ministry: Essays in Honor of Ray*

Taking up Torrance's challenge we may ask: What might a Reformed doctrine of theōsis look like? Torrance himself paints broad strokes but provides enough of a sketch for a more complete portrait to be crafted. Reformed theology, in Torrance's view, speaks of human participation in the divine nature as a union and communion with Christ in his human nature, a participation in his incarnate sonship, and as a sharing in Christ the divine life and love. "That is to say, it [Reformed theology] interprets 'deification' precisely in the same way as Athanasius in the *Contra Arianos*."[25] Quoting Calvin, Torrance argues that it is only through "real and substantial union" with Christ in his human nature that we partake of all his benefits, and it is only in the incarnate Christ that we are really made to partake of the eternal life of God himself.[26] An examination of the *imago Dei*, the Creator-creature distinction, and the concept of "reconciling exchange" in Torrance's thought, provides us with one possible way of "reforming" theōsis.

Imago Dei

Within Torrance's anthropology a subtle yet crucial distinction between *being* and *person* is offered which applies theologically and anthropologically. Theologically speaking, the Being of God refers to *ousia*, while Person refers

---

S. Anderson, eds. C. H. Kettler and T. H. Speidell (Colorado Springs: Helmers and Howard, 1990) 2–15; and *Scottish Theology from John Knox to John McLeod Campbell* (Edinburgh: T. & T. Clark, 1996).

[24] T. F. Torrance, "Come, Creator Spirit, For the Renewal of Worship and Witness," in *Theology in Reconstruction* (Grand Rapids: Eerdmans, 1965) 243.

[25] Torrance, *Theology in Reconstruction*, 184.

[26] At this point Torrance goes no further, stating: "We are unable to describe this participation in positive language any more than we can describe the hypostatic union in positive language—refusal to do so does not by itself import that a real and creative and therefore an ontological relation is not envisaged in this participation," Torrance, *Theology in Reconstruction*, 186. Torrance is appealing to some form of apophatic reticence, as Eastern Orthodoxy does. Apophaticism is a common epistemological commitment among all Eastern Orthodox writers both ancient and modern, although to different degrees with each. Amongst the various forms of apophaticism Bartos identifies a strict/radical approach and a relative approach as the two most obvious forms: E. Bartos, *Deification in Eastern Orthodoxy: An Evaluation and Critique of the Theology of Dumitru Staniloae*. Paternoster Biblical and Theological Monographs (Carlisle: Paternoster, 1999) 25.

to *hypostasis*. Torrance applies a similar distinction to his anthropology. The human creature is created in a special sense, as Gen 1:27 makes clear. The structural aspect of the human being as creature in God's image is thus posited. However, because the *imago Dei* is ultimately christological, soteriological, and eschatological, the relational aspect of the *imago* is what makes human "beings" human "persons," true men and women. Because Jesus Christ is the only true human, he is the true image of God, and so only in Christ can the human creature be fully *person*.[27] The movement within the salvation of men and women then, is from human *being* to human *person*. Anything outside of Christ falls short of true personhood.[28]

When God created humanity he created man and woman as one.[29] Torrance, clearly influenced by Barth, sees in the creation of men and women in the image of God an otherness and togetherness that is to be expressed in an inherent relatedness which is a creaturely reflection of a transcendent relatedness in the divine Being.[30] For Torrance, "this is the

---

[27] Torrance is here reliant once again upon the seminal work of Karl Barth who argued that in the strict sense it is God who is properly Person, and humans are persons in derivation from him. K. Barth, *Church Dogmatics,* 4 vols (Edinburgh: T. & T. Clark, 1956–75) II/1, 272. See T. F. Torrance, *God and Rationality* (1971; Reprint, Eugene, Ore.: Wipf & Stock, 1997) 141–42.

[28] One could even say that anyone outside of Christ falls short of true human *being*. Barth himself appears to argue this in his reinterpretation of the doctrine of election in Jesus Christ. See B. McCormack, "Grace and Being," in *The Cambridge Companion to Karl Barth*, ed. J. Webster (Cambridge: Cambridge University Press, 2000) 92–110; C. Gunton, "Karl Barth's Doctrine of Election as Part of his Doctrine of God," *Journal of Theological Studies* n.s. 25 (1974) 381–92; and H. T. Goebel, *Vom freien Wählen Gottes und des Menschen: Interpretationsübungen zur "Analogie" nach Karl Barths Lehre von der Erwählung und Bedenken ihrer Folgen für die Kirchlichen Dogmatik* (Frankfurt: Lang, 1990).

[29] Torrance follows Barth's much criticised thesis that an essential aspect of the *imago Dei* is gender. "Difference in sex is not simply a feature of the body, merely adventitious or accidental to the soul, but is intrinsic to the human soul which, far from being neutral, *is*, either male or female . . . sexuality thus determines the innermost being of people, making them either male or female in themselves," T. F. Torrance, "The Soul and Person in Theological Perspective," in *Religion, Reason, and the Self: Essays in Honour of Hywel D. Lewis*, ed. S. R. Sutherland and T. A. Roberts (Cardiff: University of Wales Press, 1989) 108–9. As with Torrance's persistent use of masculine language for humanity, he opens himself up for severe critique at this point and, also typical, he does not offer detailed rationale for his commitment to such a position.

[30] The ultimate expression of this relatedness is vertical, between God and humanity, but is also reflected horizontally in marriage and procreation. T. F. Torrance, "The Goodness and Dignity of Man in the Christian Tradition," *Modern Theology* 4 (1988) 311.

personal or *inter-personal* structure of humanity in which there is imaged the ineffable personal relations of the Holy Trinity."[31] This means that, like Barth before him, when Torrance treats humanity or, regretfully, his more customary appellation *man*, he does not mean an individual (even less a male![32]) but rather a person in ontological relation with other persons.[33] This is what Torrance means by "onto-relations" or being-constituting-relations.[34] While first applied to the intratrinitarian relations it is also applicable to intra-human relations.[35]

For Torrance it appears that as man or woman we do not image God in the strict sense, rather, as *person* we image God. It is strictly not man or woman (or man and woman together) but man or woman as *person*. Remembering that "person" is used here in the distinctively Christian sense as shaped by the intra-trinitarian relations of the three Divine Persons who are the Triune God. "It is a person in that contingent, relational sense that is the image of God .... not person as male or female human being as such."[36]

---

[31] Torrance, "The Soul and Person in Theological Perspective," 109–10.

[32] "That is to say by 'man' the biblical tradition means 'man-and-woman', for it is man and woman who constitute in their union the basic unit of humanity," Torrance, "The Goodness and Dignity of Man in the Christian Tradition," 311.

[33] The idea of person being equated with the individual is attributed by Torrance, as it is by most scholars, to Boethius, *De duabus naturis et una persona Christi, adversus Eutychen et Nestorium*, 2.1–5, cf., Torrance, "The Soul and Person in Theological Perspective," fn.12.

[34] Torrance, "The Goodness and Dignity of Man in the Christian Tradition," 311. Torrance's view of "person" is derived from the work of Richard of St Victor as opposed to that of Boethius or Aquinas, both of which are described by Torrance in his *Reality and Scientific Theology* (Edinburgh: Scottish Academic, 1985) 174–76. Contrary to Torrance, C. E. Gunton, argues that Richard's Trinitarian theology only allowed the possibility of a relational view of person, see *The Promise of Trinitarian Theology* (Edinburgh: T. & T. Clark, 1991) 93–94. Be that as it may, while Torrance interacts with the work of Richard St. Victor he develops his theology of the person based upon the insights of Athanasius and the Nicene theologians. See Torrance, "Athanasius: A Study in the Foundations of Classical Theology," in *Theology in Reconciliation: Essays Towards Evangelical and Catholic Unity in East and West* (London: Geoffrey Chapman, 1975) 215–66.

[35] T. F. Torrance, *The Christian Doctrine of God: One Being Three Persons* (Edinburgh: T. & T. Clark, 1996) 102–3.

[36] Torrance, "The Ministry of Women," 281.

Given Torrance's doctrine of onto-relations, the *imago Dei* is thus a dynamic and eschatological reflection that, while initiated and developed in time-space within creation, is ultimately only realized in the eschaton of which the Church is currently a foretaste. The onto-relations work on two levels, vertically and horizontally. Vertically one is justified and sanctified through a relationship with the triune God, and horizontally, one is formed into communion with other believers in the Body of Christ, the Church. But these two levels are one integrated whole, not two separate spheres. Theōsis, communion with God, is thus a "personal" activity and persons are defined as humans-in-relationship. The ultimate person is Jesus Christ hence mature men and women are those who have been perfected by grace as they are united to Christ by the Holy Spirit. The Church thus becomes the locus of theōsis this side of the Parousia.

Because of sin and the fall the onto-relations that exist between all personal beings, God-humanity, humanity-God, and humanity-humanity have been radically "disrupted," resulting in the breakdown of personal relating on both the horizontal and vertical levels.[37] This disruption affects the "transcendental determinism" of the human being as they refuse to listen to the Spirit of God in their alienated and sinful rebellion. The result is that only through the mediation of Christ can the Holy Spirit be poured out on human beings so that they can again come to more fully reflect the *imago Dei* that God intended them to.[38]

---

[37] Torrance, "The Goodness and Dignity of Man in the Christian Tradition," 312–13.

[38] T. F. Torrance, "The Goodness and Dignity of Man in the Christian Tradition," *Modern Theology* 4 (1988) 320–21. The idea of "transcendental determinism" is an important one for Torrance and for a doctrine of theōsis. The drive created within the human person for God is a theme that has been developed by a number of theologians. Rahner spoke of a "transcendental Christology" in which men and women are in a transcendental necessity or thirst for the absolute and the hope of a free self-communication on the part of God. This led Rahner to explicate his distinctive theology of the "anonymous Christian" and anonymous theism.

According to Rahner, whenever a person is open to the mystery that grounds human existence he or she is open to God himself. While the (Roman Catholic) Church is the visible sacrament of salvation, all sinners are in a sphere of grace. See K. Rahner, *A New Christology* (London: Burns & Oats, 1980). For a survey of Rahner's position and an interaction with the theology of T. F. Torrance see P. D. Molnar, *Divine Freedom and the Doctrine of the Immanent Trinity: In Dialogue with Karl Barth and Contemporary Theology* (London: T. & T. Clark, 2002) 181–96.

Given this definition of the *imago Dei*, one that is restored through the vicarious humanity of Jesus Christ, and mediated to us in the Spirit who unites us in Christ, we can see what Torrance means when he speaks of the doctrine of theōsis. Colyer helpfully summarizes Torrance at this point:

> *Theosis* or *theopoiesis* is not the divinising or deification of the human soul or creaturely being, Torrance contends, but rather is the Spirit of God humanizing and personalizing us by uniting us with Christ's vicarious humanity in a way that both confirms us in our creaturely reality utterly different from God, and yet also adapts us in our contingent nature for knowledge of God, for communion with God and for fellowship with one another.[39]

Thus *theōsis/theopoiēsis* is closely related to Torrance's relational *imago Dei* founded on an *analogia relationis*,[40] for in Torrance's trinitarian

---

Torrance's position is quite different from that of Rahner's at this point. For Torrance, there is no independent knowledge of God outside of God himself, hence no logical bridge can be walked from the experience of self-transcendence to the God revealed in Jesus Christ. This is in direct opposition to Rahner's basic methodology.

A similar thought to that of Torrance's is found in the Eastern Orthodox theologian D. Staniloae's theology of the *Logos*. For Staniloae, the human person is created with an inherent orientation toward the ontological pursuit of "ultimate transcendence." This ultimate transcendence is made known supremely in the person of Jesus Christ the *Logos* and it is here that theōsis, or deification, takes place. There is a need for Christ written into the very existence of men and women. See D. Staniloae, *Teologia Dogmatica Ortodoxa* (Bucuresti: EIBMBOR, 1978) 2:47. See Staniloae's critique of Rahner's position in idem, 2:14–16.

[39] E.M. Colyer, *How To Read T. F. Torrance: Understanding his Trinitarian and Scientific Theology* (Downers Grove, Ill.: IVP, 2001) 178.

[40] In an insightful essay on the ministry of women, Torrance further clarifies what it means to be created in the *imago Dei*, with special focus on the distinctive maleness and femaleness inherent in the human person. In terms of "image" this is strictly a relational term in Scripture and thus in practice, not a physical term. The image of God does not inhere in human nature, far less in specifically male or female nature, but it is a *donum superadditum*, a gift wholly contingent upon the free grace of God. T. F. Torrance, "The Ministry of Women," in *The Call to Serve: Biblical and Theological Perspectives on Ministry in Honour of Bishop Penny Jamieson*, ed. D. A. Campbell (Sheffield: Sheffield Academic, 1996) 276. From this we are not to think that human beings reflect God's uncreated Nature through some intrinsic analogy of being (*analogia entis*), but rather are destined

perspective, the Spirit unites us to Christ and through Christ with the Father, and therefore, "The Spirit makes man's being open for fellowship with God, and thereby brings his creaturely relations to their true end and fulfilment in God, He is essentially the living Spirit who, coming from the inner communion of the Holy Trinity, creates communion between man and God."[41]

Creator-Creature Distinction

Torrance uses the themes of objectivity and subjectivity to present a nuanced doctrine of theōsis.[42] For Torrance, theōsis or communion with God is achieving creaturely objectivity as opposed to sinful subjectivity. True objectivity is achieved only in the Spirit that unites the creature to the humanity of the incarnate Son.

This is important to keep in mind as it guards Torrance's doctrine of theōsis from any false view of the divinization of humanity by any mechanical, naturalistic, or ordinary human means.[43] Participation with God is achieved by grace, by God and God alone. If this point can be

---

by grace to live in faithful response to the purpose and movement of God's love toward us as his creaturely partners (*analogia relationis*).

[41] Torrance, "The Soul and Person in Theological Perspective," 112.

[42] "God does not override man but recreates, reaffirms him and stands him up before himself as his dear child, and man does not seek to use or manipulate knowledge of God for the fulfilment of his own ends in self-will and self-understanding, but loves him objectively for his own sake and is so liberated from himself that he can love his neighbour objectively also," Torrance, *Theology in Reconstruction*, 237.

[43] One false view of deification that Torrance would also rule out is noted by P. E. Hughes, *The True Image: The Origin and Destiny of Man in Christ* (Grand Rapids: Eerdmans, 1989) 232: "The incarnation as it affects our humanity is not just one more stage in an incredibly long sequence of stages from inanimate matter to biological organization, from animality to intellectuality, and thence on to spirituality and divinization. It is the grace of God intervening to lift man out of the pit which he has dug for himself and to restore him to the wholeness of his creation, so that once again he may function freely in accordance with the purpose of his being and his high calling under God. . . . Through the saving work of the incarnate Son the believer recovers both the integrity of his being and also the purpose and the power and the ultimate glory that belong to his constitution in the image of God."

maintained then many false views of divinization will be dismissed outright. As Torrance consistently maintains:

> By coming into man the Holy Spirit opens him out for God. But at the very heart of this movement is the act of God in which he became man in order to take man's place, and give man a place within the communion of the divine life. It is the act of the divine love taking the way of substitution, and opening up the way for a corresponding act on the part of man in which he renounces himself for God's sake that the divine love may have its way with him in self-less objectivity.[44]

Torrance understands God's presence in creation as communion, a communion in correspondence to the hypostatic union between God and humanity in Christ and the onto-relations that exist in the perichoretic union of the three divine Persons in the one being of God.[45] Torrance posits an immediate divine presence in creation and creation's real participation in God, however, God and humanity are never confused or mixed into one.[46] In this way Torrance distinguishes between a Christian doctrine of theōsis conceived in terms of *koinonia* and a Greek philosophical conception of divinization in terms of *methexis* (mixture of being). He clearly affirms the first and rejects the second. Much of Torrance's thought on the doctrine of theōsis revolves around making this distinction extremely clear.[47]

---

[44] Torrance, *Theology in Reconstruction*, 138.

[45] As a direct consequence of the doctrines of the *homoousion* and *perichoresis* Torrance has developed what he terms an onto-relational concept of the divine Persons. By onto-relational Torrance implies an understanding of the three divine Persons in the one God in which the ontic relations between them belong to what they essentially are in themselves in their distinctive hypostases. In short, onto-relations are being-constituting-relations. The differing relations between the Father, Son, and Spirit belong to what they are as Father, Son, and Spirit, so the *homoousial* relations between the three Divine Persons belong to what they are in themselves as Persons and in their Communion with one another. This onto-relational understanding of person defined as person-in-relationship is also applicable to inter-human relations, but in a created way reflecting the uncreated way in which it applies to the Trinitarian relations in God. See the discussion of "person" and "being" in Torrance, *The Christian Doctrine of God: One Being Three Persons* (Edinburgh: T. & T. Clark, 1996) 103–5.

[46] Torrance, *Theology in Reconstruction*, 184.

[47] He does so at times by distinguishing between a Roman Catholic doctrine of the church and grace from that of a Reformed perspective. See ibid., 169–91.

Torrance sees the idea of intimate communion developed masterfully in the theology of the Nicene Fathers and again in the Reformation. Torrance's positing of a dialogical relation between creation and God asserts a personal interaction which includes a clear distinction and close union in reciprocity. It was the Hellenistic notion of divine immutability, according to Torrance, that created a wedge between God and creation necessitating a realm of intermediation which was then conceptualized in the formation of causes. Torrance sees in the Chalcedonian notion of participation (hypostatic union) an assertion of a direct communion without mediating causes. This same idea is presented or reclaimed by Calvin's conclusion that "all nature, and the gifts and endowments of man, depend for their being upon the immediate agency of God through His Spirit and His Word."[48] Clearly Torrance is advocating a reforming of theōsis which, as a Reformed theology, questions the very basis of *the essentia-energeia* schema of Palamite theology. Communion for Torrance acts as a cognate for *theōsis*. Accordingly,

> by encountering us as personal Being God at once brings us into a personal relation with himself and prevents us from including him within our own subjectivity, for it is as the Thou, the transcendent Other, that he meets us and makes himself known. He both distinguishes himself from us as independent Reality over against us, and indeed as Lord God of our very being, and at the same time posits and upholds us before him as persons in relations of mutuality and freedom with God and with one another.[49]

It is clear that Torrance does not confuse the distinction between God and creation. Rather, communion has the idea of encounter between two distinct but not separate entities. To maintain the strongly personalist force of this communion between God and human beings Torrance adopts Calvin's stress on the importance of the Holy Spirit as "God's creative personal presence."[50] What the Spirit creates is a real personal relation

---

[48] T. F. Torrance, *Calvin's Doctrine of Man* (London: Lutterworth, 1949) 63.

[49] T. F. Torrance, *Reality and Scientific Theology* (Edinburgh: Scottish Academic, 1985) 179.

[50] Torrance, *Theology in Reconstruction*, 96–97.

between the human person and God that "posits us as subjects over against the divine Subject."[51] This is an onto-relational view of human persons partaking in the divine nature.

As with much of Eastern Orthodox theology, for Torrance the goal of theōsis is not to become "God" or to become "gods." It is not in any literal sense a matter of transcending the confines of the human nature but is, rather, the process and means by which the human can achieve true human personhood. Theōsis does not do away with our creatureliness; rather, it fulfils it. In similar vein the Eastern Orthodox theologian Staniloae suggests that theōsis cannot be taken literally. One cannot literally become God since that would be as absurd as if we were to state that God is a creature.[52] The "transcendental determination" implanted within each human person and realized by those united to Christ Jesus is that men and women will be able to be and do what they were created to be and do—be mirrors of God back to God, in Christ by the Holy Spirit. This is the goal of humanity summarized by the term *theōsis* within the patristic writers, Eastern Orthodoxy, and Torrance's own Reformed theology.

According to Torrance theōsis is prescriptive of a relation between God and creation which consistently holds together two distinct aspects of this relationship: first; the complete distinction between Creator and creature is maintained with vigorous lucidity; second, theōsis represents a dynamic relationship between God and humanity in which a real—even, according to Torrance, an ontological (onto-relational)—participation of the creature in God is made possible inherently in the creation of humanity in the *imago Dei*. By means of the language of participation in the divine life, union, and communion with God, a defense of the transcendence of God and the humanizing of persons we have entered the specific realm of theōsis language. Torrance deals with each of these specific points and is thus outlining a doctrine of theōsis, even if the technical vocabulary is used only sparingly.

---

[51] Ibid., 97. R. Spjuth summarises Torrance's "communion theology" thus: "Communion as personal interaction means that God can be present as transcendent without being confused with creation; 'union without mixture,'" R. Spjuth, *Creation, Contingency and Divine Presence: In the Theologies of Thomas F. Torrance and Eberhard Jüngel* (Lund: Lund University Press, 1995) 36–37.
[52] See Bartos, *Deification in Eastern Orthodoxy*, 145.

Reconciling Exchange

Of signal importance to Torrance's theology is the integral link between Christology and soteriology or incarnation and atonement.[53] Those writers, theologians, and preachers who, according to Torrance, can hold the work and person of Christ together, while clearly developing the organic unity of the two, will be standing on solid biblical and historical ground.[54] Torrance takes this solid and "high" ground in his own theology by making the incarnation the central feature of his soteriology.[55] The centerpiece of Torrance's soteriology is the concept of "exchange" which he employs countless times throughout his theological *oeuvre*.[56] By means of a

---

[53] See a concise summary of his position in T. F. Torrance, *Preaching Christ Today* (Grand Rapids: Eerdmans, 1994) 41–71. W. Pannenberg, *Jesus—God and Man,* trs. L. L. Wilkins and D. A. Priebe, (London: SCM, 1968) 38–49 surveys a number of soteriological models to highlight the danger of allowing our subjective views of soteriology to dictate our Christology. Viewing the "work" as paramount risks reducing the person of Christ to a mere symbol of reconciliation. A doctrine of the person of Christ separate from his work would lead eventually to the question whether this work could not have been accomplished by another agent. Cf., K. Barth, *Church Dogmatics.* 4 vols (Edinburgh: T. & T. Clark, 1956–75) IV/1, 127f.

[54] See for instance the criteria outlined in K. Rahner, *Theological Investigations. Volume 17: Jesus, Man and the Church,* tr. M. Kohl (London: Darton, Longman & Todd, 1981) 17.28–31.

[55] This is one of the more important contributions Torrance has made to contemporary theology, his articulation of the saving significance of the incarnation. See G. Pratz, "The Relationship Between Incarnation and Atonement in the Theology of Thomas F. Torrance," *Journal for Christian Theological Research* 3/2 (1998) http://apu.edu/~CTRF/articles/1998_articles/pratz.html. Cf. T. F. Torrance, "The Christ Who Loves Me," in *A Passion for Christ: Vision that Ignites Ministry*, eds. G. Dawson and J. Stein (Edinburgh: Handsel, 1999) 10. This is also one of the most highly contested areas of Torrance's theology. See for instance R. A. Muller, "The Barth Legacy: New Athanasius or Origen Redivivus? A Response to T. F. Torrance," *Thomist* 54 (1990) 673–704.

[56] Torrance repeatedly introduces this theme into his theology at key points, and uses 2 Cor 8:9 as a key text: "You know the grace of our Lord Jesus Christ, that though he was rich, yet for your sakes became poor, that you through his poverty might be rich." Here we find the doctrine of theōsis explicitly dealt with, right at the heart of Torrance's theology. A failure to understand this aspect of Torrance's theology is a failure to understand any of it. The doctrine of theōsis thus provides a window into the centre of Torrance's soteriology. See T. F. Torrance, *Preaching Christ Today* (Grand Rapids: Eerdmans, 1994) 32–34; *Theology in Reconciliation*, 167. As Yeung so rightly noted, "in this way a set of intrinsic relations between God, Christ and humanity becomes the main pattern of the

"reconciling exchange," an "atoning exchange," a "sweet exchange," or "atoning propitiation," Christ takes what is his and gives it to fallen humanity and takes what is ours and heals, restores, forgives, and judges it within his own being and life.[57] The language of "exchange" along with the concepts employed to present the idea, its historical origins and development, and the applications Torrance derives from it are all evidence that Torrance is committed to a highly stylized doctrine of theōsis which forms a *leitmotif* running throughout his soteriology.

When applied to human persons the atoning or "sweet exchange" that occurred in the person of the incarnate Son takes on the character of a "soteriological exchange." Torrance appeals to Gregory Nazianzen to speak on his behalf when he writes:

> Let us become like Christ, since Christ became like us. Let us become divine for his sake, since he for ours became man. He assumed the worst that he might give us the better; he became poor that we through his poverty might be rich; he took upon himself the form of a servant that we might be exalted; he was tempted that we might conquer; he was dishonoured that he might glorify us; he ascended that he might draw us to himself, who were lying low in the fall of sin. Let us give all, offer all, to him who gave himself a ransom and reconciliation for us.[58]

To this Torrance adds: "this atoning exchange then, embraces the whole relationship between Christ and ourselves."[59] In a "saving interchange" Christ worked out our reconciliation within the saving economy of the incarnation, and in the ontological depths of the humanity which he made his own, and now, by participating in his humanity, we too can be lifted

---

faith, with the dynamics of reconciling exchange at its heart," J. H.-K. Yeung, *Being and Knowing: An Examination of T. F. Torrance's Christological Science*, Jian Dao Dissertation Series 3, Theology and Culture 1 (Hong Kong: China Alliance, 1996) 205.

[57] Torrance identifies this "wonderful exchange" with certain elements of Irenaeus' doctrine of recapitulation: Irenaeus, *Adv. Haer.*, 5. *praef.*, "Out of his measureless love our Lord Jesus Christ has become what we are in order to make us what he is himself," cited in T. F. Torrance, *The Trinitarian Faith: The Evangelical Theology of the Ancient Catholic Church* (1988. Edinburgh: T. & T. Clark, 1995) 156, 179; and Calvin's *mirifica commutatio* in *Institutes*, 4.17.2.

[58] Torrance, *The Trinitarian Faith*, 181. Cf., Gregory Nazianzus, *Or.* 1.5.

[59] *Ibid.* See our comments on Calvin on the third page of this article.

up to the immediate presence of the Father in Christ through the Spirit. In this way Torrance presents his Reformed doctrine of theōsis.

Torrance is insistent that, against his reading of certain tendencies of scholastic Protestantism, justification is not simply a declaratory act, but an actualisation of what is declared. Justification has to do with forgiveness, and when forgiven, sinners are forgiven.[60] Accordingly, "forgiveness" is not just a word of pardon but a reality translated into our existence by crucifixion and resurrection, by judgment and recreation. It means that the sinner is now given a right standing before God and is holy— "justified."[61] Torrance suggests precisely that the believer is now holy (*hagios, iustus*) in Christ. In stressing the "in Christ" dimension Torrance is constructing the very "paradigm shift" which Trevor Hart calls for when he states: "What would seem to be required . . . is for Western theology to undergo a 'paradigm shift,' to leave behind the outlook which has been predominant ever since the writings of Tertullian, and to seek to recapture the missing dimension in our soteriology, namely the person of the Saviour himself."[62] Torrance attempts to do just this partly by means of reforming theōsis.

"It is an outstanding characteristic of all the documents of the Scottish Reformation," writes Torrance, "that a place of centrality is given to the union of God and Man in Christ, and therefore our 'blessed conjunction' or 'society' or 'fraternity' with Christ. That union with Christ lies at the heart of our righteousness in him, for it is through that union that we actually participate in his holy life."[63] It is this participation or union with God which makes us truly holy, not just legally so. "Justification is not only the forgiveness of sins, but the bestowal of a positive righteousness that derives from beyond us, and which we have through union with Christ."[64]

---

[60] Torrance uses the healing of the paralytic in Mark 2.1–12 (pars) to bear this out. See T. F. Torrance, *Space, Time and Resurrection* (Edinburgh: T. & T. Clark, 1998) 62.

[61] Ibid., 61.

[62] T. A. Hart, "Humankind in Christ and Christ in Humankind: Salvation as Participation in Our Substitute in the Theology of John Calvin," *Scottish Journal of Theology* 42 (1989) 70.

[63] T. F. Torrance, "Justification: Its Radical Nature and Place in Reformed Doctrine and Life," in *Theology in Reconstruction*, 151.

[64] Ibid., 151–52.

Because incarnation and atonement are intimately linked in the one person of the Mediator then his entire life is one of atoning reconciliation, from conception to the cross. We see this in Torrance's understanding of the active and passive obedience of Christ and how they are distinct but separate so that we can and must speak of the active obedience as *actio passiva* and the passive obedience as *passio activa*. It is on the basis of the unity between the active and passive obedience of Christ that Torrance contends that in our justification "we have imputed to us not only the passive righteousness of Christ in which he satisfied for our sins in suffering the judgement of God in his death on the Cross, but the active righteousness of Christ in which he positively fulfilled the Father's holy will in an obedient life."[65] The only correct conclusion for Torrance therefore is that justification cannot simply refer to the non-imputation of our sins through the pardon of Christ, but also to the positive sharing in his divine-human righteousness. Sanctification is correlative with justification: to receive one is to receive the other.

Through the appeal to justification as involving both declaration and deification[66] Torrance anticipates the move within Lutheran scholarship to see Luther's doctrine of justification as more than a declaratory "legal fiction," but as actually involving the making righteous of the sinner through deification. Like Torrance, Luther does not separate the person of Christ from his work. Rather, Christ himself, both his person and his work, is the ground of Christian righteousness as the believer participates in the divine nature through Christ. As we have already noted, this became a hallmark of Luther's own theology: Christ is really present in the faith of the Christian (*in ipsa fide Christus adest*).

In a return to the theology of Athanasius, Torrance recalls the threefold distinction in union and communion of which patristic theology speaks and in so doing clarifies his own doctrine of theōsis. There is first of all a consubstantial communion between the Father and the Son in the Holy Spirit who is the love that God is. In the second place, there is the hypostatic union between the divine and human natures in the one Person of Christ which takes place through the operation of the Holy Spirit who is the love

---

[65] Ibid., 155.

[66] See the useful discussion of this in B. D. Marshall, "Justification as Declaration and Deification," *International Journal of Systematic Theology* 4 (2002) 3–28.

of God. The third feature is the communion or *koinonia* of the Spirit who is mediated to us from the Father through the Son, and who is the love of God poured into our hearts. In light of this three-fold distinction Torrance maintains, "It is in virtue of our union with Christ by the power of the Son that in and through him we are made to partake of the very Love which God himself is, and are thus partakers of the divine nature."[67] Here the technical language and the citation of 2 Pet 1:4 puts us in no doubt that Torrance is again advocating a nuanced doctrine of theōsis by which, through Christ, the human person is lifted up to participate in the Triune communion in Christ by the Holy Spirit. This doctrine is again seen to be a central component within Torrance's soteriology, here acting as the heart of his doctrine of reconciliation in the midst of his *ordo salutis.*

Conclusion

For much of Western theology the concept of theōsis creates unease and often hostile rejection as it appears to make humans into "gods." Reformed and Evangelical Christians in particular have been wary of accepting or even entertaining a doctrine of theōsis. Torrance is aware of this unease and while his doctrine of theōsis never comes remotely close to affirming the apotheosis of humanity, or the divinization of humans, he does speak of the "danger of vertigo" that can overwhelm some people when they contemplate being exalted in Christ to partake of the divine nature (theōsis).[68] The vertigo of which Torrance speaks is the kind of mysticism or pantheism which identifies human being with the Divine Being. Torrance argues that this is the exact antithesis of the Christian Gospel. This is important to note for it shows the lengths to which Torrance will go in clearly stating what he does and does not mean by the adoption of theotic doctrine. "The hypostatic union of the divine and human natures in Jesus preserves the human and creaturely being he took from us, and it is in and through our sharing in that human and creaturely being, sanctified and blessed with him, that we share in the life of God while remaining what we are made to be, humans and not Gods."[69]

---

[67] Torrance, *Space, Time and Resurrection,* 70.
[68] Ibid., 136–39.
[69] Ibid., 136.

This is an emphatic rejection of any reading of the doctrine of *theōsis* which argues that the human is swallowed up by the divine, a charge often unfairly leveled at an Eastern Orthodox presentation of the tradition.

Theōsis is the work of the Triune God in making human persons participate in or partake of the divine nature, a participation in the Triune communion or *perichoresis*. Through being united to Jesus Christ the God-man, we are united to his divinized humanity and through that relationship we enjoy fellowship with God. Torrance has written that this is the goal of the incarnation, that we may be gathered up in Christ Jesus and included in his own self-presentation before the Father, and in that relationship partake of the divine nature.[70] But importantly, as Torrance acknowledges, "the staggering thing about this is that the exaltation of human nature into the life of God does not mean the disappearance of man or the swallowing up of human and creaturely being in the finite ocean of the divine being, but rather that human nature, remaining creaturely and human, is yet exalted in Christ to share in God's life and glory."[71]

It is clear that Torrance, as one example of an influential Reformed thinker, has articulated a vision of theōsis that is at once deeply respectful of Eastern Orthodoxy and indelibly Reformed. While Torrance's articulation of a Reformed doctrine of theōsis lacks development and is only one of many potential entry-points for reforming theōsis, it is our hope that further reflection on theology of this nature, focused on such a central theme as theōsis, will result in further truly ecumenical works which contribute to the healing and rapprochement of the three streams of the Great Tradition.[72]

soli Deo gloria

---

[70] Ibid., 135.

[71] Ibid.

[72] See for instance the important work of V-M. Kärkkäinen, "The Doctrine of Theosis and its Ecumenical Potential," *Sobornost* 23/2 (2001) 45–77.

The Comedy of Divinization in Soloviev

Stephen Finlan

I understand *comedy* to have three common meanings:

- a literary *genre* featuring triumphant outcomes; the opposite of tragedy;
- a literary *style* utilized in exposing the folly, immaturity, or baseness of much human behavior, communicated through irony, satire, exaggeration, and sarcasm;
- an artistic *genre* where *humor* dominates, although a serious message is possible.[1]

Of course, the three meanings often overlap. Kornblatt ably shows the presence of the last two meanings in Soloviev's final book, *Three Conversations*,[2] which has been published under three different titles in

---

[1] *The Random House Dictionary of the English Language* (Ed. Jess Stein [New York, 1967] 294) seems to combine my meanings 1 and 3: "light and humorous . . . with triumph over adverse circumstances, resulting in a successful or happy conclusion."

[2] Judith Kornblatt, "Soloviev on Salvation: The Story of the 'Short Story of the Antichrist,'" in *Russian Religious Thought*, eds. Judith Kornblatt and Richard F. Gustafson (Madison: University of Wisconsin Press, 1996) 68–87.

English.[3] She documents how effectively Soloviev uses humor to convey the most serious message.[4]

I will focus on the first two meanings of "comedy," both of which involve some recognition of the foolishness and pain of the earthly level of existence, one of which contrasts this level with an anticipated level where good always triumphs, the other of which delights in exposing human folly and greed. One produces a laugh that is understanding and optimistic; the other produces a laugh that is either bittersweet (if it has some anticipation of the higher level) or bitter (if it does not).

Triumphant comedy is seen in Soloviev's insight that "There is no life situation, even if arising according to our own fault, out of which it would not be possible to come out in a dignified way with good will."[5] Of course, this requires the willing cooperation of the person, and such cooperation is an essential ingredient in Soloviev's concept of spiritual triumph. Soloviev's article on the motives that led Pushkin into his fatal duel, is comedic, in that it shows that Pushkin learned his lesson, learned that he had been foolish to give in to rage and vanity. At the last moment, after already being wounded, Pushkin chose a Christian response, and commanded his seconds not to seek revenge against the duel's victor.[6] In his three days of dying from his wounds, the rage that had filled him disappeared, and he was finally liberated, Soloviev says, "from the captivity of passion."[7] Given his final enlightenment, and his not having to live with the burden of having killed someone out of rage and vanity, Pushkin's death was really a triumph, and his *fate* is better described as *providence*.[8] This is truly a comedic, that is a *spiritually triumphant*, interpretation. Pushkin came finally to realize that

---

[3] I will refer to *War, Progress, and the End of History: Three Conversations Including a Short Story of the Anti-Christ*, tr. A. Bakshy, rev. Thomas R. Beyer, Jr. (Hudson, N.Y.: Lindisfarne, 1990). The original edition of Bakshy's translation was called *Three Conversations Concerning War, Progress, and the End of History, Including a Short Tale of the Antichrist*. There is also the Constable and Co. edition of 1915, entitled *War and Christianity from the Russian Point of View—Three Conversations* by Vladimir Solovyof.

[4] Kornblatt, "Soloviev on Salvation," 73, 83–84.

[5] Vladimir Soloviev, "The Fate of Pushkin," from *The Heart of Reality: Essays on Beauty, Love and Ethics*, tr. Vladimir Wozniuk (Notre Dame: University of Notre Dame Press, 2000) 164.

[6] Soloviev, "Fate of Pushkin," 166.

[7] Ibid., 165.

[8] Ibid., 170.

"service to the muse does not tolerate vanity," and that "before it can be pleasant, beauty must be worthy."[9] From the spiritual viewpoint, this insight is a great triumph, although, from the earthly viewpoint, it is sad to see the realization only coming on the deathbed. But if the Christian teaching of an afterlife is true, then the sadness will itself be absorbed into the triumph, and the triumph itself consists in spiritual progress.

In one place, Soloviev focuses on the second meaning of comedy, which I gave above. He sees comedy as the expose of human contentment with selfish and ignoble existence; he "defin[es] comedy as a negative presentiment of life's beauty through the typical portrayal of anti-ideal reality *in its complacency*."[10] He sees this approach to be particularly appropriate to poetry, whose "main subject . . . is the moral and social life of humanity, infinitely far from the realization of its ideal."[11] The classical (my first) meaning of the word "comedy" also applies; God's project will ultimately unfold as a story of triumphant resolution and universal unification.

Of course, Soloviev has the biblical tradition upon which to draw. The fundamental biblical comic sources are the Psalms and the Gospels. Even the psalm that Jesus recited while on the cross, and which begins so dismally, ends in triumph: "he did not hide his face from me, but heard when I cried. . . . May your hearts live forever" (Ps 22:24, 26). And the Gospels, although so full of tragedy, are all triumphant at the end.

Triumph, in Soloviev, combines biblical and philosophical principles. There is not only a reversal of isolation and selfishness, but of cosmic Chaos as well. God "must distinguish His perfect totality from the chaotic plurality . . . . He must be able to embrace in His unity the opposite principle itself . . . . with a grace penetrating and transforming it and so drawing it back to unity."[12] This philosophic idea finds a biblical parallel, where "God's will . . . knows no envy. . . . 'I have loved thee with an everlasting love.'"[13] There is a "new divine-human covenant, based upon the inner law of love."[14]

---

[9] Ibid., 155.

[10] Soloviev, "The Universal Meaning of Art," from *The Heart of Reality*, 78.

[11] Ibid., 79–80.

[12] Soloviev, *Russia and the Universal Church* (London: Geoffrey Bless, 1948) 158.

[13] Soloviev is quoting Jer 31:3; *Lectures on Divine Humanity*, rev., ed. Boris Jakim (Hudson, N.Y.: Lindisfarne, 1995) 70.

[14] Ibid., 71. In support, he cites Jer 31:31–34 and Isaiah chapters 2, 11, and 56.

Divinization and Comedy

To explain comedy in Soloviev, it is necessary to sketch out his philosophy of divinization, however inadequate our sketch may be. Soloviev gave new life to the important orthodox (not just "Orthodox") doctrine of theōsis, giving it a particular emphasis on repair, reconciliation, and harmonization. Theōsis was to be understood *philosophically* and *ethically*, more than *mystically* (as with the Eastern Orthodox tradition). Divinization for Soloviev does not mean monastic self-cultivation, but human participation in the divine project of transforming persons, institutions, society, and even the physical world.

The key to deification or Divine Humanity is voluntary human cooperation in the divine plan.[15] Soloviev does not envision passive human acceptance of divine manipulation, nor proud and self-directed rationalism, but rational and sincere cooperation.

What Soloviev seems to find most interesting is reconciliation and harmonization, helping God to achieve, "a universal *restoration* of all things . . . . Mankind has to *co-operate* with God in this work, for otherwise there cannot be a complete oneing of God with his creatures and a full expression of the meaning of existence . . . . a materialization of spirit and spiritualization of matter—a new union of these two elements."[16] Theōsis involves a literal transformation of the human body (more on this later), and also a real reconciliation between religions, which he sees as entirely possible, at least for the estranged branches of Christianity, and for Judaism as well. In a move that horrified many of his contemporaries, Soloviev says that Russia must learn to recognize the truths of the Catholics and Jews.[17] By affirming this unprecedented openness to other religions, Soloviev is, in fact, criticizing his friend Dostoevsky, though trying his best to paint the latter as already knowing all these things.[18]

Thus, there is a strong social side to theōsis in Soloviev. He is decidedly shy about developing the repercussions of such participation for the

---

[15] Kornblatt, "Soloviev on Salvation," 68.

[16] Vladimir Soloviev (here spelled Solovyev), *God, Man and the Church: The Spiritual Foundations of Life*, tr. Donald Attwater (London: James Clarke, 1938) 134.

[17] Judith Deutsch Kornblatt and Gary Rosenshield, "Vladimir Soloviev: Confronting Dostoevsky on the Jewish and Christian Questions," *JAAR* 68 (2000) 78.

[18] Kornblatt and Rosenshield, "Vladimir Soloviev: Confronting," 73–74, 79.

individual. This resistance to the temptations of spiritual egotism is one of the essentials of the divinizing process: a divinizing person needs to be aware of the comical (that is, absurd) pretensions of human pride. In his "Story of the Antichrist," he is "poking fun at himself," quoting his own earlier poetry and attributing it to the "all-wise" monk Pansofius.[19] Soloviev is maturely aware of the danger of self-centered religious imagination, and the Anti-Christ figure in his "story" embodies exactly this. He is a charming, humanistic, persuasive *writer*[20] who has allowed his spiritual powers to go to his head: probably Soloviev's imaginative picture of what he would look like if he had gone a certain direction.

Kornblatt is correct to insist that this is not a repudiation of his earlier belief; it is self-parody but not self-negation, since the key idea of theōsis— God making use of human cooperation—is still central.[21] Despite the humor, though, Soloviev is issuing a severe warning about how a popular but false theōsis can temporarily delay the coming of real theōsis. Soloviev has not lost his dream, but has foreseen that a nightmare would assault that dream. A monstrous caricature of spiritual unity will precede the emergence of real unity.

Trinitarianism

Soloviev's ideas are Trinitarian. Spiritual realities will always reflect the Trinitarian originating pattern. In deification, God's purpose finds embodiment in the incarnation of the Son, and comes to fruition socially in the incarnation of the Spirit in the lives of believers. In both humans and in nature, there is an innate tendency toward reunification with the source, a "tendency toward the incarnation of Divinity in the world."[22] The work of Christ and of the church is "the *restoration* of mankind and the universe . . . in which all creation becomes a faithful likeness of the Godhead."[23]

---

[19] Kornblatt, "Soloviev on Salvation," 76–77.

[20] Soloviev, *War, Progress*, 165, 169. Anti-Christ writes of "distributive justice," of "universal peace and prosperity," and "the equality of universal satiety"; he is a vegetarian (166, 169, 173).

[21] Kornblatt, "Soloviev on Salvation," 70.

[22] Soloviev, *Lectures on Divine*, 136.

[23] Soloviev, *God, Man*, 168.

The threefold Deity is reflected in the threefold reality of human experience in doing, thinking, and feeling; or will, representation (thought), and feeling. These three realms of experience are illuminated, respectively, by divine goodness, truth, and beauty, which are promulgated by, respectively, the Father, Son, and Spirit.[24]

God is "that which is," and we find the Trinity again summarized in this clause: "That which is thus wills its essence or content, represents it, and feels it."[25] The Son *represents* or *expresses* the Father, while the Spirit echoes, fulfills, and feels what has been willed and expressed. Of course, Soloviev knows that will, thought, and feeling overlap and intertwine in human experience—and also in divine experience. He is not saying that each person of the Trinity embodies one of these modes in complete separation from the others, but that one manifests "as *preeminently willing*," one "as *preeminently representing*," and one "as *preeminently feeling*."[26]

God, or "the all,"[27] has a different form of expression in each of the three modes or persons: as (predominantly) goodness, truth, or beauty.[28] Love, or unity, which is the same thing, underlies each of these. Goodness is love *in essence*, Truth is love *in ideality*, beauty is love in *outward reality*: "beauty is also love . . . . as manifested or made available to the senses."[29] Love's cycle, then, is to be willed, to be ideally conceived, and to be really experienced. Tying this together is the insight that divinity is unity.

Faith and creativity are primarily (though not exclusively) identified with the latter realm, the realm of feeling.[30] This means that he saw faith largely as an intuitive response to inward spiritual gifts. The third level "may, to distinguish it from the first, be called *soul*. . . . The soul [is] the spirit in the process of being realized."[31] Despite being highly theoretical, Soloviev's philosophy calls most of all for vigorous action.

---

[24] Robert Slesinski, "V. S. Soloviev's Unfinished Project of Free Theurgy," in *Diakonia* 29 (1996) 139.

[25] Soloviev, *Lectures on Divine*, 97.

[26] Ibid., 100.

[27] Ibid., 99.

[28] Ibid., 100.

[29] Ibid., 103.

[30] Slesinski, "Unfinished Project," 137–38, where he unfairly criticizes Soloviev for restricting creativity to the realm of feeling, though noting on the next page that Soloviev could also link creativity with the will ("the creative act of the *will*," 139).

[31] Soloviev, *Lectures on Divine*, 101.

Sophiology

Soloviev's Christology and theōsis can be quite complicated. He speaks of the unity that produces, and the unity that *is produced*;[32] the former is the Word or Logos, the latter is the Sophia; and Christ "is both Logos and Sophia."[33] Here he attempts to combine doctrine with philosophy: the teaching that Christ is fully divine and fully human, with the philosophic notion that spirituality arises from potentials, and is achieved in actuals. Sophia is "the principle of humanity . . . . ideal or perfect humanity"[34]— *in potential*; it still needs to be actualized through human choice.

This is both Chalcedonian and Hegelian. Too many commentators dismiss Soloviev with the label "Hegelian." But why should not philosophic models be used to fill out theological truth, to give it greater explanatory power? After all, this is also what happened at Nicaea and Chalcedon. Philosophic concepts that were not available to Peter and Paul were used to fill out the apostolic teaching. Such new expressions must, of course, be judged by their moral worth, intellectual coherence, and beauty of exposition. It is only fitting that Soloviev should be subjected to a triune test.

It is true that Soloviev's Sophiology draws upon a colorful and eclectic range of mysticism and philosophy. In his young manhood he looked deeply into medieval and Platonic mysticism, Hermeticism, Gnosticism, theosophy,[35] and even the occult, looking into many concepts of Sophia or other feminine images of the divine. He picks up on popular Christian reverence for Sophia and for Mary, which had its own roots in Jewish philosophic speculation about Wisdom as God's partner in creation (based on Prov 3:19; 8:22–31 and Wis 7:25–8:1), but also in the Hellenistic theology of the Isis cult,[36] which had an all-embracing mother figure.

Soloviev also draws upon the alchemical tradition "in which Mary-Sophia was the Great Mother" and was considered the discoverer of

---

[32] Ibid., 107. This may borrow from Stoicism's idea of active reason and passive matter.

[33] Ibid., 108.

[34] Ibid., 113.

[35] Kristi A. Groberg, "The Feminine Occult Sophia in the Russian Religious Renaissance: a Bibliographical Essay," in *Canadian-American Slavic Studies* 26 (1992) 204–6.

[36] Groberg, "Feminine Occult," 206–7.

alchemy.[37] Linked with alchemy is Hermeticism, a Gnostic philosophy, which transmits the idea that Sophia descended to earth, but was rejected by people.[38] Add to this some notions of the Eternal Feminine that Soloviev drew from Dante and Petrarch,[39] Soloviev's studies of Jewish Kabala (which has a divine Sophia[40]), and his interest in mystics such as Böhme,[41] Swedenborg, and Blavatsky (although he ended up repudiating the latter),[42] and one gets the picture of how thoroughly syncretistic his early Sophiology was.

Yet he is able to subject this exotic cauldron of influences to a Christianizing synthesis. It hardly matters what he reads, he assimilates everything to his own transformative vision, and Christ is a focal point of that vision. In at least two of his books, he insists that the essence of Christianity "is uniquely and exclusively Christ"—it is the incarnation of deity in/as Jesus. He cites Jesus' "reference to Himself as living incarnate truth" in John 14:6.[43] Christ can do this because he embodies the threefold unity mentioned earlier.

He takes the pantheism of ancient Stoic thought and Christianizes it in such statements as this: "the world-soul feels a vague but profound desire for unity. By this desire it attracts the action of the Word."[44] The world-soul, the sum of "all living entities," can choose to reject the divine guidance, or to become "the body of Christ, Sophia,"[45] by allowing "the incarnation of the divine Idea"[46] in it. Christ's divine humanity begins to be mirrored in humanity when the world-soul grows up into Sophia, when its unconscious striving for unity becomes a mature loyalty to the real source of unity. All of this depends upon humanity fulfilling its divine goal:

---

[37] Ibid., 202, 205, 210.

[38] Ibid., 202 and n. 19.

[39] Whom Soloviev translated; ibid., 203.

[40] Ibid., 202, 204.

[41] Ibid., 200, 205, 235, 236 n.132.

[42] Ibid., 211.

[43] Soloviev, *Lectures on Divine*, 105; cf. idem, "what we value most in Christianity is Christ himself," a comment that greatly upsets the Anti-Christ in *War, Progress*, 183–84.

[44] Soloviev, *Russia*, 163.

[45] Soloviev, *Lectures*, 132.

[46] Ibid. 138.

As the intermediary between heaven and earth, Man was destined to be the universal Messiah who should save the world from chaos by uniting to God and incarnating the eternal Wisdom in created forms. . . . Man . . . was to be priest of God, king of the lower world, and prophet of their absolute union: priest of God in sacrificing to Him his own arbitrariness, the egoism of humanity.[47]

So this superman is not a Nietzschean egomaniac. But the mission of humanity is divine. In fact, "the periphery of Divinity—is humanity."[48]

Following the Christ Pattern

Under Christ's direction, the believer becomes a "new spiritual man" who unites divinity with nature in himself.[49] But this is not an individualist endeavor; in fact, deification is the real mission of the Church.

The free divinization of mankind is effected when the divine mother, the Church, is made fruitful by the action of the human power.[50]

The Church is mankind deified by Christ. . . . to believe in mankind means only to believe in its *capacity for deification*, to believe in the words of Saint Athanasius the Great, that in Christ God became man in order to make man God.[51]

Christian divinization follows the pattern of Christ "divinizing his humanity after his Divinity became man."[52] The key is human cooperation

---

[47] Soloviev, *Russia*, 179.

[48] Soloviev, *Lectures on Divine*, 114.

[49] Translating from Soloviev's collected works (Brussels) 3:166, is Richard F. Gustafson, "Soloviev's Doctrine of Salvation," in *Russian Religious Thought*, eds. Judith Kornblatt and Richard F. Gustafson (Madison: University of Wisconsin Press, 1996) 37.

[50] Soloviev, *God, Man*, 169–70.

[51] Gustafson, "Doctrine," 41–42, translating from the collected works 3:222. Athanasius says this in *De inc. Verbe* 54. It had aldready been expressed by Irenaeus in *A.H.* V preface, and would be expressed later by Gregory Nyssa in *Orat. Cat.* XXV and these authors would be widely cited by later ones.

[52] Gustafson, "Doctrine," 37; translating from the collected works 3:170.

with God. The "active action of God [*theourgia*]" is to be a "cooperative action of Divinity and humanity for the re-creation of the latter from the fleshly or natural into the spiritual or divine."[53] This leads to the ultimate goal, when the "Kingdom of God be not only *above* all, which it already is, but also *in all*. . . . God will be *all in all*."[54] Theōsis fulfills individual, social, and cosmic destinies.

The repercussion on the individual is an experience of spiritual enlightenment, even a *transfiguration*: a recovery of one's natural and original connection with God. "Salvation is a restoration of unity,"[55] which is, of course, a Platonic idea, but one that goes much further than the pre-Christian philosopher could imagine:

> Another principle of death abolished by the higher pathway of love is the contrast of the spirit to the body. In this respect as well, the issue is the whole person, and the true principle of its restoration is a *spiritual-corporeal* principle. . . . Man can *become* divine only by the actual power of an eternally existing Divinity [and by] a *divinely human* process.[56]

This can be described as "the Origenist restoration of all things."[57] It is a dynamic philosophy with tremendous potential, and could fill a long-standing void in Western theology, which has suppressed the notion of spiritual transformation, has hammered home a sense of shame and guilt, thus diminishing the *felt* connection with the Divine.

Yet we cannot deny that this side of Soloviev's thought also lends itself to a kind of magical spirituality, possibly influenced by the "Neoplatonic view" of matter being penetrated by the active force of divinity.[58] Is Soloviev taking literally the notion of the "spiritualization and divinization of the flesh"[59]? Is this a kind of alchemy, a literal transformation of matter?

---

[53] Ibid., 39; collected works, 3:377.

[54] Ibid., 41; collected works 3:318–19.

[55] Ibid., 33.

[56] Soloviev, "Plato's Life-Drama" XXVI, from *Politics, Law, and Morality: Essays by V. S. Soloviev*, ed. and tr. Vladimir Wozniuk (New Haven: Yale University Press, 2000) 248; see also Kornblatt, "Transfiguration of Plato," 43.

[57] Gustafson, "Doctrine," 41.

[58] Ibid., 39.

[59] Ibid., 38.

Probably some of his remarks do envision some kind of physical transformation, but others seem to be metaphorical, as in this instance: "this new flesh, spiritualized, deified, is the divine substance of the Church."[60]

Since the church is "*a real, living being* growing continuously in spiritual power,"[61] there has to be real growth in Christian understanding of dogmatic truth, even as the great theologian, Gregory of Nazianzen had explained. While arguing for the personality of the Holy Spirit, Gregory had said that some Christians could not grasp it because they were still grappling with the Son's personality and divinity. First the Father had to be revealed, then the Son, and finally the Spirit.[62]

Soloviev also has a concept of spiritual evolution or development, but it is not a naïve and simplistic notion of inevitable progress, as can be seen in his final work. We should remember that, in his day, theologians both East and West were ignoring or minimizing apocalyptic literature, while Soloviev was exploring its remarkable appropriateness for depicting the confrontation between truth and falsehood, between principle and politics, between honest religion (whether christological or Jewish) and a certain kind of dishonest modernism. His story picks up on the fact that people must have a Messiah, either a true one or a sham one (or, in the Jewish case, a Messianic hope).

Anti-Gnostic Triumph

The "Story of the Antichrist" rings true because we do hunger for, and need, a revelation of the "Humanity of God."[63] Of course divinization is a dangerous subject, but so is love, so is marriage, so is organization, so is everything that

---

[60] Soloviev, *God, Man*, 170.

[61] Soloviev, quoted by Paul Valliere, *Modern Russian Theology—Bukharev, Soloviev, Bulgakov: Orthodox Theology in a New Key* (Grand Rapids: Eerdmans, 2000) 190.

[62] Valliere, *Modern Russian Theology*, 189; he cites Gregory from *Christology of the Later Fathers*, ed. Edward R. Hardy, Library of Christian Classics 3 (Philadelphia: Westminster, 1954) 209–10.

[63] The phrase is Valliere's translation for *bogochelovechestvo* (*Modern Russian Theology*, 11–12), emphasizing the incarnation of the Son, God's invasion of the human sphere—an interesting idea, whether or not his translation is better than "divine humanity," which most translators prefer.

matters in human life, for it can be done ethically or dishonestly, can be motivated by religious feeling or by greed, can be backed with a love of truth or with lazy nihilism. From the good side of these choices comes comedy, an intuition of triumph in the face of adversity, an intuition that is based on real experience of love in the centers of the personality, from whence arise motivation, feeling, and reflection. True religion is inherently prophetic. Goodness is so bold as to sense that the meek will inherit the earth, despite all evidence to the contrary. Beauty is so hopeful as to foresee a time when knowledge of God will fill the earth, as the waters fill the sea (Isa 11:9). And truth is so generous as to patiently work for the time when its divided foes tire of their raging, and come to Jerusalem to be taught of God, so to speak. Actually, "Isaiah and Jeremiah herald the coming revelation as the banner . . . to which all nations shall come. . . . a universalization of a positive national idea, not an empty and indifferent cosmopolitanism."[64]

An important conclusion to be drawn from Soloviev's comedic view of life is that he is not, despite his reading tastes in his twenties, a Gnostic, at least not in the sense of second century Gnosticism, with its paranoid resentment and dread of the Creator. The fundamental instinct of comedy is the goodness of the creator, and Soloviev affirms this. This illuminates his understanding of sin and suffering. He makes an observation that others, such as C. S. Lewis, have made, that "If ugly reality were the sole reality, then how would it be possible for man *to feel the burden* of this . . . to reproach and deny it?"; suffering is evidence of "the authentic power of the ideal living within him."[65] The presence of God within, the promise of divinization, provides comedy with its hope. When Soloviev calls himself a Gnostic, he means what Clement of Alexandria means when he also calls himself a Gnostic: one who seeks knowledge of God.

What is unique in the Gospel is its affirmation of comedic triumph overarching and even embracing the stuff of tragedy. What is unique is the incarnation of the Godhead (not just "a god"), making possible the millions of incarnations in the lives of divinizing humans. Jesus, "the God-man is individual," but regenerated humanity, "divinized man, man-God, is necessarily oecumenical or catholic."[66] Soloviev's vision was broad enough

---

[64] Soloviev, *Lectures on Divine*, 73–74.
[65] Soloviev, "Fate of Pushkin," 153.
[66] Soloviev, *God, Man*, 171.

to connect individual creativity with universal harmonization. He affirms the ending of separatism and the emergence of "catholicity as an inner perfection."[67] This process always relies upon divine guidance; if one ever forgets this, one's spirituality becomes a caricature.

It is such a sham spirituality that Soloviev exposes in his story of the Antichrist. This charming writer and political leader brings about peace on earth, and is made world emperor. He then seeks to be recognized as the world's religious leader. He offers to preserve all the "icons and rituals," and to establish "a world museum of Christian archaeology."[68] But the Elder John (who stands for Eastern Orthodoxy) says, "what we value most in Christianity is Christ himself . . . . in him dwells all the fullness of the Godhead bodily" (Col 2:9); he then challenges the Emperor to "confess his name." When the Emperor becomes angrily silent, the Elder John says, "Little children, it is Anti-Christ!"[69] In the same vein, Pope Peter (representing Catholicism) rejects the "ecumenical" claims of the Antichrist and anathematizes him, while Professor Pauli (representing Protestantism) affirms the Elder's identification and the Pope's expulsion of "the arch deceiver."[70]

Such a warning about false and egotistical self-theōsis is a powerful and necessary aspect of any mature teaching. Theōsis is not meant to be a way to diminish or undermine Christology. It is Christ who revealed the way, and who *is* the way. Theōsis is hardly more than a by-product of walking the way that he showed us. Christ is "God incarnate in humanity . . . . the new spiritual Man."[71] Soloviev spends much more time on ethics, social progress, and the divinization of humanity than he does on Christology, but his arguments in these other areas depend on recognition of the unique divinity of Christ:

> For there to be an actual union of Divinity with nature, a person in whom this union might take place is necessary. . . . Both natures are necessary. . . . In Christ . . . we have an actual divine-human person . . . accomplishing the double exploit of divine and human self-renunciation

---

[67] Ibid., 168.

[68] Soloviev, *War, Progress,* 181.

[69] Ibid., 183–84.

[70] Ibid., 185–86. Here I leave out the story's intense drama.

[71] Soloviev, *Lectures on Divine,* 154–55.

. . . . Christ, as God, freely renounces the glory of God and thereby, as a human being, acquires the possibility of *attaining* that glory.[72]

By so doing, Christ enables others to attain glory. That this is accomplished by God's grace is obvious (except to the egotistical person); what Soloviev wishes to emphasize is the necessity for human cooperation: "God acts only with and through man . . . . God's work has become the work of man also."[73] God's whole plan would be defeated if God were to arbitrarily divinize humanity and the world. The divinization process needs human loyalty to be voluntary, mature, and love-motivated.

Abbreviations

A.H. – *Against Heresies* (Irenaeus)
De inc. Verbe – *On the Incanation of the Word* (Athanasius)
JAAR – Journal of the American Academy of Religion
Orat. Cat. – *Catechetical Orations* (Gregory of Nyssa)
TT – *Theology Today*

Bibliography

Carlson, Maria. "Gnostic Elements in the Cosmogony of Vladimir Soloviev." In *Russian Religious Thought*, edited by Judith Deutsch Kornblatt and Richard F. Gustafson, 49–67. Madison: University of Wisconsin Press, 1996.

Gregory of Nazianzen. "The Theological Orations." In *Christology of the Later Fathers*, edited by Edward R. Hardy, 128–214. Library of Christian Classics 3. Philadelphia: Westminster, 1954.

Groberg, Kristi A. "The Feminine Occult Sophia in the Russian Religious Renaissance: a Bibliographical Essay." *Canadian-American Slavic Studies* 26 (1992) 197–240.

---

[72] Ibid., 158–61.
[73] Soloviev, "On Counterfeits," from *A Solovyov Anthology*, ed. S. L. Frank, tr. Natalie Duddington (London: SCM, 1950) 47–48.

Gustafson, Richard F. "Soloviev's Doctrine of Salvation." In *Russian Religious Thought*, edited by Judith Deutsch Kornblatt and Richard F. Gustafson, 31–48. Madison: University of Wisconsin Press, 1996.

Hare, Richard. "East Moves West—The Enigma of Vladimir Soloviev." *The Russian Review* 17 (1958) 29–40.

Johnson, Matthew R. "Political Writings of Vladimir Solov'yev." *Religion, State, and Society* 30 (2002) 347–55.

Kornblatt, Judith Deutsch. "The Transfiguration of Plato in the Erotic Philosophy of Vladimir Solov'ev." *Religion and Literature* 24.2 (1992) 35–50.

—————. "Soloviev on Salvation: The Story of the 'Short Story of the Antichrist.'" In *Russian Religious Thought*, edited by Judith Deutsch Kornblatt and Richard F. Gustafson, 68–87. Madison: University of Wisconsin Press, 1996.

Kornblatt, Judith Deutsch, and Gary Rosenshield. "Vladimir Soloviev: Confronting Dostoevsky on the Jewish and Christian Questions." *Journal of the American Academy of Religion* 68 (2000) 69–98.

Lossky, Vladimir. *The Mystical Theology of the Eastern Church*. London: James Clarke, 1957. (First published in Paris in 1944.)

Slesinski, Robert. "V. S. Soloviev's Unfinished Project of Free Theurgy." *Diakonia* 29 (1996) 133–41.

Soloviev, Vladimir—*Some English editions spell his name Solovyev or Solovyov, but we are using Soloviev as our standard.*

—————. *God, Man and the Church: The Spiritual Foundations of Life*. Translated by Donald Attwater. London: James Clarke, 1938.

—————. *The Heart of Reality: Essays on Beauty, Love and Ethics*. Translated by Vladimir Wozniuk. Notre Dame: University of Notre Dame Press, 2000.

—————. *Lectures on Divine Humanity*. Revised and edited by Boris Jakim, based on the translation by Peter Zouboff and published by Dennis Dobson, London, 1948. Hudson, New York: Lindisfarne, 1995. (From his lectures of 1878–1881, given in various European cities.)

—————. *The Meaning of Love*. Translated by Jane Marshall. New York: International Universities, 1947.

—————. "On Counterfeits." In *A Solovyov Anthology*. Edited by S. L. Frank. Translated by Natalie Duddington. London: SCM, 1950.

—————. *Politics, Law, and Morality: Essays by V. S. Soloviev*. Edited and translated by Vladimir Wozniuk. Russian Literature and Thought. New Haven: Yale University Press, 2002.

—————. *Russia and the Universal Church*. London: Geoffrey Bless, 1948.

————. *War, Progress, and the End of History: Three Conversations Including a Short Story of the Anti-Christ*. Translated by Alexander Bakshy. Revised by Thomas R. Beyer, Jr. Hudson, N.Y.: Lindisfarne, 1990.

Starr, James M. *Sharers in Divine Nature: 2 Peter 1:4 in Its Hellenistic Context*. Coniectanea Biblical NT Series 33. Stockholm: Almqvist & Wiksell, 2003.

Stein, Jess, editor. *The Random House Dictionary of the English Language*. New York: Random House, 1967.

Valliere, Paul. *Modern Russian Theology—Bukharev, Soloviev, Bulgakov: Orthodox Theology in a New Key*. Grand Rapids: Eerdmans, 2000.

List of Contributors

Stephen Finlan (Ph.D., Durham [U.K.]; M.Phil., Drew; M.A., Pacific School of Religion) has published *The Background and Content of Paul's Cultic Atonement Metaphors* with Society of Biblical Literature, and *Problems with Atonement: The Origins of, and Controversy about, the Atonement Doctrine* with Liturgical Press. He teaches at Seton Hall University and is a research assistant with the Ancient Christian Commentary on Scripture at Drew University.

Vladimir Kharlamov (M.Phil., Drew; M.Div., Southern Baptist Theological Seminary; M.A., Odessa Theological Seminary) has several academic articles published, teaches at Fairleigh Dickinson University, and is working on a Ph.D. at Drew University. Kharlamov is a research assistant with the Ancient Christian Commentary on Scripture at Drew.

Gregory Glazov has a D.Phil. from Oxford's Oriental Institute and has published *The 'Bridling of the Tongue' and the 'Opening of the Mouth' in Biblical Prophecy* with Sheffield Academic Press, along with numerous articles. He taught at Oxford, and is now an Assistant Professor in Old Testament Studies at Immaculate Conception Seminary, Seton Hall University, South Orange, New Jersey.

Jeffrey Finch (Ph.D., Drew) has several articles published, and is in training to be ordained a Roman Catholic priest.

Robert Puchniak is a Ph.D. candidate at Drew University.

Elena Vishnevskaya (Ph.D., Drew) teaches at Fairleigh Dickinson University.

Myk Habets has taught Systematic Theology since 1999, and is a Ph.D. candidate at Otago, New Zealand.